Bioethics and the Hur

Many medical schools are now . ...ng the umanities (philosophy, literature, creative writing, medical history) with the aim of broadening the education of doctors. This book attempts to show how the humanities can extend the scope of bioethics beyond regulation, and how they can affect the attitudes of doctors towards patients and the perceptions of medicine, health and disease which have become part of contemporary culture.

The book rattles the medical cage by offering a critique of certain aspects of medical practice and research. For example, the idea that patient status or the doctor/patient relationship can be understood via quantitative scales is shown both to rest on a misunderstanding of numbers, and to create a distorted perception of human beings. The book offers an alternative way of understanding the qualitative research producing this distortion, an understanding akin to the sort we acquire from good literature. Again, much medical ethics would have us believe that doctors, unlike plumbers, teachers and the rest of us, are uniquely beneficent, indeed altruistic. This professional delusion diverts us from the real ethical achievements and problems of medicine. The central aim of this book is to expose the half-truths of contemporary medicine and to celebrate the Greek belief that Apollo was god of both medicine and the arts.

Professor R.S. Downie is Emeritus Professor of Moral Philosophy at Glasgow University and Professorial Research Fellow. He has specialised in applying philosophical techniques to practical problems. In particular, he is interested in biomedical ethics and in the use of literature and the arts as vehicles for developing medical perceptions and attitudes.

Dr Jane Macnaughton is the Director of the Centre for Arts and Humanities in Health and Medicine and Clinical Senior Lecturer in the School for Health at the University of Durham. She is a qualified GP and has a PhD in philosophy. Her main interests are in literature and medicine, philosophy and history of medicine and in the applications of the humanities to medical education.

Biomedical Law and Ethics Library
Series Editor: Sheila A.M. McLean

Scientific and clinical advances, social and political developments and the impact of healthcare on our lives raise profound ethical and legal questions. Medical law and ethics have become central to our understanding of these problems, and are important tools for the analysis and resolution of problems – real or imagined.

In this series, scholars at the forefront of biomedical law and ethics contribute to the debates in this area, with accessible, thought-provoking, and sometimes controversial ideas. Each book in the series develops an independent hypothesis and argues cogently for a particular position. One of the major contributions of this series is the extent to which both law and ethics are utilised in the content of the books, and the shape of the series itself.

The books in this series are analytical, with a key target audience of lawyers, doctors, nurses, and the intelligent lay public.

Forthcoming titles:

Horsey and Biggs, *Human Fertilisation and Embryology* (2007)
McLean and Williamson, *Impairment and Disability* (2007)
Gavaghan, *Defending the Genetic Supermarket* (2007)
Priaulx, *The Harm Paradox* (2007)
Downie and Macnaughton, *Bioethics and the Humanities* (2007)
McLean, *Assisted Dying* (2007)
Huxtable, *Euthanasia, Ethics and the Law* (2007)
Elliston, *Best Interests of the Child in Healthcare* (2007)

About the Series Editor

Professor Sheila Mclean is International Bar Association Professor of Law and Ethics in Medicine and Director of the Institute of Law and Ethics in Medicine at the University of Glasgow.

Bioethics and the Humanities

Attitudes and perceptions

R.S. Downie and
Jane Macnaughton

Routledge·Cavendish
Taylor & Francis Group

First published 2007
by Routledge-Cavendish
2 Park Square, Milton Park, Abingdon, Oxon OX14 4RN

Simultaneously published in the USA and Canada
by Routledge-Cavendish
270 Madison Ave, New York, NY 10016

*Routledge-Cavendish is an imprint of the Taylor & Francis Group,
an informa business*

© 2007 R.S. Downie and Jane Macnaughton

Typeset in Times New Roman by
Newgen Imaging Systems (P) Ltd, Chennai, India
Printed and bound in Great Britain by
MPG Books Ltd, Bodmin, Cornwall

British Library Cataloguing in Publication Data
A catalogue record for this book is available
from the British Library

Library of Congress Cataloging in Publication Data
A catalog record for this book has been requested

ISBN10: 1–84472–052–7 (pbk)
ISBN10: 1–84472–053–5 (hbk)

ISBN13: 978–1–84472–052–1 (pbk)
ISBN13: 978–1–84472–053–8 (hbk)

Contents

Foreword

It is fascinating to watch the coming of age of an area of academic study. The history of the arts and humanities movement as it affects health care and health-care ethics is a good example of such a development. The process usually begins in a small way, for example, with a seminar or a series of lectures, and then a group of enthusiasts meet nationally or internationally, a journal appears and books are written defining the boundaries of the subject and its content. Both the authors of this book were in at the beginning of the arts and humanities in health and medicine movement and the book itself is a mature reflection on the process and the current state of play in relation to ethical issues in health care. If the regulation of practice is the central concern of medical ethics (or bioethics) this book greatly enlarges that concern. At its heart is the suggestion that 'the arts and humanities can perform both a critical and a supplementary function in the ethical education of at least some health professionals'. Philosophy sharpens critical perceptions and literature and other arts supplement by maturing attitudes. In this way the arts and humanities are relevant to making difficult judgements and to developing a broader perspective on human illness and suffering than can be offered by ethical regulation.

The authors are not suggesting that every medical or nursing student can benefit from the study of the arts and humanities, nor that such courses be essential parts of the curriculum. Others of course have argued differently. This book contends that logic and moral philosophy provide ways of thinking, arguing and justifying decision making, and that the loss of these subjects is to be regretted. At present, however, it would be almost impossible to add such subjects as compulsory components in an already overburdened curriculum. But it is an interesting thought.

A study of the arts and humanities enables us to see clinical issues in different ways, illuminating familiar problems and giving them new meaning. The arts can also arm health professionals and others working in community contexts with creative ways of thinking about and delivering public health messages. For health-care professionals such insights can provide the impetus for fresh thinking but can also give support and comfort to those in the front line of health care. In ethical decision making in clinical medicine and public health the issues are rarely straightforward and therefore in most instances judgements are required. The arts and humanities provide three major ways of assisting such decision making in the field of bioethics. First, they can provide a framework (or frameworks) of ethics which can place a problem in a particular context and help with decision making. Second, using the processes of logic and argument they can help to clarify a problem and assist in justifying a particular decision to a patient or in a public forum. Third, specific illustrations from the arts and literature can illuminate a problem and suggest novel ways of dealing with it. This book is helpful in all these ways, but goes further and places bioethics in a wider cultural context.

Professor Sir Kenneth Calman
Vice Chancellor and Warden
University of Durham

Preface

There are many books on the subject of bioethics, both general and on specific areas of medical and nursing practice, and there are some, although not quite so many, in the area of what has come to be called the 'medical humanities'. But we know of no book which concentrates directly on the relationship between the humanities and bioethics. Of course, it is sometimes significant when no books exist in a given area – a cruel reviewer once said of a book that it filled a much-needed gap! But we think that there is a gap in the literature of bioethics which can helpfully be filled by some attention to the humanities. In particular, bioethics is now mainly concerned with the *regulation* of medical practice, but that focus leaves two areas in the shadows. These areas concern, first, the *perceptions* which doctors and nurses have of the practice of medicine, of its scientific credentials, and of the whole idea of health care as the paradigm profession. Such perceptions inevitably affect, second, the *attitudes* which doctors and nurses adopt towards their patients and themselves. Indeed, the public is encouraged by doctors' leaders and governments to have similar perceptions and to adopt similar attitudes to health care as a profession.

In discussing these perceptions and attitudes we shall suggest that the humanities have two main functions: a *critical* function and a *supplementary* function. The *critical* function is mainly fulfilled by the various branches of philosophy. Bioethics as a regulatory activity tends to accept medical practice and research as given and it attempts to deliver them to the public in an acceptable format. But it may also be enlightening to offer more radical challenges to medical practice and research. Are they quite as scientific as doctors would like to claim, and what ethical view of human beings do their assumptions imply? Are doctors uniquely altruistic, or even beneficent, as the dominant views in medical ethics suggest? Philosophical challenges of this sort will occupy us in Chapters 2–5, and they concern the perceptions which doctors have, and encourage the public to have, of the practice and scope of medicine.

Second, the humanities can have what we shall call a *supplementary* function in the broad church of bioethics. As we stressed, the main function of bioethics is to regulate, specifying the duties of doctors and the rights of patients. But complaints about doctors do not always suggest that they have failed in their duties. Sometimes the suggestion is rather that their attitudes are less than desirable, that they are rude or unsympathetic, or that the letters they write are peremptory or arrogant. The failure here is attitudinal. Perhaps the attitude can never wholly be put right, because it is created by the total medical situation in which the patient is vulnerable (and easily takes offence), and the doctor is perceived to have the answers (and therefore to wield power). But if anything can improve attitudes it is the humanities. They are able to make us see ourselves as others see us and to make us vividly aware of what it must be like to be in the vulnerable position of a patient. This ability we shall call the 'supplementary' function of the medical humanities. In Chapter 7 we shall suggest that this supplementary function can even be fulfilled by placing artists in hospital or community settings.

This book is written with two hopes: that we can extend and enrich the scope of bioethics, and that the medical student who said in his evaluation 'I only read *The Sun* cos we are all different' can be encouraged to be more adventurous.

Robin Downie, University of Glasgow
Jane Macnaughton, University of Durham
Autumn 2006

Acknowledgements

We gratefully acknowledge help from many quarters. Principally we must thank Sir Kenneth Calman for writing the Foreword. It is particularly fitting that he should do so since as Postgraduate Dean of Medicine at Glasgow University he was perhaps the first in the United Kingdom in recent times to see the importance of the humanities in the education of medical students. As Chief Medical Officer he continued his enthusiasm and organised several meetings on a national scale on the value of the arts and humanities in health-care education and in the wider life of the community. As Vice-Chancellor of the University of Durham he has been in a position to establish the Centre for Arts and Humanities in Health and Medicine (CAHHM), which has encouraged the use of the humanities in undergraduate medical education, and has organised many successful ventures in which communities have participated in arts projects. It is fitting that the collaboration between the Universities of Glasgow and Durham should continue in this book.

We are grateful to some colleagues who have commented on parts of the book or who have helped to clarify our ideas. We mention in particular Fiona Randall, Consultant in Palliative Medicine in Bournemouth and Christchurch Hospital Trust, Mike White, Director for Arts in Health at CAHHM, Martyn Evans, Professor of Humanities in Medicine at CAHHM, Emma Storr, Senior Tutor in General Practice at the University of Leeds and experienced organiser of Special Study Modules in the Humanities, Karen Elliott, who produced accurate documents from messy originals, and our long-suffering spouses Eileen and Andrew.

RSD
RJM

Introduction

There is the story of a young man who was cautioned by a policeman for his exuberant behaviour. The young man suggested (with what colourfulness of language history does not relate) that the policeman was being over-zealous. The policeman then said, 'You have an attitude problem', whereupon the young man (doubtless a student) replied, 'You have a perception problem'. We will not comment on the relevance of this anecdote to the Government's Anti-social Behaviour Orders, but it is highly relevant to the themes of this book. It will be our central contention that the humanities can contribute to the ethical improvement of health care in two main ways: by improving the attitudes of professionals, and by widening their perceptions. The humanities can also perform a similar function with respect to our perceptions of and attitudes to our own health. Let us explain.

Bioethics – health-care ethics, medical ethics (we shall use the terms interchangeably) – is now mainly concerned with the business of the regulation of professional practice, whether medical, nursing or related professional activity. The core of professional regulation is in medical law, and medical ethics represents an attempt to regulate those aspects of professional practice which are too detailed for the broad brush of the law. Indeed, it is common for university departments or textbooks concerned with these to have 'law and ethics' in their titles, thus linking the two and asserting their continuity. We shall not dispute that the regulatory function of bioethics should remain its dominant one. What then is left out?

To answer this question we shall refer to a novella by Graham Greene entitled *The Tenth Man.*[1] The story opens towards the end of the Second World War. The Nazis have taken hostages in a small French town, and intend to shoot three of them as a reprisal against murders by the Resistance. The Nazis leave it to the hostages to pick the victims. They draw lots and one of the unlucky ones is Chavel, a rich lawyer. The fearful Chavel offers his large house and all his wealth to anyone who will face the firing squad in his place. To everyone's surprise his

---

1 Greene G, *The Tenth Man*, 1985, Harmondsworth: Penguin Books.

offer is accepted, by a poor man, Janvier, who plans to leave all the wealth he will inherit to his impoverished sister and mother. The contracts are duly signed and witnessed, and the execution carried out. All this takes place in the first chapter, and the remainder of the story is concerned with events after the war, and especially with the attitude of Chavel to himself. In brief, he is consumed with guilt and shame.

The relevance of this story (and we have not mentioned its many subtleties) to our themes is this.[2] The regulation of professional practice through law and ethics lays down the duties of the professional and the correlative rights of the patient. For example, one of the central concepts of health-care ethics is consent. If treatment is to be ethically acceptable the patient must be given adequate information on its likely outcome and possible side effects, and in the light of that information the patient must freely agree to the treatment. The contract becomes even more stringent and formal where non-therapeutic research is concerned. In other words, there is a framework of rights and duties supported by information and free choice.

But these conditions are met in the case of Chavel – he made an offer which Janvier freely accepted on the basis of full information. The agreement was witnessed and formalised. So what has Chavel done wrong? Something serious, certainly, for we can all sympathise with his feelings about himself, his desire for concealment of what he has done and his subsequent haunted life. Indeed, he comes to see that his action, his offer of the deal, was the outcome of his long-term and ingrained attitude to human relationships. But if we perceive ethics as solely a matter of rights and duties Chavel's guilt and shame become irrational. It will be a central contention of this book that Chavel's guilt and shame are not irrational, because the mesh of rights and duties is too wide to catch all the nuances of ethics. As Chavel came to see, our attitudes to others are as important from the perspective of ethics as the performance of our duties. We shall argue that the arts and humanities are vehicles for developing and maturing our attitudes. They offer a condensation of life, and in their immediacy and intensity can affect our attitudes.

We spoke not just of the relevance of attitudes to bioethics but also of the relevance of perceptions. What are the connections between attitudes and perceptions? The answer is that attitudes logically depend on perceptions. Attitudes necessarily have a cognitive core, in the sense that they depend on beliefs, or on the way we see a situation, a person or a relationship. We have the attitudes we do because we perceive the world, including other people, in a certain way. For example, if we have a cynical atttitude to politicians it will be because we perceive them in a certain way, or have certain beliefs about them – perhaps that they are all self-seeking, or that all they want is a place in history or that they never admit to being wrong.

---

2 The relevance of this story to medicine is discussed in detail in Elliott C, 'Doing harm: living organ donors, clinical research and *The Tenth Man*', *Journal of Medical Ethics* 1995, 21: 91–96.

In the case of medicine there are many such perceptions which directly affect the attitudes which doctors have to patients, to themselves and to medicine itself. For example, many doctors believe that the practice of medicine is the practice of an applied science, and that randomised control trials are the 'gold standard' of such science. Now we have criticised this position in a previous work from the point of view of the philosophy of science,[3] but from the ethical point of view a less than desirable perception of human beings emerges. Human beings are seen as consisting of quantifiable elements which are generalisable and can be measured in 'scales'. (One size fits all.) Moreover, many doctors believe that in illness patients have the sole aim of prolonging their lives and 'fighting' disease. In terms of this perception patients are often provided with information consisting of dubious statistics, and accompanied by the assumption that the offered treatment will be accepted. For example, the information that chemotherapy has a 15% chance of prolonging your life may be provided with the assumption that the patient would be wrong-headed not to accept it. But 15% of what, for how long, with what accompanying discomfort? Perceptions of this kind – of medicine as simply an applied science with the quantification and generalisation which go with that, and of human beings as ones who above all want to be kept alive – create a common sort of attitude which doctors have to patients. Such perceptions are bound to affect the choices patients are offered and the manner in which they are offered. This is an unnoticed aspect of ethics on which we shall comment in Chapter 3.

The perceptions which the public have of their own health can also be affected by the arts. As we shall show, there is some evidence that attempts to write or draw can release creative energies in at least some patients, which they did not realise they had. The release of creative energy can be an important causal factor in healing or making whole, so it would seem to be an ethically good thing to employ artists where they can be helpful. Of course the employment of artists and writers in hospitals or general practices can give rise to ethical problems, for they are not bound by the regulations of medical ethics. Yet it is precisely because such artists are not seen by patients as part of the professional establishment that they can, sometimes, have a healing effect. This effect comes partly, as we said, from the release of creative energies, but it also comes from the idea of an equal partnership. The partnership between artist and patient or artist and community can be a model for an ethically good relationship between doctor and patient or public health doctor and community. There are ethical lessons to be learned here, as we shall show in Chapter 7.

In conclusion, we must stress again that we are not suggesting that the regulatory function of medical ethics should be replaced; it remains central. Moreover, we are not suggesting that every medical student, doctor or community can benefit ethically, or in any other way, from the arts and

3 Downie RS and Macnaughton J, *Clinical Judgement: Evidence in Practice*, 2000, Oxford: Oxford University Press.

humanities (as we shall see, p 167). But we are suggesting, more modestly, that the arts and humanities can perform both a critical and a supplementary function in the ethical education of at least some health professionals. They can provide a reasoned ethical critique of the nature of contemporary medicine and make suggestions about the directions in which it ought (and ought not) to go; and they can enrich the ethical judgements of professionals by assisting them to develop a broad and humane perspective. We have tried to capture these points in our sub-title: attitudes and perceptions.

Part 1

Bioethics and the humanities

Chapter 1

Bioethics and the medical humanities

The title of this book requires answers to two questions: what are the 'medical humanities'? What light can they shed on the practice of medicine in general and bioethics in particular? In this chapter we shall suggest preliminary answers to both questions as an introduction to the more sustained discussions in the rest of the book.

What are the 'medical humanities'?

We should note that the term 'medical humanities' tends to be used in three senses. These senses refer to three movements which may overlap, but are distinct in their aims, methodologies and participants. First, there is what we may term 'the arts as therapy'. This is perhaps the oldest strand, for the use of music or the graphic arts or creative writing has been around for many years as a recognised part of health-care therapy. This movement has its own training courses concerned with the therapeutic uses of the arts. We shall not in this book be discussing this movement, which has its own extensive literature and distinctive philosophy.

Second, and more recently, there has developed a movement often called 'arts in health'. This movement has two subdivisions: one concerned with the arts in community settings, and the other with the arts in hospitals, general practices, schools and other institutional settings. Community artists have often made alliances with health promotion campaigns, and there have been successful ventures in some inner cities and socially deprived areas. The employment of artists or writers in health care and other institutional contexts is also common. Both these movements within 'arts in health' are currently flourishing. They differ from the first movement – the arts as therapy – in that the artists concerned are not trained as and do not see themselves as primarily therapists. Healing energies are certainly released by the interaction of artists and patients or artists and community, but paradoxically this will happen only if the participants – artist and patient or community – are aiming at the creation of art rather than at therapy. We shall discuss the benefits and ethical problems of the 'arts in health' movement in Chapter 7.

There is however a third strand in the medical humanities movement – the use of the arts and humanities in the education of medical and nursing students and in postgraduate or continuing medical education. Sometimes the term 'medical humanities' is used in a narrow sense to refer just to this movement, and sometimes it covers all three. It is the third sense with which we shall mainly be concerned, and our concern will be the contribution it can make to the ethical dimension in medicine.

In more detail the medical humanities in this third sense are arts and humanities disciplines which can have some bearing on the practice of medicine. There are of course many arts and humanities and most can shed some light on medicine, but for the purposes of this book we shall concentrate on those which have most bearing on the ethical aspects of medicine. In particular, we shall concentrate on: philosophy (including its branches, such as moral philosophy, logic and epistemology, political philosophy and aesthetics); literature (including poetry, prose and drama); the fine arts and architecture.

What can the medical humanities contribute to bioethics?

These disciplines do not all have the same kind of bearing on bioethics. Basically and crudely we shall draw an initial distinction between the two types of function they have in relation to bioethics. We shall call them the *critical function* and the *supplementary function*. These functions overlap and are mutually enhancing. Philosophy has mainly, although by no means exclusively, a critical role, and literature and the fine arts have mainly, although by no means exclusively, a supplementary role.

Philosophy: the critical function

Philosophy can be characterised as a discipline which is directed at the critical examination of arguments and assumptions. It is what we may describe as a second-order or 'meta-' activity. In other words, to philosophise is to stand back from first-order activities such as the practice of science or of politics or of art or of morality and to try to uncover their assumptions and to understand them by placing them in a wider scheme of things.

The nature of philosophy is perhaps easiest to understand via its branches of logic and epistemology. We discuss the bearing of these disciplines on medicine and especially medical ethics in Chapter 3. Beginning with the theory of definition we draw attention to the complexity of the concept and the indiscriminate way it is used in medical writings. For example, as a result of a notoriously confused definition of health by the World Health Organisation (WHO) in 1946 – 'Health is a state of complete physical, mental and social well-being, and not merely the absence of disease or infirmity'[1] – medical interventions have moved into spheres where, arguably, they have no useful role, such as the pursuit of individual and social well-being. At the very least the ethical assumption and implications of a definition require critical examination. So too the exposure of weak or individual arguments is very much one critical function of philosophy which is performed by logic. This function has a direct relevance to ethics, because bad arguments can confuse complex ethical issues. For example, it is sometimes argued that, because death frequently *follows* the withdrawing of artificial ventilation or tube feeding, such withdrawals are the *cause* of the patient's death, and have therefore violated the patient's right to life. This is the logical fallacy of *post hoc ergo propter hoc* – the fact that B follows A does not establish that A caused B. In the example of tube feeding the death is caused by the underlying pathology which has not changed despite the tube feeding.

Epistemology or theory of knowledge is that branch of philosophy concerned with what we can know to be true, or what we can be certain of. When this branch of philosophy is directed at medicine we find the widespread view held by doctors or medical researchers that we can be certain only of those factors which can be counted. Thus, the idea of the measurement scale is all-pervasive in medicine. Even if we ignore the more ludicrous side of this – the spirituality scale,[2] the empathy scale,[3] the demoralisation scale[4] and so on – we must note that this kind of epistemological assumption has ethical implications. It encourages us to see human beings in a certain way as having a certain sort of personal identity – our identity is assumed to be constituted by discrete factors which can be isolated and measured. A critical examination of these assumptions will shed a new light on the way in which doctors see patients, and the way in which they see patients determines their view of patients' best interests or ethically required treatments.

The relevance of moral philosophy to bioethics might seem much more obvious than that of logic and epistemology, but in fact it is much more liable to misunderstanding; indeed, the misunderstanding is all-pervasive. Moral philosophy, like other branches of philosophy, is a second-order activity. It is detached from our first-order moral life, whether as moral agents in everyday life or as doctors. Its true function is to comment on the first-order activities of the moral life with the aim of understanding them by investigating their assumptions and the strength or weakness of the arguments used in their

1 World Health Organisation, *Constitution*, 1946, New York.
2 Speck P, Higginson I and Addington-Hall J, 'Spiritual needs in health care', *British Medical Journal*, 2004, 329, pp 123–124.
3 Hojat M et al. 'The Jefferson scale of physician empathy: development and preliminary psychometric data', *Educational and Psychological Measurement*, 2001, 61, pp 349–365.
4 Kissane DW et al. 'The demoralization scale: a report of its development and preliminary validation', *Journal of Palliative Care*, 2004, 20, pp 269–276.

justification. Moral philosophy cannot tell us whether the embryo is a person or not, or whether euthanasia should be legalised. What it can do is to examine critically assumptions which may be made by those advocating positions on these issues. This may of course have some practical relevance but the relevance is indirect.

Confusion arises because of the use of the word 'ethics'. For 'ethics' is used to refer either to the second-order and theoretical activity of moral philosophy or to the first-order and practical activity of morality. Thus, philosophers write books with titles such as *Foundations of* Ethics,[5] and doctors are guided by codes and handbooks of ethics. But these are two very different senses of 'ethics' and the differences have caused much confusion in discussions of medical ethics. Doctors and nurses who have attended a week of lectures on medical ethics are apt to use terms such as 'deontology' or 'rule-utilitarianism' or 'Kantianism' with only a poor understanding of what they might mean. Certainly the use of such terms does not solve any practical first-order problems. Indeed, the slogan 'Respect the patient's autonomous decisions' has been ripped from its Kantian context and is used in radically ambiguous ways in medical ethics. For example, it does not distinguish between a patient's competent refusal of a treatment and a patient's demand for a given treatment, and it does not make clear whether 'respecting an autonomous decision' means carrying it out, or just taking it into account. The ethical confusions these ambiguities have caused are discussed in detail in Chapter 2.

In our opinion, then, moral philosophers, to the extent that they are philosophers, should remain in their ivory tower and keep out of the dust of the arena. But this position must be modified to prevent misunderstanding. It is possible to see more and to see more clearly from an ivory tower than from the dust of the arena. The moral philosopher can comment from a good vantage point on what is going on in the practice of first-order bioethics. In Chapter 2 we shall be critical of some methods and assumptions of the practice of medical ethics and make recommendations of methods we can see working successfully if we look from another window in the ivory tower. In this way moral philosophy can make a contribution to bioethics, and in this way it is a medical humanity.

Something similar can be said about the contribution which political philosophy can make as a medical humanity. Political philosophy has its most direct impact on the ethical problems of public health. Here we find the ethical significance of distinctions between equality and equity, and the need for a detached and critical approach to concepts such as 'positive health'.

The importance of distancing philosophy, as a critical second-order discipline, from bioethics is brought out in a recent article by Carl Elliott.[6] Elliott is

5 Ross WD, *Foundations of Ethics*, 1939, Oxford: Clarendon Press.

6 Elliott C, 'The soul of a new machine: bioethicists in the bureaucracy', *Cambridge Quarterly of Healthcare Ethics*, 2005, 14, pp 379–384.

speaking mainly of the United States but much of what he says applies also to the United Kingdom and other Western countries. His main point concerns the way in which bioethics has become detached from the academic subjects which gave rise to it and has become a kind of advice provider to the bureaucracies which fund it. He writes:

> As American bioethics has grown, it has developed into a self-contained, semi-professional entity whose place in the bureaucratic structures which house it has become distinct – both from the traditional academic disciplines from which it emerged and from the clinical disciplines that it has sometimes aspired to resemble.[7]

What this means is that 'the duties, allegiances, professional identities of bioethicists will be shaped by the institutions in which they are employed'. The crucial point for our present purpose – which is to highlight the need for the critical function of philosophy – is that '[b]ioethicists will probably produce even fewer critiques of the biomedical enterprise as a whole. They will be more likely to produce arguments about how to make the system better, rather than to challenge the system itself'.[8] One consequence of this is that '[b]ioethics is no longer just about saying "no" to technology. It is often about saying an enthusiastic "yes" '[9] The point we wish to take out of Elliott's article is that, in addition to the advice-giving and regulatory roles of such bureaucratic bodies as the Ethics Committee of the British Medical Association (BMA) or the General Medical Council (GMC) or their counterparts in other countries, it is important that the critical function of philosophy should be retained. It is important sometimes to stand back from actual professional practices and consider their assumptions and the kinds of arguments they employ. This we shall try to do in Chapters 2–4.

Literature and the fine arts: the supplementary functions

For expository purposes we drew a basic distinction between the critical function of the medical humanities (contributed mainly by philosophical disciplines) and what we have termed the supplementary (contributed mainly by literature and the fine arts including architecture). Let us turn now to the supplementary function. Perhaps we might begin with a very brief headline survey of the history of bioethics.

Ethical considerations have governed medical practice from the earliest; Hippocrates is remembered as much for his 'Oath' as for his writings on

---

7 Ibid., p 380.
8 Ibid., p 381.
9 Ibid.

diagnoses and treatments. We need not concern ourselves here with scholarly investigations into authenticity and authorship, for the point is the general one that the practice of medicine has always been associated with ethical considerations. Yet in the period from Hippocrates until the 1950s medical ethics remained largely static, and its main tenets would have been quite recognisable to Hippocrates – that the doctor should not harm the patient but should always seek the patient's best interests, that the doctor should maintain confidentiality, should not take a sexual interest in patients, should not procure abortions, and in various ways should show solidarity with the profession. It is certainly possible to find writers on medicine over its long history who developed these points or saw other aspects of medical ethics.[10] But as a broad generalisation it is not unfair to say that medical ethics with the above characteristics – a small number of ethical principles plus professional etiquette – sufficed for the regulation of medical practice until after the Second World War. The activities and concerns we now associate with medical ethics did not really get going until the 1960s.

Various causes contributed to the development of this area of public and medical concern. One was certainly the abuses of medical research during the Nazi regime. Concerns here culminated in various 'Declarations' and new codes – for example, the Declaration of Geneva and the Declaration of Helsinki. A second cause was the appearance of new and more effective medical treatments. It became possible for doctors actually to prolong life with surgery and new drugs. Naturally that gave rise to the question of whether it is always appropriate to do so. A third cause is the rise of what very broadly we might call 'consumerism'. The general public, at least in the West, wished to be better informed and consulted about the medical treatments they were offered. For two thousand years it was thought to be sufficient if the doctor made his own judgement about what was in the best interests of the patient and was allowed to proceed along these lines without even informing the patient of what was proposed. But increasingly from the 1960s the patient's informed consent was required for medical treatment.

Despite these developments however it is true to say that medical ethics or bioethics remains a narrow discipline. Basically it accepts medical practice as a given and attempts to regulate it. For instance, surgical developments from the 1960s gave rise to the practice of organ transplant, and such has been the success of this that there is now a widespread shortage of human organs for transplant. One way to try to alleviate this shortage has been to attempt to transplant organs from animals, mainly pigs, to human beings. Pharmaceutical companies have invested millions of pounds in this research into 'xenotransplantation'. The reaction of governments has been to set up committees of medical lawyers,

10 Baker R, Porter D and Porter R (eds), *The Codification of Medical Morality: Historical and Philosophical Studies of the Formalization of Western Medical Morality in the 18th and 19th Centuries*, vols 1 and 2, 1993, Dordrecht/Boston: Kluwer Academic Publishers.

ethicists and scientists to monitor and regulate such research and possible treatments. The same reaction is to be found in respect to all major medical advances such as genetic testing, human stem cell research, cloning and 'artificial' reproduction. Where there is uncertainty of an ethical sort a committee is established with the aim of producing regulations based on a consensus. This is Carl Elliott's point that in such circumstances the bioethicists on the committee 'will be more likely to produce arguments about how to make the system better, rather than to challenge the system itself'.[11]

Now this forensic approach to problems of medical ethics is rightly regarded as basic: there can be no substitute for the rules, rights and duties, guidelines and codes used to regulate medicine. But the forensic approach is the better with some supplementation — its mesh is too wide to catch some of the issues which are reasonably within the sphere of the ethical. Adam Smith draws a distinction between what he terms the 'good style' of ethics and its 'grammar'.[12] These two aspects of ethics he thinks are written about by two different styles of moralist. The first group includes Cicero and Aristotle (no less). He says of them that

> by the vivacity of their descriptions they inflame our natural love of virtue... by the justness as well as delicacy of their observations they may often help both to correct and to ascertain our natural sentiments with regard to the propriety of conduct, and suggesting many nice and delicate attentions, form us to a more exact justness of behaviour than what, without such instruction, we should have been apt to think of.... The second set of moralists...among whom we may count...all those who in this and the preceding century have treated of what is called natural jurisprudence do not content themselves with characterizing in this general manner that tenor of conduct which they would recommend to us, but endeavour to lay down exact and precise rules for the direction of every circumstance of our behaviour.[13]

If we translate or transfer Smith's distinction into the present context we might say that the codes and guidelines which regulate medical practice are its grammar, its foundations in justice, whereas the medical humanities, especially literature and the fine arts, can provide its good style; they are able to suggest 'many nice and delicate attentions'.[14]

Yet this 'good style' or 'supplement' is not just an optional extra. Many of the complaints which patients make about doctors involve issues which have slipped

11 Elliott, op cit., p 381.
12 Smith, Adam, *The Theory of Moral Sentiments* (1776), Raphael DD and Macfie AL (eds), 1974, Oxford: Clarendon Press, pp 327–330.
13 Ibid., pp 328–329.
14 Ibid.

through the loose mesh of regulation. For example, letters or telephone calls or interviews can leave vulnerable patients feeling stunned. When taxed with this, doctors are often surprised, having no idea of the effect their words were likely to have. Awareness of the nuances of spoken or written language is one of the supplementary contributions which literature can make to ethics.

A doctor who is accused of rudeness by a patient might well offer an excuse that he/she was overworked and over-tired. And certainly 'burn-out' and high suicide rates among doctors are above the national average. The cure for this may be the taking of some interest in the arts. Doctors not infrequently see themselves as acting in a supererogatory manner (an issue we shall discuss in Chapter 2). But perhaps they might be better doctors if they were able to come across to their patients as balanced human beings, rather than as supererogatory martyrs. It is a matter of ethical importance that patients feel they can trust their doctor. Trust is encouraged if patients feel that apart from their skills doctors are human beings like themselves.

This point is brought out in a recent study of doctors' communication with patients with breast cancer. The study indicated that patients valued a 'relationship' with the doctor – they wanted to be seen as individuals. 'The perception of being regarded as an individual was communicated in several ways. Non-verbal cues included eye contact, smiling and touching. The simplest verbal strategy was for the patient to be told she was special. The most common strategy was brief conversation unrelated to disease.'[15]

Being a balanced human being requires a broad outlook on life. But medicine tends to be an inward-looking discipline. There are many reasons for this. For instance, the nature of medical education encourages a certain ethos. Students rapidly become 'medical students' and form friendships mainly with other medical students. Bonding is encouraged. Now this process of professionalisation is in many ways a good thing in view of the many unpleasant aspects of medical life. But it has the disadvantage that the entire personality of the doctor becomes colonised by the medical ethos. Leaving aside the burn-out issues we have mentioned we may also find that the doctor's perspective is narrowed to the extent that the patient's 'best interests' become the patient's best *medical* interests. The doctor may then genuinely believe that (for example) it is in the patient's best interests to undergo yet another round of chemotherapy when the evidence of effectiveness is less than 15 per cent. Of course it might be said that a patient can always refuse the treatment. But a doctor committed to medical best interests might well provide the information in a manner that would encourage acceptance. A broader humane perspective might enable a doctor to see the patient's situation in a more balanced way. Literature is one means of broadening a perspective and can provide a supplement for the ethics of regulation.

15 Wright EB, Holcombe C and Salmon P, 'Doctors' communication of trust, care and respect in breast cancer: a qualitative study', *British Medical Journal*, 2004. 328, pp 864–867.

Some history: Dr John Gregory

The idea that the humanities can have a beneficial influence on the way a doctor approaches his/her discipline is by no means a new one. An excellent illustration of the points we have been making is provided by the writings of the eighteenth-century physician Dr John Gregory. In his lecture on 'The Duties and Qualifications of a Physician' Dr Gregory writes:

> In the prosecution of this subject, I shall, in the first place, consider what kind of genius, understanding and temper naturally fit a man for being a physician. In the second place, what are the moral qualities to be expected of him in the exercise of his profession, viz. the obligation to humanity, patience, attention, discretion, secrecy and honour, which he lies under to his patients. In the third place, I shall take notice of the decorums and attentions peculiarly incumbent on him as a physician and which tend most effectually to support the dignity of the profession; as likewise the general propriety of his manners, his behaviour to his patients, to his brethren, and to apothecaries. In the fourth place, I shall particularly describe that course of education which is necessary for qualifying a physician to practise with success and reputation; and shall, at the same time, mention those ornamental qualifications expected from the physician as a gentleman of a liberal education, and without which it is difficult to support the honour and rank of the profession.[16]

If we ignore the education of the physician it may be permissible to divide Gregory's other points into two, which he himself refers to as 'the exertion of genius' and the 'exercise of humanity'.[17] Let us consider 'the exertion of genius'. Gregory gives a surprisingly up-to-date account of 'the exertion of genius', by which he means the knowledge-base or evidence-base of medicine. 'Perhaps no profession requires so comprehensive a mind as medicine'.[18] Indeed, Gregory explicitly acknowledges the importance of basing medical knowledge on evidence. He writes:

> Among the infinite variety of facts and theories with which his [the physician's] memory has been filled in the course of a liberal education, it is his business to make a judicious separation between those founded in nature and experience, and those which owe their birth to ignorance, fraud, or the capricious systems of a heated and deluded imagination. He will likewise find it necessary to distinguish between important facts, and such as, though

16 Gregory, John, *Lectures on the Duties and Qualifications of a Physician*, 1772, London: W Strahan and T Cadell, p 11.
17 Ibid., p 10.
18 Ibid., p 12.

they may be founded in truth, are notwithstanding trivial or utterly useless to the main ends of his profession. Supposing all these difficulties surmounted, he will find it no easy matter to apply his knowledge to practice.[19]

In this passage Gregory is asserting the importance of establishing a secure evidence-base (he distinguishes 'nature and experience' from 'ignorance and fraud'), of distinguishing 'important facts' from 'trivial' ones, and of being able to 'apply his [the physician's] knowledge to practice' (or in the clinic). In all this, Gregory is stating with admirable brevity the points much stressed in contemporary medical research.

More relevant to our present concerns is what Gregory calls 'the exercise of humanity'. Gregory writes:

> In the second place, medicine presents a no less extensive field for the exercise of humanity. A physician has numberless opportunities of giving that relief to distress, which is not to be purchased by the wealth of India. This, to a benevolent mind, must be one of the greatest pleasures. But besides the good which a physician has it often in his power to do, in consequence of skill in his profession, there are many occasions that call for his assistance as a man, as a man who feels for the misfortunes of his fellow-creatures. In this respect he has many opportunities of displaying patience, good-nature, generosity, compassion, and all the gentler virtues that do honour to human nature.[20]

It is clear that by 'the exercise of humanity' Gregory means the exercise of moral virtues. He writes:

> I come now to mention the moral qualities peculiarly required in the character of a physician. The chief of these is humanity; that sensibility of heart which makes us feel for the distresses of our fellow-creatures, and which of consequence incites us in the most powerful manner to relieve them. Sympathy produces an anxious attention to a thousand little circumstances that may tend to relieve the patient; an attention which money can never purchase; hence the inexpressible comfort of having a friend for a physician. Sympathy naturally engages the affection and confidence of a patient, which in many cases is of the utmost consequence to his recovery.[21]

Three points are worth stressing in Gregory's account of the humane physician. First, the qualities he mentions are virtues or good dispositions. In the

---

19 Gregory, John, *Lectures on the Duties and Qualifications of a Physician*, 1772, London: W Strahan and T Cadell, p 6.
20 Ibid., p 8.
21 Ibid., p 19.

field of medical ethics there has been an explosion of what is called 'virtue theory'. The view is that 'ethics' requires doctors to have a range of virtues. It is clear however that Gregory was aware in the eighteenth century of the importance of virtues to the humane physician.

Second, the virtues mentioned by Gregory are not all 'moral' virtues in the narrow sense. He realised that there is more to the humane attitude than what we have called 'regulatory medical ethics'. Thus, he mentions 'good-nature', 'gentleness', 'flexibility' and 'apparent cheerfulness'. Gregory is surely correct in this. There is more to the humane attitude than the ethics of regulation. Third, Gregory does *also* see the importance of a framework of regulatory ethical rules or principles. He writes:

> A physician, by the nature of his profession, has many opportunities of knowing the private characters and concerns of the families in which he is employed. Besides what he may learn from his own observation, he is often admitted to the confidence of those, who perhaps think they owe their life to his care. He sees people in the most disadvantageous circumstances, very different from those in which the world views them; – oppressed with pain, sickness, and low spirits. In these humiliating situations, instead of wonted cheerfulness, evenness of temper, and vigour of mind, he meets with peevishness, impatience, and timidity. Hence it appears how much the character of individuals, and the credit of families may sometimes depend on the discretion, secrecy, and honour of a physician. Secrecy is particularly requisite where women are concerned. Independent of the peculiar tenderness with which a woman's character should be treated, there are certain circumstances of health, which, though in no respect connected with her reputation, every woman, from the natural delicacy of her sex, is anxious to conceal; and, in some cases, the concealment of these circumstances may be of consequence to her health, her interest, and to her happiness.[22]

Hence he is concerned with the rule of keeping confidentiality which, of course, goes back to the Hippocratic Oath. He clearly distinguishes the imperatival nature of the rule from the more flexible display of the humane attitude. As he says,

> Independent of the peculiar tenderness with which a woman's character should be treated...there are certain circumstances of health...every woman...is anxious to conceal.[23]

In sum, then, there is much to be said in favour of retaining Gregory's distinction between the 'genius' of the profession and its 'humanity'. Under the

22 Ibid., p 26.
23 Ibid.

first heading we can place the scientific evidence base, the clinical and the communication skills which are essential to the good doctor, and under the second heading we can include both the regulatory aspects of ethics and the 'gentler' virtues which we regard as a necessary supplement. Our argument is that the 'gentler virtues' are highlighted by the humanities, especially literature.

There is a danger to which any doctor writing about the nature of medical practice may succumb, and that is offering an elevated account of it which is easy for outsiders to ridicule. Once again, Gregory is aware of the danger. He writes:

> Physicians, considered as a body of men, who live by medicine as a profession, have an interest separate and distinct from the honour of the science. In pursuit of this interest, some have acted with candour, with honour, with the ingenious and liberal manners of gentlemen. Conspicuous of their own worth, they disdained every artifice, and depended for success on their real merit. But such men are not the most numerous in the profession. Some impelled by necessity, some stimulated by vanity, and others anxious to conceal ignorance, have had recourse to various mean and unworthy acts to raise their importance among the ignorant, who are always the most numerous part of mankind. Some of these arts have been an affectation of mystery in all their writings and conversations relating to their profession, an affectation of knowledge, inscrutable to all, except the adepts in the science; an air of perfect confidence in their own skill and abilities; and a demeanour solemn, contemptuous, and highly expressive of self-sufficiency. These arts, however well they might succeed with the rest of mankind, could not escape the censure of the more judicious, nor elude the ridicule of men of wit and humour. The stage, in particular, has used freedom with the professors of the salutary art; but it is evident, that most of the satire is levelled against the particular notions, or manners of individuals, and not against the science itself.[24]

Gregory is here stressing the importance of self-awareness or self-perception and this is another aspect of the balanced individual. But Gregory is not claiming that self-awareness, lack of pomposity and the gentler virtues are substitutes for the regulatory role of medical ethics. But they are supplements, and they can be supplied by the medical humanities, especially literature, as we shall see in Chapter 6.

A mind of one's own: independence, individuality and personal development

We have claimed that philosophy, as a second-order critical activity, can make a contribution to medical ethics by examining arguments, assumptions and

---

24 Gregory, John, *Lectures on the Duties and Qualifications of a Physician*, 1772, London: W Strahan and T Cadell, p 4.

methods. We have also claimed that the medical humanities such as literature can provide an important supplement to the regulatory function of forensic medical ethics. We shall sum this up by saying that the humanities enable us to develop a mind of our own. What does it mean to have 'a mind of your own'?[25] There are two elements in it which we shall call independence of mind and individuality of mind.

Independence of mind is shown in the kind of support and justification a person might offer for a belief. In more detail, independent-minded persons exhibit three qualities. First, their beliefs, medical and otherwise, are based on *evidence* or *argument*. This sweeping statement must of course be qualified and developed. Different types of evidence are needed in different sorts of situation, and sometimes, if the matter is very technical, we ourselves may not be able to state the evidence, and may need to rely on the word of experts. But even here we may be able to assess whether the person really is an expert in that field, or whether the 'evidence' is really just ideology or pharmaceutical hard-selling.

Second, independent-mindedness requires an ability *to understand* what we claim to have in our minds. For example, suppose someone is told that the structure of the DNA molecule consists of a double helix. How does he make that statement 'his own'? He would need to understand the claim in several different senses. Thus he would need to understand some concepts of biochemistry and some concepts of mathematics and how they might be linked. He might also need to understand the wider context and significance of the claim. Understanding here is clearly something we have more or less of, and to the extent that we have it we are more or less independent-minded. Understanding is important in medical ethics, in two ways. First, the technical issues are often complex and easy to misrepresent. Second, the human issues can be difficult to understand by those who have not been in the situation themselves.

Third, we are independent-minded if we are *critical* of the evidence or argument for a belief. We may come to hold that the evidence is insufficient, or of the wrong kind, or that the side-effects or the costs of the evidence-based treatment have not been mentioned. Critical appraisal of appropriate evidence is indeed one of the characteristics common to any respectable academic discipline, and typically goes on at lunchtime meetings in hospitals and postgraduate centres. Independence of mind is something which is developed by the critical function of philosophy.

Individuality of mind concerns differences in the content of people's beliefs, rather than the evidence or rational basis of belief. The beliefs of an independent mind purport to be well founded, whereas those of a mind with individuality purport to be distinctive, unusual, original, challenging, idiosyncratic or unique.

---

25 Downie RS, 'Personal and professional development: a mind of one's own', *Clinical Medicine*, 2004, 4, pp 332–335.

Three features are characteristic of individuality of mind. First, it shows itself in an *unusual direction* of interest. The person with the individual mind may know about unusual or less commonly known things, such as the science of John of Norfolk, or the songs of troubadours. Moreover, specialised or unusual directions of interest can be displayed just as much in the sciences or medicine as in the arts and humanities.

Second, the person of individual mind may have a greater *depth of knowledge* on some subject. He/she may concentrate to the point of obsession on just one area of knowledge or skill – in this direction lies the specialised surgeon, or the medieval historian. Sometimes this kind of knowledge is dismissed by saying, 'He knows more and more about less and less'. But a highly specialised direction of knowledge and skills is obviously a good thing. In medicine we require the specialists, say for treating the back of the eye, as well as the generalists. As a gesture towards allowing individuality of mind to develop, the medical curriculum in the United Kingdom now allows Special Study Modules (SSMs) or Student-Selected Components (SSCs), in which students can follow their interests in science, medicine or the humanities through short periods of in-depth studies which may lie in unusual directions of interest.

The third aspect of individuality of mind shows itself in a variety of ways. Perhaps it is best expressed by the term *lateral thinking*, a term which was introduced by a former Lecturer in Medicine at the University of Oxford – Edward de Bono.[26] The main point made by de Bono is that we tend to see the world, including the areas of it which constitute our professional lives, in terms of certain patterns or groupings. But these are only some of the many possible patterns or groupings. The person who has a disposition to lateral thinking is the person who can break away from the familiar patterning of the world and suggest new ways of looking at things, or non-routine ways of behaving. Intellectually, lateral thinking may emerge as a sceptical disposition towards received opinion and ways of doing things. This is highly relevant to ethics.

Lateral thinking of the kind relevant to individuality of mind is illustrated in Wittgenstein's anecdote about the fly in the bottle.[27] The fly buzzes against the glass and cannot escape, but there is not a stopper on the bottle. If the fly changes direction it can escape. The person of individual mind who thinks laterally can show the fly the way out of the bottle!

The term 'originality' can be used for certain forms of this kind of individuality. It is of course above all in the arts that it can be shown, although it can also be shown in science, medicine and philosophy. Some artists reveal their originality in their ability to make us see the familiar in a new light. For example, Wordsworth and Coleridge, in their Preface to the *Lyrical ballads* of 1803, said that in their poetry they intended to remove the film of familiarity

26 De Bono E, *Lateral Thinking*, 1990, London: Penguin Books.
27 Wittgenstein, L, *Philosophical Investigations*, 1953, Oxford: Blackwell, paragraph 309.

which everyday experience spreads over things.[28] The person of individual mind can make us appreciate afresh what we already know. For example, the arts might help a doctor to look afresh at patients, when after some years they have acquired an anonymous sameness.

Another sort of originality can consist of the creation of new ideas or styles. For example, Wagner and Schoenberg might be said to be great innovators in music, Galileo and Einstein in science, Harvey and Bernard in medicine, and Kant and Wittgenstein in philosophy. The point is that whether the innovation is in science, medicine, the arts or philosophy, the result is the same – the human *imagination* is enriched and we can see the world in fresh ways.[29]

It is, of course, important that the criteria for independence of mind, and for individuality of mind, should be used only where it is appropriate and in appropriate ways. For example, the Dean of Medicine who asks, 'How can you measure the benefit for a doctor of reading novels?' is looking for the wrong sort of evidence. It is not that the humanities ought to be immune from evaluation, but anyone who uses the language of measurement about novels does not understand measurement or novels. Equally, it is important that individuality of mind should at the very least be constrained by the criteria for independence of mind; we can ignore the individuality of the flat-earthers. And of course in its behavioural aspects individuality can become disruptive of good teamwork.

What are the connections between independence of mind and individuality of mind and personal and professional development or continuing medical education? The classic text which guides us here is JS Mill's essay, *On liberty*.[30] In Chapter 3 of this essay Mill tells us that the end of man is 'the highest and most harmonious development of his powers to a complete and consistent whole'.[31] These powers are developed by pursuing ends which are rich and complex and therefore suitable for bringing out the potentialities within us. In more detail, Mill argues that we all have what he calls a 'distinctive human endowment', which can be developed. The qualities which he thinks make up the endowment are: 'the human faculties of perception, judgment, discriminative feeling, mental activity, and even moral preference which are exercised only in making a choice'.[32] We might say that these qualities are distinctive of what can be called the 'generic human self'. These qualities, Mill holds, can be developed, and it is incumbent on us as human beings to exercise choice to develop them. It is our claim that developing this endowment and developing independence of mind are one and the same, and are one essential component in personal and professional development.

28 Coleridge ST, *Biographia Literaria* (1803) 1949, London: Dent, Chapter 14.
29 Downie RS, Science and imagination in the age of reason', *Journal of Medical Ethics: Medical Humanities*, 2001, 27, 2, pp 58–63.
30 Mill JS, *On Liberty* (1859) 1969, London: Collins, Chapter 3.
31 Ibid., p 187.
32 Ibid.

Individuality of mind by contrast is concerned with the development of at least some of those qualities and interests which are peculiar to a given person. Now the development of those idiosyncratic qualities will make use of the generic features of the human endowment, the features on Mill's list, but will turn them in a direction unique to a given individual person. Mill argues for this in a second and complementary strand to his thinking. When the second strand is uppermost he stresses the importance of the conscious and discriminatory pursuit of objectives which express authentically one's own uniqueness as a person. According to this strand in his thought, it is important to 'be oneself' as opposed to 'conforming to custom'. A custom may be a good one, he says, but 'to conform to custom merely as custom does not educate or develop [in a person] any of the qualities which are the distinctive endowment of a human being'.[33]

Independence of mind and individuality of mind will both therefore find their ultimate justification in self-development (or personal and professional development), but in different ways: independence of mind leads to the development of our distinctive human endowment, the generic aspects of the self, whereas individuality of mind leads to the development of our personal uniqueness, our individuality, the idiosyncratic aspects of the self. The two aspects of development are necessary and sufficient for total self-development.

In conclusion, we should like to take a few examples of aspects of medicine which can be challenged, using the distinctions we have drawn. The first example concerns the current medical obsession with randomised trials – the gold standard. Observational or descriptive studies are depicted as second-rate, or 'anecdotal' until they are validated by a trial. This position is delightfully mocked by Gordon Smith and Jill Pell in the *British Medical Journal*.[34] They point out that the evidence that people do better with a parachute when they jump out of an aeroplane is only anecdotal! It should also be noted that while doctors seem to be fixated on the evidence of randomised trials, the term 'evidence' is used in many other ways in other respectable disciplines. A laboratory scientist, or a detective, or a lawyer look at evidence in ways which might be illuminating for medical research, were it not for the current obsession.[35] Indeed, even if the generalisations which emerge from the trial are valid, there remains the problem of how their results should be applied to individual patients. For example, for any of a number of good reasons, a given patient may refuse consent for the best evidence-based treatment and prefer another.[36] In such cases it might be good medical practice to harness the placebo

33 Mill JS, *On Liberty* (1859) 1969, London: Collins, Chapter 3.
34 Smith GCS and Pell JP, 'Parachute use to prevent death and major trauma to gravitational challenge: systematic review of randomised trials', *British Medical Journal*, 2003, 327, pp 1459–1461.
35 Downie RS, Macnaughton, Jane, *Clinical Judgement: Evidence in Practice*, 2000, Oxford: Oxford University Press, pp 8–15.
36 Ibid., pp 51–60.

effect of the patient's beliefs, rather then persist with what the evidence is alleged to say. A more critical, not to say sceptical, turn of mind is what is needed here. There is more to independence of mind than citing trials.

Turning now to medical education at all levels, we would argue that it can be impeded by the ideas that every lecture or presentation requires aims and objectives, visual aids and bullet points. This produces a dreary sameness. Obviously, visual aids may be needed for diagrams or tables, but surely every point in every presentation does not require visual aids. Indeed, to an outsider, it seems fairly comic that during a period when medical education and the public are rightly insisting on the importance of communication and listening for good patient care, doctors themselves seem unable to give or to follow a talk without visual aids. The teachers one remembers are the ones with the individual or even the eccentric approach; they enrich one's imagination as well as develop one's knowledge. Anecdotes and enthusiasm are more memorable than bullet points.[37] The power of stories over statistics has recently been examined in the *British Medical Journal* by Thomas Newman, writing from the hard-nosed end of medicine as an epidemiologist and biostatistician.[38]

As far as communicating with patients is concerned, individuality comes into its own; there is no such thing as scientific expertise in human relationships. Certainly, some people are better than others at communicating, but this is not because they have acquired some mysterious 'skill' but because they are more authentic human beings. Whether the doctor is gruff or charming, patients can distinguish the voice of an honest and sincere individual from that of someone who has been on a course. As Mill puts it: 'It really is of importance not only what men do, but also what manner of men they are that do it.'[39] This of the first importance from the ethical point of view.

The growth of the medical humanities has provided a partial remedy for this grey uniformity. For what the humanities can do above all is bring out the multiplicity of ways in which one human being can be in a relationship with another, or in which birth, life and death can be viewed. In other words, the humanities can help medicine to get away from the idea that in education, in communication, or in treatment, one size fits all. Again, Mill puts the point in a striking way. He writes that human nature

> Is not a machine to be built after a model...but a tree, which requires to grow and develop itself on all sides, according to the tendency of the inward forces which make it a living thing.[40]

37 Ibid.
38 Newman TN, 'The power of stories over statistics', *British Medical Journal*, 2003, 327, pp 1424–1427.
39 Mill JS, op cit., p 188.
40 Ibid.

Continual challenges to the false finalities of medical or educational orthodoxy are necessary if a discipline is not to stagnate, and it is those with individuality of mind who are most likely to mount such challenges.

Means or ends?

We have made a case for the kind of light which medical humanities can throw on medicine in general and medical ethics in particular. Does this mean that the humanities are merely a means, are simply instrumental to the broader aims of ethics?

A humanist is likely to adopt the position that the humanities are worthwhile for their own sake. The humanist could cite Aristotle who develops a distinction between activities which are justified by their instrumentality in bringing about further ends, and the highest good, a good-in-itself, an intrinsic good or a 'final end'.[41] One criterion for belonging to that category is that the activity in question must be totally useless! Aristotle's argument is that if an activity is useful its justification is in terms of what it produces, so it cannot be good-in-itself. It follows that the highest good must be good in and for itself and not for its usefulness. Now Aristotle places 'contemplation' or *theoria* (which means something like pure philosophy) in that category (although not ethics, which for Aristotle is a guide to a good life). It is plausible to place the arts in the same category as contemplation.

In the light of this distinction between an instrumental good – something good as a means – and an intrinsic good – something good as an end – what can we say about the place of the humanities in medical education? We have so far categorised the aims of humanities teaching and their evaluation in terms of an apparent instrumentality. Does that mean that the literature, drama and so on in these courses are not worthwhile for their own sake?

In her contribution to the first number of *Medical Humanities* Dr Jane Macnaughton distinguishes between the instrumental uses of the humanities in medical education and their non-instrumental aspects.[42] She mentions three of what she considers the non-instrumental values: broadening education horizons, for example by introducing students to alternative ways of seeing the world; assisting in the personal development of students and doctors, and by the introduction of a 'counterculture'. We might also add the ability to understand human beings and their interactions in a irreducibly qualitative way, an ability which can be developed by appreciation of the arts, as we shall argue later (p 86ff). The points Dr Macnaughton is making are that certain humanities studies are worthwhile for their own sake but should be included in medical education despite the fact, or even because of the fact, that they are non-instrumental.

41 Aristotle, *Nicomachean Ethics*, 1942, New York: Random House, 1097a–b.
42 Macnaughton J, 'The humanities in medical education: context, outcomes and structures', *Journal of Medical Ethics: Medical Humanities*, 2000, 26, pp 23–30.

Now in the *Journal of Medical Ethics* Professor Gillon has written a very generous editorial welcoming the appearance of *Medical Humanities*.[43] In this he takes Dr Macnaughton to task over her instrumental and non-instrumental distinction. He is not denying the intrinsic value of the arts and humanities; indeed, he is asserting that they have such an intrinsic value. He is making two points: that the humanities should not be included in medical education unless they have an instrumental value, but that *in addition* to their intrinsic value the humanities do in fact have an instrumental value for medical education. And he goes on to claim that Dr Macnaughton's three examples of the non-instrumental values of the arts for doctors are in fact 'surely open to interpretation as being highly "instrumentally" valuable (quite apart from their intrinsic value) in the simple sense of being likely to produce better doctors and therefore appropriately introduced in medical education for that purpose'. He then goes on to show how this is the case in her three types of examples. Professor Gillon's argument seems plausible, but only if we grant him two assumptions, that we can stretch the meaning of 'instrumental' until it is really very thin, and that something can be at one and the same time instrumentally good and a 'final end'.

If we take his first assumption we can see the 'thinness' of his use of the concept of instrumentality when he says that something is 'instrumental' if it conduces to human flourishing or to a better understanding of the outside world or to personal development. This application of 'instrumental' is far removed from baseline applications of the concept, as when we say that a hacksaw was instrumental in the prisoner's escape or that the headmaster was instrumental in influencing the pupil's choice of career. The baseline use of 'instrumental' as illustrated in these typical examples has two features: it implies that there is a causal connection between the instrument and what its use leads to, and it implies that the instrument has no place in the end brought about by its use. Neither of these conditions holds when we say, for example, that the appreciation of the arts conduces to human development. The term 'conduces' does not here indicate a causal connection, for a causal connection would imply that the appreciation of the arts was one thing and human development something different. The point is, however, that an appreciation of the arts is a necessary component part of the final end state of human development or educatedness. Hence, the language of instrumentality is misleading because of its associations with causality.

The second assumption is also debatable – that something can be causally instrumental and also a final end. We do not want to press this, however, partly because we do not wish to engage in a discussion about the interpretation of Aristotle, but mainly because we believe the entire controversy is misconceived; it seems real only because of the terminology in which it is stated. In short, we

---

43 Gillon R, 'Welcome to medical humanities – and why' (editorial), *Journal of Medical Ethics*, 2000, 26, pp 155–156.

wish to maintain that the distinction between an instrumental means and an intrinsic or final end is misleading.

Consider the following example, that of the creation of a painting. In painting a picture the artist will use assorted instrumental means, such as paint brushes, an easel and, say, a model. These are instruments whose justification lies in the final end or product – the painting. They are causally or productively connected with the painting and when it is completed they have no further part to play (unless, of course, the painting is being entered for the Turner Prize!). As instrumental means they are only contingently connected with the painting and are removed leaving no trace when it is finished. Is Professor Gillon saying that Dr Macnaughton's examples are instrumental in that sense? That literature and so on are only causally or contingently or extrinsically connected with producing a flourishing or educated human being and when they have done their work they will be removed like the easel, etc.? Obviously not! But that is the implication of using the terminology of instrumentality. What then should be said? Let us return to the example of the painting. The paint brushes, easel, model, etc. are instrumental means to the painting and have no part to play when it is completed. But the canvas, paint and the shapes created are also means to the creation of the painting. The difference is that they do have a necessary part in the finished product. We can therefore call them component (as distinct from instrumental) means to the painting. In Aristotle's terminology, the paint brushes, etc. are efficient causes of the painting whereas the canvas, paint and shapes are the material and formal causes of the painting, which itself is the final cause, the ultimate aim of the whole process.[44]

If we apply these distinctions to the question of the relationship between the humanities, the educated person and the good doctor it might be possible to take the following line. We can say that the enjoyment and practice of the humanities are activities worthwhile for their own sake and that they are means to creating an educated, developed and flourishing human life. But they are not instrumental in that process; they are essential components of such a life. To put it another way, we can say that part of what it *means* to be an educated developed human being is to able to enjoy at least some humanities for their own sake. Of course, that is only part of what it means; there are other essential components in the educated life, such as some appreciation of science, some interest in current affairs, some general curiosity, and so on. For the developed or flourishing life other aspects would also be needed, such as friends.

It is a separate question (often overlooked by those teaching the humanities) whether it is necessary for a good doctor to be an educated, developed human being. Perhaps doctors should simply be highly trained with highly specialised skills. Perhaps the ability to look before and after just gets in the way and distracts from the technical business of medicine. Certainly, some scientists have

---

44 Aristotle, *Physics*, 1941, New York: Random House, Book II, Chapter 3.

devoted their entire lives to pursuing a scientific or mathematical goal at the cost of every other side of their nature. This is one kind of good life from which we all benefit. Can the same be true of some doctors? Perhaps of some doctors in some specialities, but to the extent that doctors must deal with patients, with other human beings, they differ from scientists or mathematicians. This does not mean that they must be overflowing with compassion or empathy, because these are inward-looking concepts.

An analogy with playing an instrument might help. The good musician, giving a moving performance, is not brimming with emotion – he would lose the place if he were! His feelings are, as it were, in his fingers. So with the doctor; his gaze should be outward, away from himself. The doctor needs to be aware of what is on the whole likely to be good for this particular patient and requires sensitivity to the patient's wishes, consent or refusal and so on. In other words, the doctor needs to be able to make considered judgements, and a developed sense of judgement has a humanistic element as a component means. That is why we have argued that the humanities can offer an essential supplement to the regulatory function of medical ethics.

Conclusions

In this introductory chapter we have outlined in general terms what the medical humanities are and what they can contribute to medical ethics. In particular, we have suggested two main functions of the humanities, which we have called the critical and the supplementary. These do not, cannot, supplant the ongoing regulatory function of medical ethics but they can draw attention to neglected areas and new perspectives. Above all they comprise essential components in the educated, developed judgements of the humane doctor.

Part II

Medical humanities

The critical function of philosophy

Chapter 2

Moral philosophy and bioethics

Moral philosophy has been interpreted in various ways in its long history. In Chapter 1 we have accepted the dominant contemporary philosophical approach which depicts moral philosophy as a second-order activity concerned with uncovering and examining critically the assumptions we make and the arguments we use when as moral agents we engage in moral discussion and make practical decisions. Since bioethics from one point of view is simply ordinary first-order morality in a medical context its assumptions and arguments should be open to the second-order scrutiny of moral philosophy. Scrutiny of this critical kind will be the main aim of this chapter. Our hope is that out of this critical examination will come some positive suggestions for methods of argument which can be used by those who, unlike moral philosophers, actually face these problems. As a way into these questions we shall offer some observations on the recent history of bioethics.

Bioethics: recent history

Medical ethics or, as it is often called, bioethics or health-care ethics, is of recent origin. Of course it is possible to point to passages in Greek writing and to occasional writings thereafter which deal with issues which are recognisably bioethical. But there is little doubt that the rumblings which became the explosion of writing on bioethics were first clearly heard in the United States in the early 1960s. Something of the nature of that genesis is traced by Albert R Jonsen.[1] There are three features of Jonsen's account to which we should like to draw attention. First, bioethics arose out of public concerns, such as the selection of patients for chronic haemodialysis in Seattle in 1962. Second, the cultural context in which it was formed was what Jonsen calls 'American Moralism' – a species of Calvinism. Third, that particular sort of moralism encouraged the view that moral problems can be solved by applying principles whereby an ordering is given to complex medical scientific facts.

---

1 Jonsen AR, 'American moralism and the origin of bioethics in the United States', *Journal of Medicine and Philosophy*, 1991, 16, pp 113–130.

Granted these features of bioethics as it emerged in the 1960s, it is easy to explain its appeal to moral philosophers. Moral philosophy in the post-war period was criticised for being arid, trivial and removed from the moral problems of real life. It was treated by philosophers as no more than the application of logical techniques to the analysis of moral language. This approach to moral philosophy was shaped by two assumptions: that moral philosophy must be sharply distinguished from anything empirical, and that it had no bearing on any first-order moral issues. Some philosophers were (and are) happy with these assumptions, but others felt that, if moral philosophy were to justify its centrality in a humane education, then it would need to engage more fully with the moral problems of real life. Bioethics had an obvious appeal to moral philosophers looking for a role in the shaping of their culture: it had an obvious first-order relevance, and discussion was conducted in a manner familiar to moral philosophers – in terms of principles. It is against this background that we are to understand Stephen Toulmin's essay, 'How Medicine Saved the Life of Ethics'.[2]

It is worth noting here – although the points are of sociological rather than philosophical interest – that there are two other reasons which encouraged philosophers to become involved with bioethics. The first is that, increasingly from 1980, university departments were obliged to seek funding from outside sources, and it is easier to obtain funding for projects with an obvious practical relevance. The second is that doctors were themselves perplexed as to when to use the new technology which had been created, and were being challenged by patients and fund allocators to justify their decisions. They therefore appealed for help to philosophers in the belief (perhaps mistaken) that the latter had a special sort of expertise which would help them with their problems: if you need an analysis, then send the urine to the biochemist and the ethics to the philosopher.

Implicit in the second point is the ambiguity in the term 'ethics'. As we said in Chapter 1, there are three main senses of the term 'ethics'. First, 'ethics' can refer to that branch of philosophy also called 'moral philosophy'. Ethics in this sense is a theoretical, 'second-order' study of practical morality and its aim is to discover, analyse and relate to each other the fundamental concepts and principles of 'first-order' ordinary practical morality. This chapter is an essay in moral philosophy or 'ethics' in this sense.

The second main sense of 'ethics' is ordinary morality or value judgements as they are found in a professional context. This usage brings out the continuity between the moral problems of everyday life and those encountered in hospitals or other spheres of professional practice. Morality or ethics must be seen broadly as including the whole of value judgements about good and harm.

The third sense of 'ethics' refers to codes of procedures, guidelines and professional advice generally, or ethics narrowly conceived. Ethics in this sense

---

2 Toulmin S, 'How medicine saved the life of ethics', in Downie RS (ed), *Medical Ethics*, 1996, Aldershot and Brookfield USA: Dartmouth, Chapter 2.

is regulatory for the profession. Ethical regulation of this sort is important for it provides some of the principles which underlie professional activity across cultural and national boundaries.

It is worth stressing the difference between the second broad sense of ethics, as the value judgements of everyday life, and the narrow sense which refers simply to the specific items of professional regulation. For example, in the wide sense it is a moral or value judgement that a given patient, all factors considered, ought to be allowed home despite the risk of recurrence of her problem because this is her wish. But this decision does not raise a question of ethics narrowly conceived. It is because many health-care professionals assume that ethics is simply professional regulation (or restrict the scope of ethics to what is implied by its narrow sense) that they are unaware of the extent to which they are continually making moral or value judgements in the broad sense.

There are certainly technical – scientific and social – factors involved in deciding whether or not a given patient ought to be allowed home. But the decision about what in the end ought to be done goes beyond the technical and encompasses the professional's overall judgement as to what is for the total good of the patient. This overall, all things considered, judgement of the patient's good is what we mean by a moral or value judgement. One of the central aims of teaching ethics is to make the professional aware of the all-pervasive nature of such value judgements and the extent to which the professional's own values affect decisions. It is here that the humanities have a supplementary function in raising the awareness of professionals to the wider implications of their decisions.

Bioethics: the four principles

However that may be, the historical origins of bioethics and the keen interest which moral philosophers began to show in the issues gave rise to a certain way of conducting bioethical discussion known as the 'four-principles' approach. This approach was given its definitive form in a work by James F Childress and Tom L Beauchamp entitled *The Principles of Biomedical Ethics*, first published in 1976.[3] This approach dominated Anglo-American bioethics in the 1980s and has been stated, criticised and defended in a large work edited by Professor R Gillon. According to Gillon,

> the four principles plus scope approach claims that whatever your personal philosophy, politics, religion, moral theory or life stance, you will find no difficulty in committing yourself to four *prima facie* moral principles plus a concern for their scope of application. Moreover, these four principles plus attention to their scope of application can be seen to encompass most if not all

3 Childress JF and Beauchamp TL, *The Principles of Biomedical Ethics*, 1976, Oxford: Oxford University Press.

of the moral issues that arise in health care (I am increasingly inclined to believe that the approach can, if sympathetically interpreted, be seen to encompass *all* moral issues, not merely those arising in health care). The principles are respect for autonomy, beneficence, non-maleficence and justice. '*Prima facie*', a term introduced by the English philosopher W.D. Ross, means that the principle is binding unless it conflicts with another moral principle – if it does then you have to choose between them. The four principles approach does not claim to provide a method for doing so – a source of much dissatisfaction to those who suppose that ethics can be boiled down to a set of prioritized rules such that once the relevant information is fed into the algorithm (or computer) out will pop The Answer. What the principles plus scope *can* provide is a common set of moral commitments, a common moral language, and a common set of moral issues to be considered in particular cases, before coming to your own answer, using your preferred moral theory or other approach to choosing between these principles when they conflict.[4]

The problem of scope is that of deciding to whom or to what we owe these *prima facie* moral obligations. For example, supposing we agree that we have a *prima facie* moral obligation to benefit people, we still have the problem of deciding who these people are and how much they should be benefited. Again, we must respect autonomy, but are children or the mentally deranged autonomous? What counts as an autonomous agent? For example, if a 14 year-old boy refuses consent for a life-saving operation, does this count as an autonomous decision to be respected? If a 22 year-old (or indeed a 62 year-old) takes an overdose and leaves a note saying 'let me die', does this constitute an autonomous decision? These are issues of scope.

One question which will occur immediately to moral philosophers concerns the surprising absence of the principle of utility. The principle of justice, which is concerned with the distribution of resources, is included as one of the four because the distribution of resources is of current ethical concern. But utility also is (at least) a principle of distribution, so why not include it as a fifth principle?

Defenders of the four-principles approach can offer two replies. The first is to depict the principle of utility simply as an extended version of beneficence. Indeed, historically, this was the way in which utility entered moral philosophy. Francis Hutcheson, an early exponent of the principle of utility, took the view that there are three kinds of (in his language) 'benevolence':

> Sometimes it denotes a calm, extensive affection, or good-will towards all beings capable of happiness or misery: sometimes, a calm deliberate affection of the soul toward the happiness of smaller systems of individuals: such as patriotism ... parental affection. ... Or, the several kinds of particular

---

4 Gillon R (ed), *The Principles of Health Care Ethics*, 1994, Chichester: John Wiley, p xxii.

passions of love, pity, sympathy, congratulations.... The first sort is above all amiable and excellent: it is perhaps the sole moral perfection of some superior natures...[5]

On this line, then, utility is simply benevolence or beneficence with a universal scope.

The other reply is to think of the principle of utility as that which underlies the other four principles, which are then seen simply as expressions of utility in different circumstances. This line has the advantage of providing a (theoretical) decision-procedure when the four principles conflict. For some philosophers however it will have the general and well-known disadvantages of utilitarianism, such as the awkwardness of squaring utility and justice.

How are the four principles meant to work in the solving of bioethical problems? One way of seeing their function borrows from a general account of moral reasoning which was common in the period 1960–90 (although it goes back to Aristotle). In this view, one of the four principles either itself features as a major premise in a moral argument or gives rise to more specific principles (or rules) which do feature. For example, the general principle that we ought to respect the autonomy of patients might plausibly be said to give rise to specific principles, for instance, that we ought to obtain consent for treatment, ought not to deceive a patient about his/her condition, ought to maintain confidentiality and so on. The minor premise was thought to be factual, and the two premises combined were said to entail a practical conclusion. For example:

Major premise	It is wrong (one ought not) to deceive someone about a matter which is important for his future welfare
Minor premise	Failure to disclose to Mr X the full facts about his disease deceives him about a matter important for his future welfare
Conclusion	Therefore, it is wrong to fail to disclose to Mr X the full facts about his disease

In the passage cited (p 34) Gillon seems to be denying that this is how the principles feature in moral argument, preferring to see them as providing 'a common language'. Nevertheless, principles are often used as the major premises of moral arguments and were certainly used as such in medical ethics. Debate about such arguments can be directed at either the minor premise (i.e., the alleged facts) or at the major premise (the principle or rule derived from 'respect for autonomy').

As far as the minor premise is concerned, it might be maintained that the alleged facts are inaccurate, mistaken, incomplete, not fully known or that they

5 Hutcheson, Francis (1725), 'An inquiry concerning the original of our ideas of virtue or moral good', in Downie RS (ed), *Francis Hutcheson: Philosophical Writings*, 1994, London: Dent, Everyman Library, pp 88–95.

do not constitute a case to which the principle applies (scope). In the example given, it might be maintained that Mr X *was* told, or that he was too ill to take in what was said, or that it was not yet certain that he had the disease, or that a failure to go into the full facts (which he would not understand) did not really constitute a case of deception.

Dispute can also break out over the major premise (the principle). In the given case someone might defend the major premise by showing how it is derived from respect for autonomy which (it is hoped) we all accept. But an opponent might argue that disclosure of the full facts of his case might upset Mr X and so lead to a worsening of his disease, and that the principle of beneficence would forbid full disclosure. Once again there might be factual dispute over the minor premise – whether full disclosure would in fact lead to deterioration. Even if the facts were agreed, there might remain conflict between the two major premises: the principle of respect for autonomy and that of beneficence (or perhaps non-maleficence). This in turn might be resolved (if one were a utilitarian at heart) by arguing that greater general utility will result if doctors are believed to disclose the full facts rather than if they are thought sometimes to withhold information.

The four-principles approach to reasoning in bioethics, which reigned supreme for many years, is now heavily under attack from several quarters. These attacks on the four principles in bioethics are sometimes derived from, influenced or paralleled by, discussions of reasoning and, indeed, of philosophical method more generally. The syllogistic paradigm of practical reasoning handed down from Aristotle has been criticised along with the Kantian (or Calvinistic) idea of the centrality of principles in the moral life.

Before discussing the adequacy of this form of moral reasoning we shall consider a prior question – the *meaning* of three of the principles, as they are used in medical ethics – non-maleficence, beneficence and respect for autonomy. The fourth principle – justice – and its ambiguities will be discussed in Chapter 4 on political philosophy and public health. We shall discuss non-maleficence and beneficence together, as they are often lumped together as the duty of seeking the best interests of the patient.

Beneficence, supererogation and altruism

It is widely assumed in medical ethics circles that doctors are beneficent, and that the beneficent activities of medicine make it a morally good activity. Some writers go even further and maintain that doctors' duties are supererogatory, that is, that they exceed the requirements of duty. Others again maintain that 'medicine is one of the few spheres of human activity in which the purposes are unambiguously altruistic'.[6] These claims raise three questions. First, what is the difference between supererogation and altruism? Second, are the duties of

6 Editors, 'Looking back on the millennium in medicine', *New England Journal of Medicine*, 2000, 42, pp 42–49.

doctors supererogatory? Third, is 'beneficence' as used in medical ethics a moral category at all?

In a Symposium in the *Journal of Medical Ethics* Dr AC McKay maintains that the duties of the doctor are supererogatory,[7] and Drs Glannon and Ross maintain that doctors are not altruistic (although patients sometimes are).[8] What is the difference between supererogation and altruism?

Dr McKay offers a number of accounts of supererogation, of which the most persuasive is that by Onora O'Neill:

> [supererogation] is not required but is measured by that which is required; in supererogation the ordinary measures of duty rather than the categories of duty are exceeded.[9]

Drs Glannon and Ross seem to equate supererogation with altruism (for example, in their abstract, where they say that an act of altruism is supererogatory and is 'beyond obligation').

We think they are making a conceptual error here. The error arises from the ambiguity in the expression 'beyond obligation', which can mean 'in the category of obligation, but exceeding what strict obligation requires', or 'in a different moral category from obligation and perhaps (*pace* Kant) a morally superior one'. Our contention is that the first interpretation of 'beyond obligation' captures the meaning of 'supererogation', and the second captures 'altruism'. For example, if you are having a very busy morning in the clinic and decide to work through your coffee break in order to minimise patient waiting times you are showing supererogation. It is your professional duty to treat patients, but in missing your coffee break you are exceeding what strict duty requires, although you are still in the category of duty. On the other hand, if you decide to take a short coffee break and on your way to the canteen you encounter lost visitors looking for Ward G in the south east wing and you take some trouble to guide them to Ward G, thus missing your break, then you are altruistic. You had no duty to act in this way but were showing kindness at some inconvenience to yourself.

If that is a correct account of the difference between supererogation and altruism then (necessarily) doctors do not act altruistically in their professional work because in their work they are acting in the category of professional duty. Of course, they can act altruistically in what we might term the 'context' of their professional duties. For example, a general practitioner (GP) or family doctor, as a professional with public legitimacy, is entitled to sign a passport photograph as

7 McKay AC, 'Supererogation and the profession of medicine', *Journal of Medical Ethics*, 2002, 28, pp 70–73.
8 Glannon W and Ross LF, 'Are doctors altruistic?', *Journal of Medical Ethics*, 2002, 28, pp 70–73.
9 O'Neill O, *Towards Justice and Virtue*, 1996, Cambridge: Cambridge University Press.

being a 'true likeness'. This is not exactly a professional duty, but it could be seen as altruistic (although the halo is a little tarnished in that general practitioners are instructed by their professional body to charge £25 for carrying out this skilled task). But, as Glannon and Ross point out, patients do act altruistically when they agree (normally without payment) to participate in tests. Granted that doctors do not act altruistically in their mainstream professional lives the question posed by McKay remains: do they act in a supererogatory fashion? This is our second question.

When McKay argues that doctors' duties are supererogatory he is not claiming that doctors judge themselves to be supererogatory, far less that they all live up to the ideal. His point is that the duties they agree to and internalise when they join the profession are supererogatory as compared with the duties of most other occupations. He is claiming that the entire profession in comparison with (most) others is supererogatory. As far as we can understand the argument for this extreme thesis, it seems to have one central plank and a number of ancillary supports.

The central plank (on which Glannon and Ross also stand) is that the duties of medicine are fiduciary (stemming from the asymmetry of knowledge between the professional and the patient), and that doctors through an oath or covenant commit themselves to the open-ended service which follows from this kind of duty. Since McKay leans heavily on this claim about the oath or covenant it is a little surprising that he does not cite any evidence about the content of these oaths and does not consider the possibility that not all new doctors take such oaths. Indeed, such oaths as we have read are of a general and bland nature which do not in the least suggest the supererogatory. And even if we allow that the doctor–patient relationship is fiduciary it is still true that doctors are also in a contractual relationship with an employer to work so many sessions for a certain salary.

At this point McKay introduces one of his supporting arguments: that in medicine there is a dislocation between payment and service. Now of course that may simply not be true of some doctors working on a sessional basis. But even if it is true that in the British National Health Service (NHS) payment is fixed but commitment is open ended we do not have an argument for the supererogatory nature of medical duty. In the first place, medical salaries are very high and this is partly to reflect the open-ended nature of medical duties. Second, many occupations, which do not claim to be supererogatory, have a similar open-ended nature – for example, middle to senior positions in the civil service, or school teaching. Third, even if it is true that some doctors work longer hours than those in some other jobs, is this a good and admirable state of affairs? Doctors might be more humane if they attended fewer committees, took more time off, read a few novels and spent more time with family or friends. One might feel a little nervous if attended by a supererogating hero. (In fairness to doctors it might be said that many of them are aware of this, and would claim that hours spent in committee work is something imposed on them by the increasing bureaucracy of health care.)

A second supporting argument seems to be that physicians must take on the risk of failure with its accompanying guilt and fear of litigation. This argument splits into two: that outcomes in medicine are very uncertain despite the doctor's best endeavour, and that the shadow of the lawyer is at every bedside. The first strand worries doctors only because of their tendency to see themselves as heroes. Indeed, it is this tendency which has encouraged the growth of the second strand in that it has led the public to think that every medical failure is a case of negligence. In the present context, however, neither of these points puts medicine as a profession into the supererogatory category.

We should now like to comment on what seems to be the motivation behind these articles. McKay wishes to defend the profession in the UK context in which several unfortunate incidents have stirred up a campaign seemingly aimed at lowering the status of medicine in public esteem. McKay's method is to remind us that at least the ideal of medicine is supererogatory. On the other hand, Glannon and Ross wish to counter the growing tendency in the United States to depict doctors as altruistic (which they equate with being supererogatory). This they do by arguing that doctors perform the non-altruistic duties of beneficence to their patients.

Now we entirely agree with McKay on the unfairness of the current UK campaigns against doctors, but we think his attempted method of defence (even supposing it were more philosophically persuasive) is mistaken. One reason why the public has so eagerly turned against doctors is that for years the public has been subject to doctors' high opinions of themselves. McKay would now have us believe that, despite the fact that doctors have more interesting jobs than most people, more job security, and a higher salary, they are also, and by the very definition of the profession, morally superior. It doesn't take a psychologist to tell us that such a line of argument will not improve the standing of the profession in the eyes of the public.

Glannon and Ross begin their article by quoting from the *New England Journal of Medicine*, which asserted that 'medicine is one of the few spheres of human activity in which the purposes are unambiguously altruistic',[10] and from the American Board of Internal Medicine which stated that 'altruism is the essence of professionalism. The best interest of patients, not self interest, is the rule'.[11] And these quotations come from a country in which 14% of the population have no health care at all because they cannot afford to pay! If there is such a thing as professional self-deception it is illustrated by these quotations. Glannon and Ross do well to counter this smugness.

We shall now turn to our third question and take up a point assumed by Glannon and Ross, and almost universally assumed in the corpus of medical

10 See fn 6.
11 American Board of Internal Medicine, 'Project professionalism', 1998, Philadelphia: American Board of Internal Medicine, p 5.

ethics. It is that doctors (whether or not they are supererogatory) are at least beneficent. This is the most important of the three questions discussed in this section because it concerns the meaning or moral significance (if any) of the terms 'beneficence' and 'non-maleficence' (or best interests). We wish to assert that the widespread claim that doctors by being 'beneficent' or seeking the best interests of their patients are, by that very activity, morally good is either false or trivially true. Oddly, there is support here from Dr McKay. In taking up this issue we are returning to an old controversy between Professor RS Downie, the late Mr Paul Sieghart, and Professor Raanan Gillon.[12,13,14,15]

Our argument can be put simply. What is the basic professional duty of the doctor? It is to treat patients according to their best medical interests. This is not the moral duty of beneficence; it is simply a job description. Or if you want to insist that it is the moral duty of beneficence then it is one to be found in most jobs. The 'lollipop' or road crossings lady helps the children to cross the road to school. That is her job description. Call it the moral duty of beneficence if you like. The garage mechanic mends your puncture. Call it beneficence if you like, but it is just part of what he does for a living. Aristotle maintains that all actions aim at some good, but he doesn't mean a moral good.[16] The 'good' at which all actions aim is just the point of the action. In the case of medicine that point is the best medical interests of the patient. To pursue that aim does not put you in the ranks of the saints and martyrs, or even of the moderately morally good; it is just what you do for a living. Moral assessment applies to *how* doctors do their jobs, not to the bare fact that that is the job they do.

The significance of this argument, if it is accepted, is considerable. It has been a rarely questioned assumption that doctors, in pursuing the best interests of their patients or in acting towards them in a beneficent manner are showing morally good or indeed altruistic or supererogatory moral qualities. Yet every working person from the waitress to the bus driver might with as much justification claim that they aim at the best interests of whatever or whoever is the object of their activity. Why then should doctors make such a fuss about it, and claim a halo? The answer to this is complex, and we shall discuss the question in more detail in Chapter 5. But we can say now that at least part of the answer is the belief that medicine is a profession and professions have ethical characteristics which are lacking in trades, industries and business. We shall be

12 Sieghart P, 'Professions as the conscience of society', *Journal of Medical Ethics*, 1985, 11, pp 117–122.

13 Downie RS, 'Professional ethics', *Journal of Medical Ethics*, 1986, 12, pp 195–196.

14 Gillon R, 'Do doctors owe a special duty of beneficence to their patients?', *Journal of Medical Ethics*, 1986, 12, pp 171–173.

15 Downie RS, 'Professional ethics: further comments', *Journal of Medical Ethics*, 1986, 12, pp 195–196.

16 Aristotle, *Nicomachean Ethics*, Ross WD (trans), 1954, Oxford: Oxford University Press, Book 1, Chapter 1.

content in the present context with our claim that the moral meaning of beneficence, non-maleficence and best interests is less obvious than is usually supposed. Let us now examine the meaning of other terms associated with the 'four principles' – 'respect', 'autonomy' and the related term 'dignity'.

Autonomy, dignity and respect in Kant

The concept of autonomy (from the Greek, meaning 'self' + 'law', or having the capacity to be self-governing) has gradually become the dominant member of the four-principles quartet.[17] It is central to the moral philosophy of Kant, whose development of the concept has been the source of liberal ideas of morality from the eighteenth century to the present. The key idea in Kant is that moral imperatives (judgements about what we ought to do) derive from our own adoption of universal moral laws, which we apply to ourselves and others alike. The ability to be in this way self-governing Kant calls 'the autonomy of the will'. Moralities whose imperative force does not come from our own will, but from 'outside' the self, Kant calls 'heteronomous'. Examples of heteronomous moralities are those imposed by an external State, or majority social opinion, or a Church, or by our own empirical psychological desires (and here utilitarianism was very much in his sights).[18]

It is worth noting here, although we shall return to the point (p 116ff), that providing a treatment or a service purely because a patient desires it, may or may not be a good thing, but it is the very reverse of what Kant means by respecting a person's autonomy. To be autonomous for Kant is emphatically not to be able to do or have whatever one desires, but rather it is to have the capacity for rational self-governance. In another of his striking analogies, to be autonomous is to be a member of a kingdom of similar autonomous or self-legislating 'ends-in-themselves'.[19]

Granted Kant's core idea it is easy to relate the concepts of respect and dignity to autonomy and to each other, at least in Kantian terms. Since it was Kant's view that it is autonomy or the capacity to be self-governing which makes human beings unique in the scheme of things, or to be grown-up persons, it was an easy move for him to show a necessary connection between the concepts of autonomy and dignity. Those unfortunate individuals who are pushed around in a heteronomous way by others from the outside, or those who have their decisions made for them, lack dignity; but if you are able to make your own autonomous decisions then you exemplify dignity.

It is worth stressing that Kant's views on dignity are the reverse of many claims made in health care. For example, to provide a treatment solely on the

17 'Autonomy' has now become 'patient choice', a dominant ethical idea.
18 Kant I, *Groundwork of the Metaphysic of Morals* (1785), Paton HJ (trans), 1953, London: Hutchinson's University Library, pp 108–113.
19 Ibid., pp 100–102.

grounds that the patient (or relative) desires it but which the best evidence suggests will not work is far from respecting the patient's dignity; it is treating the patient as a child to be humoured. Moreover, the doctor who provides such a treatment against his own evidence-based judgement is not acting as an autonomous or dignified professional but has become merely an agent of the desires of someone else.

If to be truly autonomous or self-governing is to exemplify a true human dignity how does the idea of 'respect' fit in? Respect is basically a special kind of attitude. If we consider the deference which might be thought appropriately directed to someone of great creative ability, or perhaps to a great statesman, then we might say that we are showing an attitude of respect. For example, if Beethoven were to enter the room then music lovers would feel impelled to stand up. Or if Nelson Mandela walked in then those present would in various ways show a deference or respect. It was the moral insight of the Enlightenment, perhaps especially the insight of Kant, to suggest that such deference should be extended to persons as such because persons have the capacity to embody moral values such as honesty. In other words, respect is an attitude of deference or reverence directed at persons not just for their gifts or status, but for being the kind of creatures they are – moral beings – or for their dignity as autonomous creatures. This is the idea behind a large number of well-known sayings deriving from the eighteenth century. For example, Robert Burns says

The rank is but the guinea stamp,

[...]

A man's a man for a' that.[20]

Developing Kant's ideas: a bad way and a good way

Now Kant's views have been developed in two ways in health-care ethics. The first way involves an unfortunate narrowing of his idea of autonomy, and an unfortunate change in the meaning of 'respect'.

In health-care ethics autonomy has been narrowed to mean simply the ability of people to choose whatever they want. In contrast, for Kant autonomy means to be able to stand back from one's immediate interests or desires and to express moral values, or to be self-governing in being able to act in terms of rules which should be valid for all. The core aspect of Kant's account of autonomy has dropped out of health-care ethics and the term 'autonomy' is now used to mean more narrowly the ability to choose what one wants – 'I want' has eclipsed 'I ought'.

Going along with this unfortunate narrowing of the idea of autonomy there has been an equally unfortunate change in the meaning of the term 'respect'. For

20 Burns R, A man's a man for a' that (1790), in *The Penguin Book of Scottish Verse*, Scott T (ed), 1970, London: Penguin Books, p 330.

Kant, 'respect' means the deference which might be accorded to a high achiever; he sometimes uses the term 'reverence' instead of 'respect'. But, as we have seen, his moral insight is that this attitude should be directed towards all persons equally, to the extent that they can embody moral values. In health-care ethics, however, the object of respect has become the patient's self-determination or his/her desires or choices, and to respect a decision seems to be simply to do what the patient wants. Indeed, some writers argue that to respect the dignity of a patient is just to do what the patients want, regardless of whether it is in their best interests or of its impact on resources for other patients.[21] This seems an unfortunate way to develop Kant's ideas.

There is however a second way in which Kant's ideas can be developed which is more helpful for ethics. It can reasonably be argued against Kant that he has an unduly narrow view of human nature. He inherits a tradition of dualism from his predecessors in terms of which human beings have both a rational element in their make-up and also a desiring and sentient element. Kant identifies autonomy with our possession of the rational element. For him our rationality is the divine spark which gives us dignity. Now we do not propose here to argue against a dualistic view of human nature, but will simply assert, dogmatically, that a richer and more satisfactory view of human beings emerges if we are depicted as mind–body unities. We have a body which can suffer pain and we have emotions which shape our identities as much as or more than our rationality does. Thus, we are the persons we are because of how we feel about other people, where our loyalties lie, and the kinds of events we fear. Granted the acceptability of this modified view of Kantianism we shall later try to show that it can contribute to a fruitful and positive way of understanding the concepts of autonomy.

It is important to note that when we are dealing with competent patients the concepts of autonomy and dignity cover the same area, so that when one concept applies the other does also. But when we speak of very sick or incompetent patients, or even of the dead, we can still use the concept of dignity even when autonomy is no longer applicable. Hence, dignity is a concept with a much wider area of applicability than autonomy, and *the two concepts are different in essence.*

Unfortunately, in much contemporary writing on medical ethics the principle of respect for the patient's autonomy has moved in a consumerist direction, and the dignity of a person has collapsed into the rights of a consumer. We have just suggested other ambiguities in the term 'respect' (which is used in so many ways that it is largely meaningless), but in this section we have tried to bring out that the principle 'Respect the patient's autonomy' has moved far away from its Kantian foundation and is really now a source of confused moral messages rather than a guiding principle. Having indicated some serious problems over the

---

21 Paris J, Schreiber M, Statter M, Arenson R and Seigler M, 'Sounding board', *New England Journal of Medicine*, 1993, 329, pp 354–357.

meaning of the four principles we shall now critically examine the way they are used in ethical reasoning.

Criticisms of the 'four-principles' approach

Even if we assume that we can make the four principles clear and unambiguous there remains the problem of what to do if they conflict. Gillon claimed that they 'provide a common moral language' (see p 34), but the possession of such a language does not resolve conflicts. In fact most of those basing their moral reasoning on principles also accept, implicitly or explicitly, moral theories as the foundation of principles, and the assumption is that when our principles conflict we can appeal to the foundation theory, such as utilitarianism, to resolve the conflict. Enthusiasts for theory, such as applied philosophers, might even claim that if we start with the theory, perhaps the liberal theory of justice, or utilitarianism, we can actually deduce via subsidiary principles, granted our knowledge of the facts, what in a given case we morally ought to do.

This approach has been criticised by many writers but perhaps most effectively by Carl Elliott.[22] Elliott makes a number of points against the deductivist approach. First, there are many incompatible theories and no obvious way to adjudicate among them. Second, theorists wish to have theories which are tidy and neat, but the moral life is frequently untidy and inconsistent. Should the theorist aim at tidiness or truth? Third, the relationship between a moral theory and the judgements we make in everyday life is unclear. On the one hand, the idea seems to be that we appeal to the theory to justify or arbitrate among our particular judgements, and on the other that the theory is meant to be valid to the extent that it reflects these particular judgements and is falsified or rendered less plausible if it seems incompatible with them. Finally, Elliott points out that people don't appeal to theories in ordinary life. In ordinary life one persuades, cajoles, jokes, threatens, coerces, reminds, harasses, begs, and forgives. One tells stories, makes analogies, sermonises, moralises, holds grudges and gets righteously indignant.[23]

To say all this is by no means to say that principles have no place in moral argument. Nor is Elliott suggesting this. The point is that principles do not have the role in moral argument which deductivists and theorists suggest. Perhaps we should say that principles *ought* not to have a deductivist role, for when they do we are heading for the rigidity which leads to fanaticism. An inductive rather than deductive approach might be more helpful. Probability is the guide of life and we must not look for certainty more than the nature of the subject admits of.[24]

22 Elliott C, 'Where ethics comes from and what to do about it', *Hastings Center Report*, 1992, 22, 4, pp 28–35.
23 Ibid., p 30.
24 Aristotle, op. cit., Book 1, Chapter 3.

Casuistry

The way ahead in the search for an acceptable method for medical ethics may be to begin with the experience noted by Stephen Toulmin and Albert R Jonsen. They both served on the U.S. National Commission for the Protection of Human Subjects of Biomedical and Behavioural Research, and they noted that agreement could be reached on specific substantive points by members who held very different religious and philosophical theories of life. Out of this experience they were encouraged to return to a very ancient method of moral reasoning called 'casuistry', that is, a method based on attention to the details of specific cases.[25]

Casuistry has been defined as:

> the interpretation of moral issues, using procedures based on paradigms and analogies, leading to the formulation of expert opinion about the existence and stringency of particular moral obligations, framed in terms of rules or maxims that are general but not universal or invariable, since they hold good with certainty only in the typical conditions of the agent and circumstances of action.[26]

Casuistry has a bad name since it is associated with special pleading. As such it is totally rejected by many writers of the eighteenth century, such as Adam Smith.[27] Oddly enough, although Adam Smith rejects casuistry as a method of moral reasoning he is happy with an activity he calls 'natural jurisprudence', which is for all the world like a legal version of casuistry. Indeed, it would not be an exaggeration to say that English and American common law are casuistic in their method of case analysis. So what are the characteristics of this method of reasoning, whether we call it casuistry or natural jurisprudence?

The first characteristic is that there must be total immersion in the details, the particularities of a given case and its setting. Albert Jonsen, an influential modern writer in the revival of casuistry, calls this the 'morphology' of the case.[28] For example, before reaching a decision it is important to know the expectations of the interested parties, whether these expectations are reasonable in the context, what the institutional policies, if any, may be, what the history of the case is and so on. Now, of course, the morphology of the case will be investigated against a background of moral rules and principles. But it is too simple to say that the pressure of these rules and principles will shape the

25 Jonsen AR and Toulmin SE, *The Abuse of Casuistry*, 1988, Berkeley and Los Angeles: University of California Press.
26 Jonsen AR, 'Casuistry as methodology in clinical ethics', *Theoretical Medicine*, 1991, 12, pp 295–307.
27 Smith A, *The Theory of Moral Sentiments*, Raphael DD and Macfie AL (eds), 6th edn (1790), 1976, Oxford: Clarendon Press, Section iv.
28 Jonsen, op. cit.

structure. It is just as likely that the rules and principles will be interpreted in terms of the particular case in hand. It is all very well to parade 'respect for the autonomy of the individual', but how is this principle going to be interpreted in a case where the main party involved is a self-destructive individual who is also the provider for a family? Whose autonomy is being considered? Are there other moral principles, such as a regard for justice, also involved? In complex cases a whole range of moral considerations must be identified and sifted before a reasonable moral judgement can be made. This process of interpretation involves an integration in which the facts are interpreted in terms of rules and the rules are interpreted in terms of the particularities of the case. Jonsen calls this the 'taxonomy' of the case.[29]

The word 'taxonomy' is helpful here. The Greek work 'taxis' means the drawing up or ordering of soldiers in battle lines. Just as the best troops might be marshalled at a certain point so it is important in moral reasoning to have paradigms or clear examples where these will not be in dispute. For example, in the current controversy as to when medical treatment might be withheld or withdrawn we might begin with the maxim that it is always wrong to give medical treatment to a dead body. Moving out from that paradigm we might ask in what way a permanent vegetative state is like that of death. Or in what way advanced senility is like it. These comparisons and analogies then suggest that some forms of treatment, perhaps artificial nutrition and hydration, might be appropriate but not others. The point about the term 'taxonomy' is that it helps to make clear that the given case is not unique. It has similarities and dissimilarities to a paradigm case. An ultimate practical judgement about what to do will therefore not be based on a deduction from a principle but on how the principle might appear in the morphology of the total circumstances in comparison with other cases.

Jonsen uses the term 'kinetics' to describe the third feature of casuistical reasoning. He uses the term to indicate the way in which one case or a set of circumstances imparts a kind of moral movement to other cases. The metaphor suggests that reasons can be more or less 'weighty' or that there may be 'balancing considerations'. This 'it all depends' approach does not fit easily with ethics since the time of Kant. A true Kantian would take the line that 'Lying is always wrong' but the casuist would want to know the bearing the lie had on the 'community of trust' which is the underlying justification for truth-telling. But perhaps the lie was a 'jocose' lie, or perhaps it was part of a good story which was true for the most part.[30]

In order to illustrate Jonsen's terminology and to contrast it with the Kantian approach let us take an example from Kant.

> Suppose, for instance, that someone is holding another's property in trust (a
> deposit) whose owner is dead, and that the owner's heirs do not know and

29 Jonsen AR, 'Casuistry as methodology in clinical ethics', *Theoretical Medicine*, 1991, 12, pp 295–307.
30 Ibid.

can never know about it. Present this case even to a child of eight or nine, and add that, through no fault of his, the trustee's fortunes are at their lowest ebb, that he sees a sad family around him, a wife and children disheartened by want. From all of this he would be instantly delivered by appropriating the deposit. And further that the man is kind and charitable, while those heirs are rich, loveless, extremely extravagant spendthrifts, so that this addition to their wealth might as well be thrown into the sea. And then ask whether under these circumstances it might be deemed permissible to convert the deposit to one's own use. Without doubt, anyone asking the question will answer 'No!' – and in lieu of grounds he can merely say: 'It is wrong!, i.e. it conflicts with duty.'[31]

Kant has reached his conclusion by simple deductive reasoning:

> It is wrong to steal;
> Taking someone's deposit is a case of stealing;
> Therefore one ought not to take the deposit.

But a casuist would want to be immersed in the details of the case: how much was the deposit? what were the conditions of the trust? what was the trustee's relationship with the owner (private or professional)? what was the relationship of the owner to the relatives? and so on. This is the morphology of the case. Then the casuist would want to line up cases of stealing, cases of saving from starvation, cases of the presumptions of friendship, and so on. This is the taxonomy. Then he would consider how this particular case in these particular circumstances could be balanced against other such cases. This is the kinetics.

Casuistry, interpreted in this way, seems a possible method of moral reasoning. We have yet to consider how far, if at all, it can also be considered a branch of philosophy. But first we must examine some objections to casuistry, and also make clear the analogy between the casuist and the judge.

Some objections to casuistry

Casuistry was dealt what were thought to be fatal blows by philosophers of the Enlightenment, such as Adam Smith, Hume or Kant. It may be appropriate to examine the kind of criticisms which were made during that period and consider whether they still hold good. We shall concentrate on Adam Smith, and consider two objections which Smith makes explicitly, and a third which might be raised nowadays on the basis of Smith's assumptions.

---

31 Kant I, *On the Old Saw: That may be Right in Theory but won't work in Practice*, Aston EB (trans), 1974, p 3. There is an interesting discussion of Kant's views on casuistry in Leites E (ed), *Conscience and Casuistry in Early Modern Europe*, 1988, Cambridge: Cambridge University Press.

Objection from the content of obligation

This objection makes three connected points. First, that the casuists 'attempted, to no purpose, to direct by precise rules what it belongs to feeling and sentiment only to judge of'.[32] Smith's point here is not that rules are never appropriate but that the casuists use them for the looser virtues where rules are inappropriate. Smith's second point is that in any event it is not possible to ascertain through rules what is required in many cases, for there cannot be rule-like dividing lines between, for example, a delicate sense of justice and a weak scrupulosity of conscience, or between reserve and dissimulation – 'what would hold good in one case would scarcely do so exactly in another'.[33] A third and connected point is that even though books of casuistry contain many cases, 'yet upon account of the still greater variety of possible circumstances' it would only be a matter of chance if a case was found which was exactly parallel to the one being considered.[34] Hence, Smith concludes that books of casuistry not only try to do the impossible, but are also useless. These connected criticisms concern the content of what we ought to do.

In reply, two points can be made. First, Smith is surely wrong in thinking that any moral questions can be answered simply by appealing to our feelings and sentiments. Many moral situations are complex and immediate feelings can mislead. This is not to say that feelings are unimportant but rather that reason must lead in making moral decisions. The second point of reply is that Smith misunderstands casuistry if he thinks that casuists over-use rules. Perhaps indeed in their stress on immersion in the details of particular cases they under-use rules.

Objection from moral motivation

The second criticism which Smith makes is double-barrelled, and it concerns moral motivation. First, books of casuistry, because of their style, do not 'tend to animate us to what is generous and noble... or soften us to what is gentle and humane'.[35] Second, and more dangerously, they 'tend rather to teach us to chicane with our own consciences, and by their vain subtleties serve to authorise innumerable evasive refinements with regard to the most essential articles of our duty'.[36] Kant would be nodding his head! In view of these criticisms it is not surprising that Smith concludes that 'casuistry ought to be rejected altogether' and that the 'two useful parts of moral philosophy, therefore, are Ethics and Jurisprudence'.[37]

32 Smith, op. cit., Book VII, Section iv, para 33, pp 339–340.
33 Ibid.
34 Ibid.
35 Ibid.
36 Ibid.
37 Ibid.

The first barrel can be ducked, at least in the context of moral reasoning. Casuists are not intending to 'animate' or motivate us. That perhaps is one job for poets, writers or dramatists. We have called this aspect of medical ethics its 'supplementary' role, and we shall discuss it in Chapter 6. But the second barrel hits the mark. There is a danger, if you think every case is different, that you will 'chicane' with your conscience. Only if we underline the importance of the paradigm cases can that be avoided.

Objection to the assumption of moral expertise

The third criticism emerges if we consider what Smith takes to be the two useful parts of moral philosophy – Ethics and Jurisprudence, or what he often calls 'natural jurisprudence'. By the time of Smith lawyers had taken on the mantle of secular casuists. For example, they decided complex issues of property and rights. So why did Smith allow the practice of natural jurisprudence, which involves what he calls 'abstruse distinctions' while rejecting casuistry? The answer is that law was seen as something external to the newly discovered individual self. Certainly there were problems of collisions between individual conscience and law, and an important aspect of the history of jurisprudence is that of recording successive attempts to keep law and conscience in harmony. But to the extent that law was perceived to be external to the self, it was regarded as legitimate for there to be 'experts' who considered precise applications of natural jurisprudence in system of positive law.

But what of the modern casuist, the ethics consultant in medicine or business or the environment? Is such a person a moral expert? The third criticism of modern casuistry then is that it assumes that there can be the kind of expert we are willing to allow in law, but are not willing to allow in morality. Do the modern casuists in medicine or public affairs assume that they are moral experts? Can there be moral experts, and if so, where does that leave the autonomy of the individual conscience?

To take the first question, it is true to say that in the practice of casuistry, ancient or modern, some conception of expertise is being presupposed. If we consider the complexity of the issues which are faced in bioethics, such as problems in surrogacy, the transplanting of foetal tissue, cloning and so on, it is apparent that we are dealing with problems where the technical and the moral are inextricably entwined so that some conception of expert judgement is being presupposed.

It might be argued that the complexity concerns the technical, empirical side to the problems and once the facts are sorted out then the purely moral element can kick in. This controversy first surfaced in the Scottish Enlightenment in the mid-eighteenth century. On the one hand it was argued by Hutcheson, Hume and Smith that in moral judgement we should first clarify the facts, what is the case, no matter how complex, and our awareness of the facts will then cause the appropriate moral sentiment to be activated. In other words, 'moral judgement' is strictly speaking an inaccurate description; the element of judgement is purely directed to sifting the facts, and the element of the moral is purely an emotional or attitudinal reaction. Thomas Reid, on the other hand, held that the facts and values could not be separated and judgement was integral to the whole process. In a witty passage he observed that if Hutcheson and Hume were correct then a judge should really be called a 'feeler'![38]

In our opinion Reid has the better of them there. The sorting of the facts in a technical matter is not simply a morally neutral activity. The question of which facts are the important ones involves value judgements. Fact and value make up a seamless garment. What are the implications of taking this line?

One implication is that there is room for the moral expert. It does not, of course, follow that this expertise is generalisable. Someone may be considered a moral expert in one area but have no special qualifications to speak on another. Nor does it follow that every moral problem needs an expert. If I see you drop your wallet on the way out of the room there is no need for an expert to tell me what I ought to do. The main area in which moral expertise might be shown may be that of the expert committee set up to deal with a problem generated by the new technology. We shall not here go into what would be appropriate qualifications for membership of such a committee, or what might disqualify. Clearly, some knowledge of the law, of the technicalities of the problem and some analytical skills might count as qualifications (not sufficient ones), and a vested interest might be a disqualification.

The second question here concerns individual autonomy. Are we suggesting that we should hand over our right to make some moral decisions for ourselves to an expert, or expert committee? The short answer is 'yes', but this must immediately be qualified. First, it is only some moral questions which admit of an expert answer. Second, we are in a sense familiar with expertise in courts of law. Judges are trained to or are experienced in sifting through complexities, have a measure of detachment from their immediate feelings, and are able to see the wider implications for the public interest of decisions one way or the other. What we are suggesting is something similar for morality in a technical sphere. There is a continuum involved from a quasi-legal expert committee such as the BMA Ethics Committee – which from time to time issues booklets expressing the expert view of the committee on a matter such as the withholding or withdrawing of treatment at the end of life – to an individual doctor who explains a proposed treatment option, perhaps recommends one, but must obtain the consent of the patient. This kind of moral expertise was perhaps not needed in the time of Adam Smith – although he recognises it in the sphere of 'natural jurisprudence' – but it is necessary to guide us throughout the moral complexities of the modern age.

---

38 Reid T, *Essays on the Active Powers* (1788), Lehrer K (ed), 1975, Indianapolis: Bobbs-Merrill, Essay V, Chapter 7.

Is casuistry (as natural jurisprudence) a branch of philosophy?

Finally, we can raise the questions of whether casuistry, granted that it is possible and can be desirable, is a branch of moral philosophy. If casuistry is a helpful approach to moral practice is it a branch of philosophy? *A fortiori*, are the many subsets of casuistry, such as medical ethics, branches of moral philosophy?

There is no one answer to this question because fashions change as to what is or is not a legitimate philosophical activity. There is however one (perhaps fatal) objection to the view that casuistry is a legitimate branch of moral philosophy, at least in terms of the second-order critical view of the discipline which we are adopting in this book. The objection is that the judgements of casuistry are directed at reaching decisions in particular first-order cases, whereas moral philosophy is a second-order or 'stand-back' or 'meta' discipline.

Our claim here derives from Aristotle, when he says that his Ethics is not philosophy.[39] Aristotle has two points: that philosophy is concerned with knowing, whereas ethics is concerned with doing; and that the objects of philosophy are universals of various sorts, whereas the objects of ethics are individual actions.

Of course, even if our view of moral philosophy as a second-order or 'meta' discipline is allowed it might still be the case that those trained in philosophy have something to contribute to the solution of practical problems via the methods of casuistry, or natural jurisprudence. Training in philosophy is training in analytical skills which are transferable to first-order activities such as bioethics.

Finally, and most importantly, the ethicist can point to the complexity of factors in moral reasoning. Principles are important, although the idea that there are just four is not very plausible. But moral judgements come into play before principles apply. For example, a decision as to which 'facts' are the salient ones in any given case requires moral judgements prior to the application of any principles. Perhaps then medical ethicists should reason in a manner analogous to that of medical lawyers. For example, the judge in a case involving medical law must sift the facts, be aware of the relevant legislation and precedents, be aware of the views of the medical governing bodies, and more generally be governed by ideas of the equitable and the public good. Bioethics is similar except that the range of relevant principles may be wider. And just as some legal training may help the doctor some philosophical training may also guide a doctor to a sound ethical decision.

Compassion, the virtues and self-development

A different line of criticism of the four-principles approach derives from feminist writers such as Carol Gilligan, filtered through the growing literature on nursing

39 Aristotle, op. cit., Book 1.

ethics.[40] Their general line is to the effect that an emphasis on principles represents a male view on ethics, including bioethics, whereas a feminist view should be based on the virtues such as compassion, or on sentiment. In this approach to bioethics, the central concept becomes that of 'care', said to be what nurses do, as opposed to 'cure', what (male) doctors are said to try to do. The professional stereotypes and oversimplifications exemplified by this contrast are discussed by Jecker and Self.[41] Nevertheless, there is no doubt that discussions in the feminist/nursing literature do successfully identify a need for the concept of care, and also that ethics involves more than an appeal to principles. This kind of criticism might also be levelled at a case-based approach to moral reasoning. For the emphasis in casuistry is still on rational argument.

The main point in this sort of criticism is that, as JS Mill says, 'It matters not only what men do but what manner of men they are that do it'.[42] In other words, whereas it is of the first importance what actions a doctor or nurse carries out, it is also important *how* they do it, their manner in doing it. And the manner in which we do something is a direct outcome of the kind of person we are. This is where the virtues and self-development come in. But, do we have moral duties to be a certain sort of person? If we do there must be a self-regarding aspect or morality.

Some philosophers deny that there can be a self-regarding side to morality, for they see morality as having an essentially social function, concerned only with regulating one's conduct *vis-à-vis* other members of society. Such a view has developed out of one strand in JS Mill's thinking. Mill in his essay *On Liberty* seemed to be arguing that moral issues arise only to the extent that one's conduct harms other people; in so far as one's conduct affects only oneself it does not raise a moral issue.[43] Yet in the same work, Mill has a chapter on 'self-development' in which the moral importance of developing certain personality traits is stressed. And this view, that there are moral duties to cultivate in oneself certain characteristic human excellences, goes back to Plato and Aristotle and is taken up in a slightly different form by the Judeo-Christian traditions. According to these traditions human nature can 'flourish' and should therefore be cultivated, or we have a duty to cultivate the talents we have in trust.

Even Kant argues that we have duties to our selves. For Kant, the principle (or attitude) which is often stated in the form of 'One ought to respect autonomous persons' is more fully stated as 'Respect human nature, whether in your own person or in that of another'.[44] In other words, Kant makes ample room for the idea of a self-regarding area of morality.

40   Gilligan C, *In a Different Voice: Psychological Theory and Women's Development*, 1982, Cambridge, MA: Harvard University Press.
41   Jecker NS and Self DJ, 'Separating care and cure: an analysis of historical and contemporary images of nursing and medicine', *The Journal of Medicine and Philosophy*, 1991, 16, pp 285–306.
42   Mill JS, *On Liberty* (1859) 1963, London: Collins, Chapter 3.
43   Ibid., Chapters 1 and 2.
44   Kant, op. cit., Chapter 2.

This is an important area of morality for those in the caring professions, and it is the more important in that its neglect can seem a virtue. It is quite common for professional carers to live a life of devotion to their patients as a result of which their own lives become empty and impoverished. They have cultivated only their medical knowledge and skills and have nothing to say on anything else.

The duty of self-development can also be justified in terms of its benefits to other people. Since so much of the success of a doctor, nurse, dentist or other health worker depends on the relationship each has with a patient, and since the nature of that relationship depends partly on the patient's perceptions of the helper, it is vital that the professional should be seen as an authentic human being who happens to be a doctor, nurse or other carer. There is a moral element in the most technical-seeming medical or nursing judgement. If that is so, then it is important that those judgements should be the products not just of a technical, scientific mind, but of a humane and compassionate one. That is why it is important for the health-care professional to be *more* than just a health-care professional; he/she should also be a morally developed person who happens to follow a professional path. Self-development, then, is good both for its own sake and for what it gives to patients, friends and families.

It is often argued[45] that bioethics stresses principles too much and feelings not enough. One quality which is thought important to remedy this alleged deficiency is called 'compassion', or the ability to suffer with someone. The natural ingredients of compassion are part of the make-up of a normal human being. We all have the capacity to feel with others, to enter to some extent into their predicaments and share their emotions. Compassion, however, is not just a matter of having informed feelings for particular others – it is not just passive. To have compassion is to be moved to act on the basis of the promptings of natural emotion. We prefer the old-fashioned term 'compassion' to the semi-technical term 'empathy' on the grounds that the latter suggests something passive and, indeed, over-professionalised. In a similar way, the term 'sympathy' is ambiguous as between passive and active modes of expression. If someone is described as 'very sympathetic' this might mean simply that he/she shared one's feelings, or that he/she went on to do something about one's predicament. To be compassionate, however, requires both responses.

We are maintaining, then, that true compassion has an *affective* aspect – we feel with others – a *cognitive* aspect – we have particularised insight into the situation of others – and a *conative* aspect – we are moved to act on behalf of others. Compassion cannot ever replace principles, but so understood it provides an essential supplement to them.

Compassion is the virtue most often stressed in health-care ethics, but other virtues are also important. For example, courage is important. Courage is most often thought to be the virtue which enables us to act as we ought when we are fearful of physical danger. But other situations can also require courage.

45 Gilligan, op. cit.

Sometimes angry relatives make demands which are unreasonable or might not be in the best interest of the patient, and threaten legal action unless their demands are met. It takes courage to face up to relatives in such situations and explain why their demands cannot be granted. Courage may also be required when dealing with senior colleagues or management, if they are pursuing policies not in the best interest of patients.

It is well known that health carers lead busy lives. Now busyness is not simply a matter of long hours; it can also mean several demands being made on one's attention at the same time. Or it can mean conflicting demands, or demands of different sorts being made at the same time. For example, there may be a need to give teaching to a less than reliable junior, while conscious that an angry or distressed relative is waiting to be interviewed and a very sick patient urgently needs a change of medication. The virtue which is needed in such situations of stress is equanimity, the disposition to stay calm and deal competently and firmly but politely with each problem. All without raising one's blood pressure.

In sum, we are arguing here that virtues are important – courage, compassion, equanimity, patience – and that self-development is important. (We have already discussed self-development in Chapter 1, and we shall pick up the theme again in Chapter 6). But the virtues, compassion or self-development are no substitutes for rational discussion in the manner of the case-based approach.

Interpretation, culture and medical ethics

The merits in casuistry, but also its problem of bias, are explained by Loretta M Kopelman. She points out that:

> The potential for bias arises at each stage of a case method of reasoning including in describing, framing, selecting and comparing of cases and paradigms. A problem of bias occurs because, to identify the relevant features for such purposes, we must use general views about what is relevant; but some of our general views are biased, both in the sense of being unwarranted inclinations and in the sense that they are one of many viable perspectives.[46]

The same kind of point is made in a broader way by Carl Elliott. Elliott writes that our ethical judgements are an integral part of the culture to which we belong.

> [Ethics] is one thread in the fabric of society, and it is intertwined with others. Ethical concepts are tied to a society's customs, manners, traditions,

---

46 Kopelman LM, 'Case method and casuistry: the problem of bias', *Theoretical Medicine*, 1994, 15, pp 21–37.

institutions – all of the concepts that structure and inform the ways in which a member of that society deals with the world. When we forget this, we are in danger of leaving the world of genuine moral experience for the world of moral fiction – a simplified, hypothetical creation suited less for practical difficulties than for intellectual convenience.[47]

To argue in this way is not of course to reject rational argument. Rather it is to insist that discussion and interpretation in different cultural settings – Britain and America, say – will reflect the influence of many factors in addition to the purely ethical. Now whereas it is true that we are all, whether doctors and nurses or not, influenced by the culture in which we live, the medical profession is more specifically influenced by what we shall call, following Albert Jonsen, the 'ethos' of medicine.[48] What is the 'ethos' of medicine? It is the spirit, the manner in which the history and traditions of medicine have encouraged doctors to see themselves and their occupation. Perhaps more than any other profession doctors are conscious of themselves as bonded and with a special vocation. Being a doctor is something which colonises the entire personality and doctors will tend to see questions of ethics in terms of this medical ethos. The analysis of this ethos is a complex matter but for our purposes we can isolate three strands.

First, there is what we might term the 'Hippocratic' strand. Doctors see themselves under an obligation to develop medical skills and knowledge. Nowadays this urge takes a scientific form, or at least a form which makes claims to objectivity via randomised trials. But from the very start of medicine, say in the Hippocratic writings, this imperative can be seen at work.

Second, there is what we might call the 'Good Samaritan' strand. There is a slight suggestion from the language of St Luke (himself a physician) that the Good Samaritan was a Greek-trained physician. (The remedy he uses – oil and wine – was a remedy in Greek medicine.) At any rate he has set an example of the good doctor who treats patients whatever the danger or the expense.

Third, there is what we might term the 'aristocratic' strand. Physicians have always been part of the well-educated section of a society and no doubt because of the mystery surrounding their profession and the vulnerability of their patients they have always had a privileged status in society and are typically rewarded with honours and a high salary.

These three strands or components – there may be others – create an ethos in which questions of ethics are interpreted in ways which to an outsider might seem odd. For example, the growth of research ethics committees with lay members is not universally approved by medical researchers. There is sometimes

47 Elliott C, 'Where ethics comes from and what to do about it', *Hastings Center Report*, 1992, 22, pp 28–35.
48 Jonsen AR, The *New Medicine and the Old Ethics*, 1990, Cambridge, MA: Harvard University Press, 1990.

the suggestion – rightly – that such committees slow down the pace of medical research. Again, the idea that doctors should do their very best for a given patient, regardless of cost, can lead to conflict with budget-holders or insurers. And the idea that patients might refuse treatments which doctors wish to try can give rise to ethical problems.

Granted the culture of medicine, the ethos, the discussion of clinical cases and research policies requires not simply the application of principles but skill in interpretation, skill in understanding another point of view. This notion of point of view or perspective was introduced by one of the early writers in hermeneutics, Johann Martin Chladenius. Hermeneutics is the study of the interpretation of text and Chladenius uses the ideas of hermeneutics in relation to historical method.[49] His ideas are sufficiently important for our purposes to justify further investigation.

In the context of science, we might say that interpretation of phenomena can be correct or incorrect. Scientific enquiries focus on things that are not yet known but are assumed to be knowable, and knowledge of them depends on there being an appropriate experiment to uncover this. In order to frame such experiments, scientists will put forward interpretations of the phenomenon. These interpretations are called hypotheses, and, if possible, they will then be subject to experiments to test their validity. The point, for the present argument, is that interpretations in this context may be correct or incorrect, but the answer is not known – and may never be known – by the interpreter. In order, then, for scientific interpretations to have some validity and for them to be taken seriously as possible explanations of phenomena, we depend on being able to say whether they are plausible or not. Nicolaus Copernicus, in postulating a sun-centred system of astronomy in the sixteenth century, was not in a position to say whether his view was correct or not. He could say that this interpretation fitted the available facts better then the old earth-centred idea, and was, therefore, a more plausible interpretation.

In some types of case, we can have situations where different interpretations of events or subjects can have equal *validity* and are not necessarily correct or incorrect. Politics gives many examples of this but literature and fine art may be the main areas where it is most commonly said that a number of different interpretations of a work may be equally plausible. For example, one of the reasons that the plays of Shakespeare continue to fascinate theatre directors is that they can be played in many different ways. For instance, *Othello* can be seen as a play about a jealous husband, or about the trusting gullibility of the simple soldier, or about racial hatred. *The Merchant of Venice* can be played as a light comedy or as a comedy verging on tragedy, if the role of Shylock is given prominence by the director. We cannot say that any one of these readings of the plays is the correct one. They are all plausible as long as the text will support them. We cannot even appeal to authorial intention to support the most plausible

49 Mueller-Vollmer K (ed), *The Hermeneutics Reader*, 1985, Oxford: Oxford University Press, p 7.

reading, as Shakespeare does not stamp his presence on the plays. Artists may or may not choose to allow their own views of a work to surface. This may be particularly so of highly abstract art, where the artist paints something and leaves it to the viewer to make up his own mind about what the painting means.

This is not to say that anything goes in literature and art. Interpretations must be supported by a sensitive reading of the text, which will involve understanding of nuances and analogies employed by the author. The poem *Felix Randal* by Gerard Manley Hopkins contains this verse:

> Sickness broke him. Impatient, he cursed at first, but mended
> Being anointed and all; though a heavenlier heart began some
> Months earlier, since I had our sweet reprieve and ransom
> Tendered to him. Ah well, God rest him all road ever he offended![50]

The poem can be seen as an account by Hopkins of this man Felix Randal, whom Hopkins ministered to as a priest in his last illness. But the poet's use of the Lancashire dialect in this verse brings Felix's voice to our ears and the poem becomes a vivid picture of this big, burly farrier at first railing against his illness and then accepting it with Northern fatalism. If our ears were not attuned to this dialect or if the style change was not pointed out to us, we would lose much of what was intended in the poem and our reading of it would be incorrect.

In summary, interpretations of things can be correct or incorrect, or more or less plausible; and it is possible to have a number of valid or plausible interpretations of the same thing. An individual's interpretation is guided by his own viewpoint. The correctness or plausibility of that interpretation will depend on how far that viewpoint is obscured by lack of knowledge or understanding of the subject.

Interpretation is, therefore, related to understanding. But what exactly is the relationship? There is no one conceptually correct answer to this. We can say either that interpretation is a process that *leads to* understanding, or we can say that interpretation *just is* understanding in a context of puzzlement.

An example of the idea of interpretation leading to understanding might be of the finding on an archaeological dig of a piece of carved flint lying amongst other such implements and animal remains. The archaeologist can see that the piece of flint has a blunt end and a broad sharp end, and its position implies that it might have been used in the process of cutting up meat. He concludes that he has found a flint axe-head. This conclusion has come about entirely by interpretation of the shape of the implement, the position it was found on the dig, and by comparison with other such finds. The axe-head is then taken to a museum and is put on view as 'flint axe-head'. Does the viewer just understand that this is what the artefact is without going through an interpretative process?

---

50 Hopkins GM, Felix Randal, in *Poems by Gerard Manley Hopkins*, MacKenzie AH (ed), 1974, London: The Folio Society, p 92.

It may be that some interpretative activity is required by the viewer, as well, before he can conclude that this is an axe-head. That activity might be almost subconscious but it is necessary for the viewer to compare this object with axes as he knows them before he can see that this object is plausible as an axe.

As an example of the second idea of the relationship between interpretation and understanding, consider the situation in which we are not sure of the import of what someone is saying. In such a situation we engage in a process of interpretation. To confirm our interpretation we might ask, 'Do I understand you correctly?' In other words, interpretation is just understanding in the context of a certain sort of puzzlement. Indeed, another of the important originators of hermeneutics, Friedrich Schleiermacher, made no clear distinction between them and saw hermeneutics as the 'art of understanding'.[51]

From the point of view of this book, it is unimportant which line is taken. The important point is that interpretation is closely related to understanding, however that relationship is to be understood.

Granted the influence of the medical ethos or culture the importance of interpretation in ethical judgement can be seen. Principles and rules appear differently in different cultural contexts and from different individual perspectives and even 'facts' can be interpreted differently. This is not to say that there cannot be rational discussion of individual cases or research policies but it is to say that patience, equanimity and tolerance (moral qualities not much mentioned in the literature of medical ethics) are required in the attempt to reach understanding and agreement. The ability to communicate with others – patients, colleagues or management – is also required, and we shall discuss this in Chapter 6.

Conclusions

We are now in a position to be able to sum up the contribution which moral philosophy, seen as a medical humanity, can make to medical ethics. Bioethics is a practical activity with the aim, as Aristotle put it, not of knowing but doing. Moral philosophy is a theoretical activity which stands back from the immediacy or the urgency of reaching practical decisions or workable policies. It is a second-order or 'meta' activity which reflects critically on the assumptions and arguments of the first-order activity, in this case of medical ethics. From this detached position our suggestions are that bioethics should not be seen as a matter of applying theories or principles, although principles may have a part to play. Moral arguments require the sifting of facts, the noting of inconsistencies, and the ability to interpret and come to an understanding of view points other than one's own. Sometimes this understanding is a self-understanding which is possible only for those who are able and willing to try to step outside a given perspective. For doctors, granted the medical ethos and a busy life, this is not always easy.

---

51   Mueller-Vollmer, op. cit., p 12.

Chapter 3

Logic and epistemology

It is not controversial to suggest that even if moral philosophy is a theoretical activity, one which stands back from first-order decisions and attempts to understand them, it might still make a contribution to first-order ethical problems. It is less obvious however how logic and epistemology or the theory of knowledge can be practically relevant in ethics. The first part of this chapter is concerned with at least some of the contributions of logic and the second part with those of epistemology.

As an introduction to both parts we shall begin with a discussion of an image which has exerted great influence on philosophy since the eighteenth century. This image originates in David Hume. He tells us that he is providing a new philosophical microscope to make ideas clear.[1] This image might be said to be one of the major influences on the whole analytic movement in philosophy. We find, for example, that in one of the seminal books of philosophical ethics of the twentieth century GE Moore distinguishes the question, 'What does "good" mean?' from the question, 'What kinds of thing are good?'[2] It is true that Moore answered the second question in the final part of his book, but most philosophers never make it to the end of the book, and moral philosophy subsequent to Moore concentrated on the question of meaning. In terms of this microscope analogy, then, philosophy helps practice by making ideas clear.

This image appealed to the desire of philosophers to have a quasi-scientific role in academic life. And there is no doubt that conceptual clarification is one central function of philosophy, and one which can have a bearing on practice. It is easy to make fun of the philosopher who, when faced with a difficult question, always begins, 'It depends what you mean by . . .'. The reality is that this is an important first step in many difficult problems (as we shall see p 63ff) Nevertheless, the microscope analogy is open to some serious objections with ethical implications when viewed as a full account of the relationship between theory and practice. We shall mention two objections.

---

1 Hume D, *An Enquiry Concerning Human Understanding* (1748) 1902, Oxford: Clarendon Press, Section 1.
2 Moore GE, *Principia Ethica*, 1903, Cambridge: Cambridge University Press.

The first is that the philosophical microscope is not so objective as its scientific counterpart. Even in science it is notorious that there is a danger that the scientist will see what he hopes to see. In philosophy there is no doubt that the philosopher's eye will have a film of theory over it. The mistake is not that of seeing a problem or concept from a given point of view, but that of being unaware that you are doing so, because you are misled by the microscope image into thinking that your analysis is more neutral or objective than it is. You are in reality presenting your analysis from a given moral position.

The second objection is that concepts are being looked at only one at a time through the microscope, whereas a full understanding of them requires the seeing of links between them, and also between the concepts and their total cultural context (as we said p 54ff). Important philosophers in the analytical tradition subsequent to Moore, such as Wittgenstein in his later writings, stressed the point that concepts have meaning only in a cultural context.[3] We shall find that the image of the philosophical microscope – and the two limitations it has – will affect problems in medical logic and epistemology, and especially the medical obsession with definition.

Logic

We shall begin by discussing a few examples of the way in which faulty logic can have major ethical implications, and then we shall proceed to examine the theory of definition, because, as we have said, the way in which a central concept is defined can affect what medicine does about it, and therefore it can affect the ethics of the situation.

Logic is the study of valid and invalid types of reasoning. It is not directly concerned with truth, which is the realm of science. It is concerned with what conclusions validly follow from certain premises. There are numerous ways in which arguments can go wrong or be fallacious, and we shall draw attention to some with ethical implications. Problems of consistency are also the concern of logic – you cannot assert A if you also hold B which is inconsistent with A. We shall also draw attention to some problems of consistency in the literature of medical ethics.

The first example of logical confusions with ethical implications concerns an argument in an editorial in the *British Medical Journal*. AC Grayling, a professor of philosophy, argues that there is no significant moral difference between killing and letting die. He writes:

> Lawyers and doctors distinguish between withholding treatment with death as the result, and giving treatment that causes death. The first is considered to be permissible in law and ethics, the second is not. But in fact there is no

3 Wittgenstein L, *Philosophical Investigations*, 1953, Oxford: Blackwell.

difference between them: for withholding treatment is an act, based on a decision, just as giving treatment is an act, based on a decision. Moreover, someone who starved another person to death would be liable for murder as if he or she had poisoned the person. Like the doctrine of double effect, which allows death hastening levels of analgesia to be given with the putative sole aim of controlling pain, the distinctions are fictitious. Death, after all, is the ultimate analgesic.[4]

This argument is a tissue of logical confusion. First, it is totally irrelevant, because it is not in dispute, that 'withholding' is an action based on a decision, or more accurately, that the doctor is as much morally responsible for withholding treatment as for providing it. But it is crass in the extreme to suggest that withholding or withdrawing a treatment on the grounds that it is providing no benefit, and may indeed be harmful, is morally equivalent to poisoning someone. If the patient dies in the one case the cause of death is the underlying pathology which treatment was unable to remedy, whereas in the other case the patient dies because poison has been administered.

Second, the ambiguous language 'withholding and withdrawing treatment with death as the result' is radically misleading because it suggests causality. If B occurs 'as a result of A' then the implication is that A has caused B. But withholding or withdrawing is entirely neutral with respect to causality. If the hotel is on fire and I withhold or withdraw my garden hose on the grounds that it will make no difference to the fire I have not caused the destruction of the hotel. Similarly, to withhold or withdraw medication or tube feeding on the grounds that it is futile does not 'result in' or cause the patient's death, even although the patient's death may shortly follow.

Third, his claim that the doctrine of double effect allows 'death hastening levels of analgesia' to be given is quite misleading both on the doctrine of double effect (which we are not defending) and on the medical guidelines. If a patient's pain cannot otherwise be controlled, then he/she may be given a measure of sedation, provided he/she consents to this. As well as deadening the pain or the awareness of it this will render the patient less mobile and breathing may be to some extent suppressed. These factors may, but do not necessarily, make death more likely. On the other hand, Grayling's loaded phrase 'death hastening levels of analgesia' smacks of the tabloids rather than logic.

The general point is that this weak logic may push unwary readers towards a particular ethical stance on withholding and withdrawing treatment, or providing sedation for extreme pain. Thus, ethics and logic are closely connected.

Another concept central to logic, indeed to communication, is consistency. Inconsistency can lead to conclusions which have ethical implications. Let us consider an important example of this. It involves a letter to the BMA News

---

4 Grayling AC, Editorial, *British Medical Journal*, 2005, 330, p 799.

Review and the reply to it from the Chairman of the BMA Ethics Committee. The letter from Dr Michael Jarmulowicz runs as follows:

> Is the BMA medical ethics committee suffering from schizophrenia? It fully supported the cries that there must be consent to take tissue for post mortem histology but is now promoting the idea of presumed consent for transplantation. Can someone explain the point of principle that I seem to have missed? Doesn't logic demand some consistency? Why should a pathologist deserve condemnation for removing a diseased, non-viable heart after death without consent, while a transplant surgeon will be allowed to remove a healthy, viable heart on the assumption that the patient would have wished this?[5]

BMA medical ethics committee chairman Michael Wilks responds:

> Logic demands consistency between like issues. There are fundamental differences between the retention of organs for research and the removal of organs for transplantation. The primary difference is that there is considerable knowledge and support within society for transplantation – the latest official survey shows 90 per cent support for transplantation – the same is not true of research. There would be widespread publicity to ensure that the 10 per cent who did not wish to donate could register that objection. The justification for this different approach is explored in the BMA's parliamentary briefing (www.bma.org.uk).[6]

He refers us also to a more sustained paper on the topic by English and Somerville.[7]

Michael Wilks seems to have missed the point of the objection. Of course 'logic demands consistency between like issues', and of course research is different from transplantation. And for all we know the public may favour transplantation (perhaps because they have not been told the details of the procedure). But these points are neither here nor there. The 'like issues' are those of consent, and in the case of research we are told that it is unethical to remove tissue without full consent but in the case of transplantation it seems to be ethically desirable to remove tissue without full consent. The relevant point is consent, not the use which will be made of the tissue. On this matter the committee is clearly inconsistent, and the inconsistency has serious ethical implications. And the same is true of the more sustained defence offered by English and Somerville.

---

5 Jarmulowicz M, *British Medical Association News Review*, 7 February 2002.

6 Wilks M, ibid.

7 English V and Somerville A, 'Presumed consent for transplantation: a dead issue after Alder Hey?' *Journal of Medical Ethics*, 2003, 29, pp 147–152.

These are just two of many possible examples of ways in which bad arguments can have serious ethical consequences. Weak logic encourages us to lump together what is logically distinct, such as killing and letting die, or to separate for doctrinal reasons what are in effect in the same logical category, such as consent for organ removal whether for research or transplantation.

Definition

Definition is the most common term from Aristotelian logic which survives in contemporary medical language. It is standard for doctors to expect a definition of any key word before entering into discussion. The point has been discussed in many articles by JG Scadding.[8] But how much can definitions achieve? Are we defining words or things? Should definitions come at the beginning, or at the end? Are there words which are indefinable? Are definitions true or false? Are they tautologies? Can they settle disputes? How do definitions affect ethical decisions? These questions raise philosophical issues well beyond the scope of this book but we shall try to provide some clarification of what it is reasonable to hope for from definitions, and touch only in passing on the wider philosophical issues.[9]

Nominal definition

The Aristotelian tradition distinguishes 'nominal' and 'real' or 'essential' definitions. To bring out this distinction one must consider answers to questions which begin: 'What is ...?' 'What does it mean to ...?' For example, 'What is "positive health"?' This question is asking for the definition of a term, a word or words; as such it is asking for a nominal definition. One way of identifying the request for a nominal definition is to consider whether what we are asking about (as in the example given) should be enclosed in inverted commas. If however, like jesting Pilate, we ask without quotation marks round the word 'truth': 'What is truth?' we are not asking about the meaning of a word – for we can use the word 'truth' correctly – but about the nature of what the word refers to. And, of course, that nature is very complex, which is why Pilate did not wait for the answer. This second sort of inquiry is an inquiry into 'realist' or 'essentialist' definitions, which we shall discuss in the next section.

There are many methods of nominal definition. One method – beloved of writers of essays – is to look the word up in a dictionary. This method of definition is called 'lexical' because it is concerned only with words, or 'reportive' since it

8 See, for example, Scadding JG, 'Health and disease: what can medicine do for philosophy?', *Journal of Medical Ethics*, 1988, 14, pp 118–124.

9 A more detailed philosophical discussion of definition can be found in Robinson R *Definition*, 1954, Oxford: Clarendon Press.

reports current usage of words in terms of their approximate synonyms. At some point, however, we must get outside the enclosure of words or we shall not really know what any word means; lexical, reportive or 'word–word' definitions presuppose the existence of 'word–thing' definitions.

A great deal of medical students' knowledge of their subject (too much in some people's opinion) consists of word–thing definitions. Students must know the names of bones, muscles and so forth, and the more advanced student must know what type of thing a term like 'compound fracture' refers to. Sometimes students are already familiar with the word, and the teacher's task is to link the word with the type of thing; at other times students are familiar with the thing and then learn the word, like the character in the play who learned to his surprise that he had been speaking prose all his life. In a third situation the word and the thing are learned as part of the same lesson, as when the professor describes a set of symptoms to the student and then gives the symptoms a name. 'These events are called a "myocardial infarction"'. In a fourth type of situation, in a clinic, say, the professor may be in a position to point to an example of the disease or injury. It is the stuff of the traditional medical cartoon to depict the professor declaiming 'A truly magnificent example of the Schneidergruppel farben syndrome' while the dismayed patient cowers in fright. But whatever the ethics of the situation the professor is engaging in the logically correct procedure of word–thing definition.

In the case just described it is possible for the professor, as we said, either to describe the syndrome or to point to an example of it. But there are types of situation where only the latter method is possible. This type of case is called 'ostensive' definition and its method is to explain the word by pointing to the thing. Obvious examples here are colour words. Of course it is possible to say ' "Green" is the colour which has such and such a wave length.' But this does not constitute a complete definition of 'green'. This point – that some words can be defined only ostensively – must be distinguished from a related question: are some words indefinable? We shall return to the latter question as part of our discussion of 'real' definition.

It is notorious that words in ordinary or indeed technical language are sometimes ambiguous, and one impetus behind the desire to define is to remove ambiguity. Definitions which select one from a range of meanings as the preferred meaning for a given purpose are called 'stipulative', and stipulations are essential for clear discussion. An excellent example of this is provided by William James. William James reported returning from a walk to find a group of friends debating about a squirrel clinging to the trunk of a tree. As someone walked around the tree it seemed that the canny squirrel edged sideways around the trunk, always keeping it between himself and the moving person. James's friends were quite sure that the person went around the tree. What they couldn't seem to agree on was whether the person went round the squirrel. Here is how James dealt with the question:

> 'Which party is right', I said, 'depends on what you practically mean by "going around" the squirrel. If you mean passing from the north of him to the east, then to the south, then to the west, and then to the north of him

again, obviously the man does go around him, for he occupies these successive positions. But if on the contrary you mean being first in front of him, then on the right of him, then behind him, then on his left, and finally in front again, it is quite obvious that the man fails to go round him, for by the compensating movements the squirrel makes, he keeps his belly turned towards the man all the time, and his back turned away. Make the distinction, and there is no occasion for any further dispute.'[10]

One disguised form of stipulative definition may be called 'persuasive definition'. For example, the word 'courage' has favourable resonances. Suppose that a teacher of small boys wishes to broaden their moral outlook so she says that true courage was shown by those who did not go off to fight but protested against the futility of war. In this way she has used the emotive force of 'courage' to bolster up a form of behaviour which her young pupils might not have thought to be typical of courageous behaviour. Again, a word such as 'cultured' means 'conversant with and appreciative of the arts'. Suppose a medical professor in a lecture tells his students that ethics and the arts are unnecessary in medical courses because medicine too is a form of culture. This would be the practice of persuasive definition, because the favourable connotations of the word are being applied to new criteria.

Our claim that a nominal definition can be achieved by a description of the type of thing the word refers to, or by pointing out an example of the thing, may encourage the view that definition is relevant only for nouns. But not only does this ignore the complex nature of language, it also misleads even about the process of defining nouns. To bring out this point consider how you would define words such as 'or' and 'damn!' The point is that language is not just indicative, as when nouns denote things, but is also expressive, as when we use expletives, and syntactical, as when we use word-order, or linking words, to convey our meaning. Definitions of syntactical words must involve rules for use, and even expressive words such as 'damn!', or parenthetical expressions, or qualifying expressions, require rules for their use and cannot be defined by a description or by pointing. So much is reasonably obvious when it is stated.

It is less obvious, but of central importance, that rules for use are explicitly or implicitly involved in *any* definition of meaning, including the nouns we might define by pointing. In describing or pointing out examples of, say, a compound fracture we are giving rules for the use of that term. Language is a public institution and the rules for its meaningful use must be publicly available. Even a word like 'pain' which may seem definable only by pointing to some private experience within the body is none the less governed by publicly understood rules; it *must* be if we are to communicate with each other. At this point it may be objected that we cannot really know what you mean when you use the word 'pain'. To discuss this question is to move from nominal definition to what the tradition calls 'real' or 'essentialist' definition.

'Real' definition

Those who were first concerned with definition were concerned with the nature of *things* and not mainly of words. For example, Plato's Dialogues are typically concerned with establishing a definition – of justice in the *Republic*, of courage in the *Laches*, of love in the *Symposium*, and of knowledge in the *Theaetetus*. But these definitions are of the things and not of the words. Similarly, Aristotle offers a range of definitions of motion, happiness, virtue and so on, but again he is concerned with what these things are and not simply with words. Indeed, Aristotle defines 'definition' as the statement which gives the essence,[11] and he is clearly thinking of the essence of the thing or the type of thing, and not mainly, or not at all, of the word. And it is not just the ancient Greeks who take this line on definition, nor indeed is it just philosophers. Linnaeus provided 'real' definition of plants through his system of botanical classification, and the WHO in 1946 offered a definition: Health is a state of complete physical, mental and social well-being, and not merely the absence of disease or infirmity.[12] Clearly, the WHO was not offering a definition of the *word* 'health', but what they take to be the very essence of health itself. What is it that Linnaeus and the WHO were trying to do?

Linnaeus was attempting to classify. In traditional logic the classification is in terms of 'genus' and 'species', where the class that is to be divided is called the 'genus' and the sub-classes are called the 'species'. Classification involves devising a process of dividing such that all the sub-classes or species are mutually exclusive. This process of classification employs some technical terms which are widely agreed: they are 'difference', 'property' and 'accident'. A quality is said to be a 'difference' if it serves to distinguish the class of entities of which it is a quality from other species of the same genus, or in other words if it is used in the definition of the class. A quality is said to be a 'property' if it is a quality possessed by every member of the class, yet is not used to distinguish the class from other species of the same genus. Finally, a quality is said to be an 'accident' if it may indifferently belong or not to all or any members of the class. This terminology may be archaic but the ideas are perfectly familiar and are perhaps expressible as 'defining characteristics', 'accompanying characteristics', and 'randomly attached characteristics'. For example, we might wonder whether certain symptoms are defining characteristics of a disease or just accompanying ones, always or sometimes. Moreover, classification can have important ethical implications, especially in psychiatry, where the way a mental illness is

---

11 Aristotle, *Topics*, Book 1, Chapter 4, in McKeon R (ed), *The Basic Works of Aristotle*, 1941, New York: Random House, p 190.
12 World Health Organization, *Constitution*, 1946, New York: WHO.

classified will affect not only the treatment but the way in which the patient may view herself and be viewed by friends and relatives. Indeed, certain moods or states of mind, such as mild depression, may be classified as treatable illnesses by some psychiatrists but not by others.

'Real' definition, as the search for watertight classifications, gives rise to many philosophical problems. Do the types we classify occur naturally in the world – *in rebus* – or do we impose classifications on the world? A great deal of ink, indeed of blood, was shed in mediaeval times over this and similar problems. And even if there are naturally occurring types in the world they are not always distinctly demarcated but sometimes overlap. Wittgenstein uses the helpful term 'family resemblance' to make the point that it is not always possible to find the necessary and sufficient conditions which constitute the essential identity of a type of thing.[13] Nature is often fuzzy at the edges of types and our concepts reflect this by being vague or 'open-textured' (to use another helpful expression). To be too rigid in defining may be to label unfairly and stigmatise – an ethical matter – and to miss new ways of seeing a medical problem.

What comes out of this is that the process of real definition in the sense of classification is sometimes arbitrary and depends in the end on stipulation. Closely connected with the idea of real definition as classification is the idea of real definition as scientific analysis. For example, it might be said that Hippocrates could not really define, did not really know, what epilepsy is. From one point of view this is absurd: he discussed the phenomenon. But what he was unable to do was provide a correct scientific *analysis* of it, whether it is physical or psychological in its causation, or what kind of malady it essentially is.

This account of real definition must be developed if it is to fit the WHO definition of health. We agreed that the WHO definition was not a definition of the *word* 'health', but neither does it seem to be an attempted classification of health. It seems more like Plato's definition of justice in the *Republic:* a statement of an ideal. Value words of all kinds are frequently defined in this way. Kant, for example, defines dutiful action as action done not with a motive of inclination or self-interest but out of pure respect for the moral law. He then confesses that there may be no actual cases of purely dutiful action, for the 'dear self' is always turning up in our motivation.[14] He must therefore be suggesting an ideal of dutiful action. In a similar way the WHO is really suggesting what it regards as an ideal of health. This of course has very important ethical implications since the WHO is suggesting that medicine ought to move in a particular direction to include lifestyle and social welfare. We shall look into this in some detail in the next two sections. There may be other processes which can be called 'real definition' but classification, analysis and the search for ideals are common forms of it.

13 Wittgenstein L, op. cit., paragraphs 65–75.
14 Kant I, *Groundwork of the Metaphysic of Morals.* Paton HJ (trans), 1948, London: Hutchison, Chapter 2.

Some problems solved

We are now in a position to deal with some of the questions which we raised at the start. First, are there indefinables? All *words* can in some way be defined, but there may be *things* or *experiences* which are indefinable. For instance, it is common to say that 'love' cannot be defined. If this means that the word cannot be defined then this is false. But if it means that the experience is not adequately analysable in words then perhaps it is true. Again, it is arguable (although we shall not begin to do so) that some philosophically important concepts are indefinable. For example, we can define the word 'knowledge', but there is no non-circular definition (classification or analysis) of what knowledge is. It is of course controversial to try to offer real definitions of value words, such as 'good'. This is very important in medicine. As we shall see (p 85) there have been attempts to devise scales of 'good' doctor/patient interaction. But to do this it must be stipulated that certain factors count as 'good' in the interaction, such as eye-contact. But not everyone may want the doctor to be staring at them all the time! In other words, it is essentially contestable what counts as a 'good' doctor/patient interaction and the attempt to settle this in advance by a stipulative definition assumes without argument or evidence the answers to controversial questions.

Second, can definition be true or false? The answer will depend on the sort of definition we are considering. Take first nominal definitions. Reportive or lexical definitions and ostensive definitions will be true or false in so far as they do or do not correctly indicate how a word is in fact used, whereas a stipulation as to how a word is going to be used cannot have truth value; it is simply telling us about how someone intends to use the term. A 'real' definition which is recommending an ideal cannot have truth value, for the function of ideals is not to state facts but to guide conduct. 'Real' definitions in the form of classifications are more problematic. We may discover at least some real sorts of thing in nature, but there can be more than one way of classifying things, and controversial borderline cases. Such problematic and contestable cases of classification exist pre-eminently in psychiatry, but also in other areas of medicine.

Third, should definitions come at the beginning or the end? The answer here will again depend on the kind of definition we are considering. It can be helpful and saving of confusion if writers make clear at the start how they are proposing to use an ambiguous term – as in the William James example – but at other times a definition can result only from prolonged argument and analysis since what is at stake is what the definition ought to be, and a premature definition may just assume the answer to a disputed position. A notorious example of this is when a fetus is defined as already having the attributes of a person, leaving the pro-abortionist to defend a murder charge; controversial moral disputes cannot be settled by plucking a definition out of the air.

Fourth, are definitions tautologies? Those who raise such a question may have in their minds definitions such as 'Bachelors are unmarried men', which has the ring of a tautology. This is not the context to investigate the difficult and controversial philosophical issues of the tautology, the analytic proposition, the synonym, or the translation, but at the commonsense level it is plausible to say that word–word definitions, as in dictionaries, approach the tautologous. But word–thing definitions are not tautologous, nor are 'real' definitions.

Pitfalls and recommendations

We can now make some suggestions of relevance to bioethics. First, many contemporary philosophers would be unhappy about retaining the label, 'definition' for what the tradition calls 'real' definition. It is good advice to follow this lead and instead to use a range of other terms, such as 'classification' or 'analysis' or 'recommendation'. To use the term 'definition' as a substitute here may mislead by implying that the analysis or recommendation is objective and neutral when in fact an ethical stance has been adopted. But it should be noted that many writers continue to use the term 'definition' in this wide and perhaps misleading way.

Second, it is important to distinguish defining characteristics of a type of thing from its accompanying characteristics. The latter may be only typical and not always present. Defining characteristics purport to provide the necessary and sufficient condition of something, whereas accompanying characteristics are simply typically true of something.

Third, note that stipulative definitions can be confusing when the writer, having stipulated a narrow and precise meaning of a word, then forgets the stipulation and later uses the word in another or in a wider sense. In particular, avoid stipulating counter to the normal meaning of the word. For example, the word 'person' in the well-known slogan 'respect for persons' is used in a Kantian sense, such that 'persons' are self-determining, self-governing creatures able to run their own lives in terms of rational laws valid for all. It follows from that stipulation that the Down's Syndrome child is not fully a person although fully a human being. But such is the emotive force of the word 'person' that to suggest that a mentally handicapped child is not fully a person is to run the risk of acrimonious and entirely needless debate over a stipulation which goes against the emotive force of ordinary language.

A recent example of confusion over the meaning or implications of a term centred on the word 'consent'. The word 'consent' is used widely in ordinary speech and indeed in the Human Tissue Act of 1961. But since 1961 it has increasingly been used in what is almost a technical sense by ethicists. This ambiguity was one source of the dispute in the United Kingdom in 1999–2000 over the retention of organs and tissues after autopsy.[15] It was alleged that pathologists and others had retained the organs and other tissues of children after

---

15 For a fuller discussion of the issues here see Downie RS, 'Research on dead infants', *Theoretical Medicine and Bioethics*, 2003, 24, 2, pp 161–175.

autopsy without obtaining full consent from the parents of these children. Many pathologists argued that they were acting in terms of the law then current – the Human Tissue Act of 1961. In terms of this Act a pathologist or other professional 'lawfully in possession of the body of a deceased person' could proceed with non-statutory autopsy and research, but only if 'having made . . . such reasonable enquiry as may be practicable . . . he has no reason to believe' that any surviving relative of the deceased objects to the body being so dealt with. In other words, the pathologists were required to ask parents and relatives if they objected to the organs or tissues of a deceased child being used for research. If the parents said 'We don't object' they were deemed to have consented. And as far as ordinary language goes they had consented. But as far as the language of bioethics goes they had not consented, because in bioethics consent is nowadays logically tied to full disclosure of all relevant facts.

To bring out the difference between consent in ordinary contexts and consent in bioethical contexts consider the following example. Suppose I invite you to meet me for a drink after work and you reply, 'Thanks, see you at the door at 6 pm'. As far as ordinary language and conventions go you have consented, and if you do not show up around 6pm I have a moderate grievance. It will not do if you try to defend yourself by saying 'You did not inform me how long the date would last, whether we would be drinking wine, beer or coffee etc.'. But all that information and much more would be required for a valid consent in bioethics. Nor is it simply in trivial contexts that the ordinary notion of consent can be seen at work. If you say 'I do' in a certain context you have consented to marry me – indeed, you have married me – even if you are not at all well informed about what you are letting yourself in for! The point in all this is not necessarily to criticise the bioethics use of 'consent' but to point out that unnecessary disputes arise when a term is taken from ordinary language and given a more precise sense than it usually has.

Fourth, consider whether a definition is always necessary. We can all meet a friend at 8 pm for dinner without being able to define time or space, and medical treatment can proceed independently of definitions of disease or health. Indeed, definitions can be undesirable if they foreclose speculation.

The central message for ethics in this discussion of definition is that experience constantly breaks through the false finalities of language, and the barriers of definition can be artificial and distracting. Apparently neutral definitions may sometimes conceal value judgements with important implications for practical medical policy.

Two examples: disease and health

To expand this message we shall take two extended examples of the difficulties to be encountered in the pursuit of definitions of terms which are not in fact definable. What will emerge is that when definitions of these terms are suggested they turn out to presuppose value judgements, and like all value judgements they have practical implications. Practical implications in medicine can be financially very costly and more importantly can determine policies. The terms we shall discuss are all central to medical discourse. They are: disease and health.

Disease

There are two main strands in discussions of disease. We shall call them the biological and the sociological.[16]

In terms of the biological strand, 'disease' is a scientific, descriptive term and diseases are *discovered* and *classified* by various biological sciences, such as biochemistry, physiology and anatomy. And, as we said, classification is one form of 'real' definition.

The origin of this approach to disease can be found in the ancient Greeks. For example, the biologist-philosopher Aristotle sees the task of the biologist as that of discovering the repeatable features of nature and then of classifying the phenomena in terms of genera and species. In a word, biological science is taxonomy.[17] This way of thinking enters the early modern world through the seventeenth-century physician Thomas Sydenham (1624–89), and the eighteenth-century botanist Carl Linnaeus (1707–78). These influential biologists believed that it was possible to classify, not only plants and animals, but also diseases, into genera and species. Types of disease can be discovered, and they exist independently of human interests. They would be identified in terms of various malformation, irregular growths, genetic irregularities and so on, which lead to the malfunctioning of an organ or a bodily system. In terms of this type of definition diseases exist as independent entities like types of plant.

It follows from this position that the fact that most people try to avoid disease, and medical scientists try to eradicate it, is completely independent of the meaning of the term disease. To put it another way, disease may be relevant to clinical medicine, but only to the extent that a disease-entity may be the cause or part-cause of a condition with which a patient presents himself to a clinician. The disease-entity exists independently of the clinical situation, and can be studied independently of it, in laboratories and so on.

Such a view is very plausible in general outline and is still very much alive. It has been given new strength with the rise of genetics and the idea that there is a 'gene for' every human ailment. None the less the biological view is open to criticism. We shall express some of these in an outline of the second approach to defining disease – the sociological.

16 There are helpful discussions of the concept of disease in Nordenfelt L and Lindahl I (eds), *Health, Disease, and Causal Explanations in Medicine*, 1984, Dordrecht: Reidel. We are especially indebted to the essay by H Tristram Engelhardt, 'Clinical Problems and the Concept of Disease', pp 27–37.
17 Aristotle, *De Partibus Animalium*, 642b–644b, in McKeon, R op. cit., pp 651–655.

The sociological view has a negative and a positive side. Negatively, it finds a range of problems in the biological view. First, its exponents point out that there are some phenomena which are regarded as diseases by some social groups but not by others. For example, there is a range of conditions associated with ageing, such as failing vision or hearing, or stiffness in the joints. Value judgements and cultural norms are the factors which determine whether these are diseases or not. From the biological standpoint they are statistically normal. A similar sort of problem concerns the fact that some conditions might count as a disease in one context, but not in another. For example, colour-blindness might seem a disease in many contexts, but colour-blind individuals can identify camouflage with greater success than colour-visual individuals. Here one might imagine an environment where the capacity to spot camouflage maximises one's own chances to survive and reproduce. Again, many people might think of deafness as a disease or disability, but the British Deaf Association denies that deafness is a disability. For them a deaf person is just one kind of normal person, and the deaf are said to have their own culture. In short, the sociological approach draws attention to the facts that disease classification may be culture relative, and certainly can involve value-judgements. It is not the neutral, descriptive activity of discovery and classification postulated by the biological approach.

More positively, we are invited to see disease in terms of the impairment of human function taken as a whole. Whereas in the biological approach disease is associated with failings in organs or parts of the body, in the sociological it is thought to apply to the whole human organism. From the sociological perspective, human beings are diseased if they cannot function normally, where 'normal' is interpreted in terms of the norms of a given culture. 'Disease' ('illness' or 'disability') characterises a life as a whole, as it is acted out in a given society, and the term applies only derivatively to an organ or part of the body. The stress in the sociological approach, then, is on the evaluative nature of the concept of disease, and the values of a given culture. For example, in some cultures obesity might be ranked as a disease but in others it might be seen as a sign of affluence and enhance reproductive status. Diseases, for the sociological way of thinking, are not *discovered*, and they have no timeless, absolute definition. Rather they are defined by the values, norms and social expectations of a given society. This approach has merits and clearly fits some of the ways in which we speak of disease. To some extent diseases and their treatments are matters of fashion. (An idea made fun of long ago by Bernard Shaw in *The Doctor's Dilemma*.)

None the less there are also real problems with the sociological line. Briefly, we shall mention two difficulties. First, science can identify particular, anatomically located diseases. These are attributable to specific organs or systems, and not to the person as a whole. For example, someone might have diseased lungs, and be dying in a palliative care unit, but overall, as a person, he might experience the well-being of someone who has made his peace with his friends and family and is ready to go. So a diseased bodily part can exist alongside overall health and well-being. Second, there is general agreement in the medical sciences about what biochemical or physiological states should be viewed as healthy and what viewed as diseased. It is true that in many cases there might be dispute at the margins. For example, there might be dispute as to whether a given cholesterol level is too high. But nevertheless there is agreement that certain levels indicate disease and others are entirely normal. This seems to suggest that disease language is at least mainly scientific, and a non-evaluative definition would therefore be appropriate.

We seem to have reached an impasse. The biological and the sociological approaches are plausible in their criticisms of each other, but neither has a fully persuasive positive theory.

In science or philosophy when an irresolvable problem is reached it is worth considering whether we are asking the right question. We wish to suggest a third way, which avoids questions of definition entirely but fits many aspects of current medical practice.

Our suggestion is that we drop the whole idea of trying to answer the question of definition: 'What is disease?', and substitute the idea of 'clinical problem'. In developing this line, we might say that language can misguide, and concepts by their very character can misdirect us. Disease-concepts have been distorted on the one hand by the assumption that they name things in the world in a value-free fashion, and on the other hand by the assumption that they are purely human value-constructs. Our suggestion is that we should see disease-concepts instead as goal-directed notions. What are the goals? They are the goals of medicine. These we might characterise in general terms as the attempt to prolong life, where that is worthwhile, to free us from pain, and to minimise impairments to everyday function. Certain physiological and anatomical states are likely to impede the achievement of these important human goals in any environment. Obvious examples are the major cancers and heart diseases. They will therefore constitute cross-culturally recognisable diseases. However, other states of affairs, such as the failings of age, will count as diseases in some societies but not in others.

We shall state the argument in a different way. There may be an error in seeking *the nature* of disease. Different sorts of answers may be appropriate for evolutionary biology and for clinical medicine. Our present concern is with clinical problems. Now, if we are correct in saying that clinical medicine is focused on resolving clinical problems connected with prolonging life, minimising pain and improving impaired everyday functioning, then it will allow with equal propriety as clinical problems: lung cancer, schizophrenia, the pains of childbirth, unwanted fertility and unwanted sterility, as well as difficulties like appendicitis or stiff joints. That list contains some problems which are classic diseases, others which are conceptually borderline, and others which don't fall under the heading of 'disease' at all. The point is that clinical medicine is interested in *reliable warrants* for *useful medical interventions*, and the question whether something is or is not a disease then becomes irrelevant. As a warrant for medical intervention we suggest that clinical judgement and the patient's consent are more reliable guides than biological disease-taxonomies or definitions.

This 'third way' has certain merits for clinical medicine, in that it side-steps the philosophical problem of definition with which we started: What is disease? What are its necessary and sufficient conditions, or its definition? These are interesting questions, but too much attention to them can move clinical medicine in the wrong direction.

But we do not want to give the impression that the 'clinical judgement' approach is without drawbacks, even from a practical point of view. We shall note two respects in which 'disease-entity' terminology may have practical advantages over the 'clinical problems' terminology. The first is the desirability of limiting what can reasonably count as a 'clinical problem'. The *British Medical Journal* ran an issue on 'non-diseases'.[18] The editor listed the top 20 non-diseases, which included boredom, baldness, freckles, jet lag, unhappiness, road rage and so on. One great merit of the disease-entity approach is that it can stop clinical medicine being forced to take over all the ills of life. The clinician can say that where there is no underlying pathological condition there is nothing for clinical medicine.

Second, patients themselves may prefer to have their condition identified with a disease-name. Armed with a disease-name they have a socially and legally validated defence against employers, a possible claim against insurance companies, immunity from ordinary social claims and conventions, and indeed a nameable alien entity against which they can be said to 'fight'. Hence, the popular, and perhaps also the scientific, belief in disease-entities may be stronger than that in clinical judgement, especially granted the new faith in genetics. Many members of our obese population feel relief at the suggestion that there may be a 'gene for' obesity! So there are problems with a 'clinical judgement' approach, and some reasons to accept the ancient Greek idea of biological disease-entities, despite its drawbacks.

The humanities may have a role in this unsatisfactory situation. Hard-nosed scientists are not allowed to indulge in a flight of fancy, they must seek 'real' definitions. But from a humanities perspective we can suggest an analogy rather than a definition. Diseases are like weeds. Weeds are plants, but if these plants are growing in the wrong place, or there are too many of them, or they kill other plants, or they are multiplying too rapidly, they become weeds. Patients are like the owners of gardens, and clinicians are like gardeners. Together they decide which plants or diseases to try to eradicate, which they can only restrain and keep in check, and which should be left alone. Moreover, just as gardeners have jobs not connected with deciding what are weeds and what should be done about them – jobs such as watering and testing the pH of the soil – so clinicians and

18   *British Medical Journal*, Letters to the Editor, 2002, 324, pp 912–914.

clinical biochemists have jobs which are not directly concerned with disease. Questions of definition are therefore not always helpful, and can mislead by pointing research in the wrong direction.

Health

Let us now turn to attempts to define health. Once again we shall find that these attempts can cause medical practice to adopt an ethical stance disguised as neutral definition. Indeed, as we shall see (p 100), some of these definitions can lead to medical authoritarianism.

Images of disease, illness, bereavement and death are common in literature, but images of health are more difficult to find, the reason being that health does not have a clear identity of its own. The experiences of disease and illness are intense and have a certain duration. Thus, they can become objects of attention in their own right and easily generate a rich variety of images. Being healthy, on the other hand, might just be a way of saying that we are not ill or diseased. If so, the lack of literature on health is not surprising, because there is nothing to write about. Medical practice seems to support this view of health, in that when treatment restores us to health it is really just removing disease or illness. Even if we say that there is some biological balance or equilibrium, we still do not have a concept that is likely to be a focus for a writer's attention. For when we are in this state of bodily equilibrium – when we are healthy – we do not notice our health but concentrate on other matters. Health is, as it were, transparent, whereas illness and disease are opaque. Health, therefore, easily escapes the attention of writers because in one sense it lacks the identity of illness or disease.

The 1946 WHO definition of health offers another sense of health: 'Health is a state of complete physical, mental and social well-being, and not just the absence of disease and infirmity.'[19] This definition has, of course, been much criticised, but the problem for the purposes of this discussion is that it does not give health a clear identity, any more than do the 'absence of disease' or the 'equilibrium' views of health. For what has come to be known as 'positive health' is a concept in perpetual disguise. It is conceptually impossible to distinguish positive health from other states such as well-being, happiness, exhilaration, fitness or vigour. In other words, we shall not find many images of health unless we look for them under other descriptions or in other guises. But these other guises tell us a great deal about health, just as we can learn a great deal about someone by noting the clothes they wear. It is therefore on some of the many guises of health that we shall concentrate, and also on the conceptual company that health keeps, such as beauty and youth.

19   See fn 12.

In whatever guise it appears, health is regarded as a value, for it frequently appears in lists alongside other values, as in phrases such as 'healthy, wealthy, and wise'. The following anonymous verse about the four-leaf clover is typical:

> One leaf for fame, one for wealth
> One for a faithful lover,
> And one leaf to bring glorious health,
> Are all in a four-leaf clover.[20]

But the health that is thought to be valuable or worth having, however varied its images, is usually more than the absence of disease or infirmity. As the Spanish-born Latin epigrammatist Martial (AD 40–104) stated, 'Non est vivere, sed valere est' ('Life's not just being alive but being well').[21] But there is a huge variation of opinion about what this 'being well' consists of. The only thing that seems to be agreed upon by writers is that there is no single state that is being well.

The same emphasis on the variable nature of states of health can be found in the writer/philosopher Nietzsche (1844–1900):

> For there is no health as such, and all attempts to define anything that way have been miserable failures. Even the determination of what health means for your body depends on your goal, your horizon, your energies, your drives, your errors, and above all on the ideals and phantasms of your soul. Thus there are innumerable healths of the body and … the more we put aside the dogma of the 'equality of men', the more must the concept of a normal health, along with a normal diet and the normal course of an illness, be abandoned by our physicians. Only then would the time have come to reflect on the health and sicknesses of the soul, and to find the peculiar virtue of each man in the health of his soul: in one person's case this health could, of course, look like the opposite of health in another person.[22]

In the case of Richard Wagner (1813–83), his 'normal' state is one of 'exultation', as a letter to August Roeckel dated 26 January 1854, shows:

> In order to become a radically healthy human being, I went two years ago to a Hydropathic establishment; I was prepared to give up Art and everything if I could once more become a child of Nature. But, my good friends, I was

---

20 Downie RS, *The Healing Arts*, 2000, Oxford: Oxford University Press, p 186.
21 Martial (Marcus Valerius Martialus), *Epigrammata*, in Porter P (ed), *After Martial*, 1972, Oxford: Oxford University Press, Book 6, no.70.
22 Nietzsche FW, *The Joyful Science*, 1967, New York: Vintage Books.

obliged to laugh at my own naiveté when I found myself almost going mad. None of us will reach the promised land – we shall all die in the wilderness. Intellect is, as someone has said, a sort of disease; it is incurable. In the present conditions of life, Nature only admits of abnormalities. At the best we can only hope to be martyrs; to refuse this vocation is to put oneself in opposition to the possibilities of life. For myself, I can no longer exist except as an artist; since I cannot encompass love and life, all else repels me, or only interests me in so far as it has a bearing on Art. The result is a life of torment, but it is the only life. Moreover, some strange experiences have come to me through my works. When I think of the pain and discomfort which are now my chronic condition I cannot but feel that my nerves are completely shattered: but marvellous to relate, on occasion, and under a happy stimulus, these nerves do wonders for me; a clearness of insight comes to me, and I experience a receptive and creative activity such as I have never known before. After this, can I say that my nerves are shattered? Certainly not. But I must admit that the normal condition of my temperament – as it has been developed through circumstances – is a state of exultation, whereas calm and repose is its abnormal condition. The fact is, it is only when I am 'beside myself' that I become my real self, and feel well and happy.[23]

On the other hand, the quiet life of honest toil is much promoted in literature as the life of true health and well-being. Oliver Goldsmith (1730–74) writes in 'The Deserted Village':

A time there was, ere England's grief began,
When every rood of ground maintained its man;
For him light labour spread her wholesome store,
Just gave what life required, but gave no more;
His best companions, innocence and health;
And his best riches, ignorance of wealth.[24]

But literature has its health cynics, such as James Thurber (1884–1961): 'Early to rise and early to bed makes a male healthy and wealthy and dead.'[25]
     More typically, images of health are presented in terms of youth and vigour and beauty. Tolstoy (1828–1910) in his masterpiece *War and Peace* uses images of youth, vigour and health as metaphors for moral goodness. In Book 1 we are

23 Wagner R, *The Musicians' World: Letters of the Great Composers*, Gifford H (ed), 1965, London: Thames and Hudson, p 290.
24 Goldsmith O, *The Deserted Village*, Masson J (ed) (1770) 1869, London: Macmillan.
25 Thurber J, 'The Shrike and the Chipmunks', *The New Yorker*, 29 April 1939.

introduced to the young people of the Rostov family and in particular to the eldest son, Nicholas, who is described as:

> short with curly hair and an open expression. Dark hairs were already showing on his upper lip, and his whole face expressed impetuosity and enthusiasm.[26]

Later, when he joins the army to campaign against Napoleon, we are again struck by his appearance:

> Rostov in his cadet uniform, with a jerk to his horse rode up to the porch, swung his leg over the saddle with a supple youthful movement, stood for a moment in the stirrup as if loath to part from his horse, and at last sprang down and called to his orderly.

His sister, Natasha, is similarly portrayed as bursting with good humour and vitality:

> She...glanced at her younger brother, who was screwing up his eyes and shaking with suppressed laughter, unable to control herself any longer, she jumped up and rushed from the room as fast as her nimble little feet would carry her.

These attractive portraits follow immediately on from the opening scenes of the novel which take place at a soirée attended by the great and the good of St Petersburg society. These characters are portrayed as older, false and manipulative. The contrast is striking.

There seems to be widespread agreement from the time of Plato to the present that diet and exercise (rather than health care or doctors) are the determinants of health.[27] John Dryden (1631–1700) is another example of this tradition:

> Better to hunt in fields, for health unbought.
> Than fee the doctor for a nauseous draught.
> The wise, for cure, on exercise depend;
> God never made his work, for man to mend.[28]

Some writers distinguish between physical and mental health. Maimonides (1135–1204), for example, writes of the two perfections of man:

> Man has two perfections: a first perfection, which is the perfection of the body, and an ultimate perfection, which is the perfection of the soul. The

26 Tolstoy L, *War and Peace*, Maude I and Maude A (trans), 1922, Oxford: Oxford University Press.

27 Plato, *Republic*, Lee D (trans), 1955, Harmondsworth: Penguin, Book 4, pp 444–445.

28 Dryden J, 'Epistle to my honoured kinsman John Driden', in Kinsley J (ed), *Collected Works of John Dryden*, 1956, Oxford: Oxford University Press.

first perfection consists in being healthy and in the very best bodily state. His ultimate perfection is to become rational in actuality.[29]

But not everyone agrees that the well-being of the mind or soul consists of the exercise of rationality. George Herbert (1593–1633) sees it as virtue:

> Only a sweet and virtuous soul,
> Like seasoned timber never gives;
> But though the whole world turn to coal,
> Then chiefly lives.[30]

Others see mental health (and indeed physical health) as a balance of elements: 'Whatever dies was not mixed equally.'[31] John Donne (1572–1631) is here writing of love, but he is using an idea of health that goes back to the Greeks. Indeed, the notion of mental health as expressed through a 'balanced personality' is still current in psychiatry. (We shall discuss the idea at much greater length in Chapter 6). But others again see mental health as an extreme. For example, William Blake (1757–1827) in *The Marriage of Heaven and Hell* represents some aspects of this point of view:

> Energy is Eternal Delight

or

> The road of excess leads to the palace of wisdom.[32]

It is noteworthy that there is a tradition that sees our mortal life as highly unsatisfactory. Bodily health, which maintains that life, is correspondingly described paradoxically as a kind of sickness. Shakespeare's disillusioned Timon of Athens is a good example:

> My long sickness / Of health and living now begins to mend, / And nothing brings me all things.[33]

> (Act V, Sc. i)

29 Maimonides, *The Guide of the Perplexed*, Pines S (trans), 1963, Chicago: Chicago University Press.
30 Herbert G, 'Virtue' in *The New Oxford Book of English Verse*, 1972, Oxford: Oxford University Press.
31 Donne J, 'The Good Morrow', in Allison J (ed), *The Norton Anthology of Poetry*, 1970, New York: Norton.
32 Blake W, The Marriage of Heaven and Hell, in Selincort, B (ed), *Selected Poems of William Blake*, 1951, Oxford: Oxford World's Classics, 1951.
33 Shakespeare W, *Timon of Athens*, in *The Oxford Shakespeare*, 1993.

Again when Socrates (469–399 BC) drinks the hemlock, which is his punishment for speaking the truth, Plato (428–348 BC) reports in the *Phaedo* that Socrates asks for a sacrifice to be made to Asclepius.[34] The point here is that he wishes to give thanks to the demigod of health for his recovery from the long sickness of life.

Our brief survey shows that the imagery of health is richer than at first it seems. It has emerged that health is a multifaceted concept and cannot be pinned down in a single definition; any attempt to do so will lead to a distortion of human values, a matter of considerable ethical significance for it involves forcing one ideal of the good life on us.

The general conclusion of this study of definition is that definitions can have ethical implications because they can suggest ways of perceiving patients and treatment policies, which in turn lead to ways of spending health resources. But definitions cannot settle ethical issues and, in the guise of neutrality or objectivity, definitions often conceal ethical positions which have no more claim on us than other positions.

Epistemology

Epistemology or theory of knowledge is an ancient branch of philosophy. It is concerned with questions such as 'What is knowledge?' or 'What can we be certain of?' or 'Do the senses give us reliable knowledge?' The general view which emerged in the modern period is that mathematics is the key to reliable knowledge. This is the view of the most influential philosopher/scientists such as Galileo (1564–1642), Descartes (1596–1650) and Newton (1642–1727). The view has dominated science, and, in its efforts to be scientific, medicine has also developed this stance. It is a stance with profound ethical implications for how doctors have come to see their profession in the twentieth century, and more importantly how they have come to see their patients. We shall find running through the scientific perspective of medicine a contrast between what is countable and is therefore 'objective' and likely to be true, and what is 'subjective', 'anecdotal' or just a 'matter of opinion', and therefore likely to be unreliable and unimportant. This emphasis on the countable has had profound implications for the way medical research has been conducted over the last 50 years. And the nature of medical research has affected the way in which doctors view their patients. In other words, the perspective has ethical significance, as we shall try to show through argument and illustration.

The main areas of medical research are: (1) the search for systematic understanding of the body in its normal workings and pathology; (2) observational studies, both descriptive and quantitative; (3) experimental studies, in particular randomised trials to establish the best treatments; and (4) qualitative research.

34   Plato, *Phaedo*, 1970, New York: Library of Liberal Arts.

The first three of these areas of medical research raise difficult problems of scientific interpretation and judgement. We have discussed these in detail elsewhere[35] and will not repeat the arguments here since the judgements involved are not mainly ethical. But qualitative research does raise ethical problems in the broad sense, since in the guise of objective science it suggests ways in which doctors should view their patients and their medical activities. In other words, qualitative research brings in certain ethical perspectives dressed up as established fact by its use of numbers. Its credentials, and especially its numerical credentials, require therefore to be examined.

Qualitative research

Research that attempts to find the meaning behind a patient's or a doctor's action, or to interpret their actions, is referred to as 'qualitative research'. In the field of research on sexually transmitted diseases, for example, a simple descriptive study would answer the question, 'What is the prevalence in young women of infection with *Chlamydia trachomatis?*', whereas qualitative methods would be required to find out what these women understood about this infection and whether the experience of having had the infection changed their behaviour in any way. Such methods might include semi-structured interviews with individual women and focus-group discussions. We have no quarrel with such research, and shall later (p 87ff) suggest a way of interpreting it. But we must discuss the arguments for a numerical interpretation.

Should researchers involved in qualitative research use numbers to present their findings? There is an increasing focus on qualitative research in medicine[36] and, whereas the results of such research used to appear only in sociological, educational and anthropological journals, medical journals are beginning to publish some examples. There is, therefore, a tendency to force qualitative research into a quantitative mould. For example, we find qualities like 'patient-centredness' being given a score of 1.45 and doctor satisfaction measured as 8.95.[37] Are such measurements meaningful or helpful? Indeed – and this is the primary consideration in this section – do they distort the doctor–patient relationship? In answering these questions we shall focus on the uses of numbers and the establishment of scales, look at the implications numbers and scales have for qualitative research, and finally, suggest a more satisfactory interpretation of the findings of qualitative research. We have therefore three questions to discuss: First, can qualitative research meaningfully use measurements and scales in the manner of quantitative research? Second, supposing we cannot meaningfully use

35 Downie RS and Macnaughton J, *Clinical Judgement: Evidence in Practice*, 2000, Oxford: Oxford University Press.
36 Jones R, 'Why do qualitative research?', *British Medical Journal*, 1995, pp 131–132.
37 Law S and Britten N, 'Factors that influence the patient-centredness of a consultation', *British Journal of General Practice*, 1995, 45, pp 520–524.

measurements and scales, how does their attempted use distort the way doctors view their patients or their consultations? (This is the question with the main ethical significance.) Third, is there some other way of interpreting qualitative research which makes it helpful for medical practice? (Here we shall find the kind of understanding typically gained from the humanities provides a good analogy.)

Qualitative research, numbers and scales

The philosopher of science, Ernest Nagel said:

> Measurement has been defined as the correlation with numbers of entities which are not numbers.[38]

The use of numbers and the mechanism of counting are essential first steps in understanding the nature of measurement. We use numbers in three distinct ways.[39] First, as a method of identification or labelling, as in the numbering of football players on a field or in labelling diagrams. In this case, the numbers have no relationship with each other and they are assigned in a totally arbitrary fashion. Letters might equally well serve this function of number-use.

Second, numbers are used to indicate the position of something in a series. Examples here might be the numbering of theatre seats or house numbers. The numbers indicate the relationship of one seat or house to the other, and enable people to find them easily. A more complex example of the same use of numbers is that of the relative hardness of wood, glass and diamond. Diamond can cut glass but glass cannot cut diamond; glass can cut wood but wood cannot cut glass. We can therefore, arrange these three objects in a series of increasing hardness, with wood at the bottom and diamond at the top. If we give wood the number 1, glass 2 and diamond 3, this tells us that wood is softer than glass, which is in turn softer than diamond. This kind of arrangement in a series is appropriate for non-additive qualities like hardness and also applied to the kinds of things that qualitative research deals with, such as patient satisfaction and quality of life. But the arrangement has a limitation: it does not tell us that diamond is three times as hard as wood because our series does not give indication of how much harder any object is in comparision to any other. The important point is that when qualities are arranged in a series and identified with numbers, the use of those numbers to perform calculations like averages or percentages is meaningless, as the relationship between points 1 and 2, and between 5 and 6 in the series, may be completely different. Distinctions between qualitative entities

---

38 Nagel E, 'Measurement', in *Philosophy of Science*, Danto A, Morgenbesser S (eds), 1960, Cleveland: Meridian Books, p 121.

39 Cohen MR and Nagel E, *An Introduction to Logic and Scientific Method*, 1934, London: Routledge and Kegan Paul, p 294.

can very often only be expressed through descriptions like 'more and less' or 'better and worse' as they have no true numerical meaning.

The third way in which numbers are used is to describe quantitative relationships between things. Examples here might be weights or distances, or amounts of things. If we take one bag of sugar to weigh 1 unit and balance a similar bag of sugar opposite it so that neither bag sinks, we can say that the second bag also weighs 1 unit. We can then take a bigger bag of sugar and balance it against the two smaller bags, such that neither side sinks, and say that the bigger bag weighs 2 units. In this way we can construct a scale of measurement for the bags of sugar. This use of numbers is appropriate for properties that are additive. It applies to the quantitative analysis of scientific research, such as the measurement of blood pressure or blood levels of a drug or cholesterol. Unlike the case of the series, the distances between the points on these scales are equal and, therefore, we can construct measurements of means with standard deviations and talk of scales and percentages with meaning.

But what if the subject of the measurement is not an additive entity? For instance, can the degree of patient satisfaction with a doctor or of quality of life be described using a scale? Most qualitative research does not deal with qualities that are additive, so what are the problems of employing scales as a method of presenting its results? There are four main ones:

1   Ensuring that it is the same quality that is being measured from the highest to the lowest points on the scale.
2   Making the quality continuum explicit, that is, is it possible to distinguish between discrete points along it?
3   Establishing 'the equality of difference', that is, that each point on a scale is the same distance from another.
4   The effect of the observer on the construction of the scale and the measurements taken by it.

Now we discuss these at greater length.

1   This problem can be illustrated by a study on doctor's modes of dress.[40] The researchers acknowledged that they might not be measuring the patients' reactions to the pictures of doctors presented to them in the study but rather attitudes based on what the patients were used to in their own doctors. It is particularly when a respondent expresses an extreme view that the attitude under consideration may turn into something different. In this example, extreme disapproval of a casual mode of dress may reflect a personal dislike of wearing jeans, rather than any view as to what it is appropriate for a doctor to wear.

---

40 McKinstry B and Wang J, 'Putting on the style: what patients think of the way their doctor dresses', *British Journal of General Practice*, 1991, 41, pp 275–278.

2   The second problem is whether it is possible to distinguish between discrete degrees of a quality along its continuum. Unless this can be done it is impossible to use numbers in any way, even as labels, as each point has to be clearly distinguishable from the next. Likert[41] encountered this problem in his description of a scale for the measurement of attitudes. His method depended on the construction of a statement to which people of different points of view would respond differentially according to the strength of their view from 'strongly approve' to 'strongly disapprove'. He gave an example of American attitudes towards Japan. A current example for the United Kingdom might be attitudes towards Europe. In a referendum on closer integration with Europe, a statement like 'Britain should follow Germany's lead and favour entering the Euro Zone' is likely to produce a predominantly negative response. It is difficult to think of a statement that would accurately reflect the spread of opinion on this subject, but suggesting that Britain should follow Germany's lead certainly would not. Likert scales are in common use in qualitative research and great care needs to be taken in the construction of the statements employed, particularly if the researcher is constructing a scale of four or more points.

3   This problem involves ensuring that the discrete points are at equal numerical distances to each other. Cohen and Nagel point out the difficulty:

> We must be on guard against a common error. It is often believed that because we can assign numbers to different degrees of a quality, the different degrees will always bear to each other the same ratio as do the numbers we have assigned to them. This is a serious mistake, and arises because it is supposed that measurement requires nothing more than the assigning of numbers.[42]

From the preceding consideration of numbers and their use it seems that the distinction between the second use (that of numbers arranged in a series) and the third (that of numbers to make quantitative distinctions) has become disregarded in some qualitative research. As an example of this, as part of a study looking at quality of care in general practice in Australia, Winefield et al.[43] measured doctor's satisfaction with a consultation using a visual analogue rating scale with points ranging from 0 = completely unsatisfying, to 5 = average in satisfaction, up to 10 = completely satisfying. The result of this analysis was expressed as a mean score of 8.95. This kind of method is valid in as much as it uses numbers in the first and second senses: both as

41 Likert R, 'A technique for the measurement of attitudes', *Archives of Psychology*, 1932, 140, pp 1–55.
42 Cohen and Nagel, op. cit., p 294.
43 Winefield HR, Murrell TG and Clifford J, 'Process and outcomes in general practice consultations: problems in defining high quality care', *Social Science and Medicine*, 1995, 41, p 969–975.

labels to stand for certain doctor responses and as a method of placing responses in a series, such that a score of 1 is considered less satisfying than a score of 2. However, this method does not establish a *scale* for the measurement of satisfaction between a score of 0 and 1 and is the same as that distinguishing a score of 2 from that of 3. To express the scores as a mean presupposes the establishment of a scale and is, therefore, invalid.

4   This problem deals with the effect of the researcher on the construction of the scale and its use in measurement. In quantitative research, measurement and the use of scales are straightforward. The scales used are generally well established and are not dependent on the factor being researched. If we want to measure blood pressure, for instance, the mercury sphygmomanometer exists and all that need concern us is the precision of the reading taken by the observer. The measurement is objective as the instrument has not been devised by those carrying out the research. This is qualified, however, by the fact that in all measurement we do not just measure x but rather the situation that combines x and the effect of the measuring instrument y. Thus with the case of blood pressure measurement we may not get a result that is the true blood pressure (x) but rather a reading (xy), which is different because of an error made by the observer or the measuring instrument.

In qualitative research, the margin for such error is much greater as the researcher is him or her self often one of the research instruments. Because qualitative research aims to 'study things in their natural settings',[44] methods of measurement may have to be devised specifically for the quality under consideration in the context in which it appears. As an example of this, Law and Britten[45] use a method of measuring patient-centredness devised by Henbest and Stewart[46] to assess doctors' consulting styles. The measurement is based on scoring doctors on the basis of their response to a 'patient offer', that is, anything patient says that is of potential significance. If a doctor does not respond, he scores 0; if he responds with a closed question, he scores 1; if he allows the patient further expression, he scores 2; and if he actively facilities the patient's expression, he scores 3. Audio-tapes of the consultations were used for analysis.

But in this study, the researchers were the most significant factor in the resulting score xy (which combines the effect of the instrument, y, with what is measured, x), as they were the ones who were analysing the audio taped consultations and deciding on scores. Thus, the researchers using this tool would listen to everything the doctor said as a reflection of his patient-centredness, and silence would score 0. But, in the true situation, silence might reflect the fact that the doctor knew the

44 Britten N, Jones R, Murphy E, Stacey R, 'Qualitative research methods in general practice and primary care', *Family Practice*, 1995, 12, pp 104–114.

45 Law and Britten op. cit.

46 Henbest RJ and Stewart MA, 'Patient-centredness in the consultation: a method of measurement', *Family Practice*, 199, 6, pp 249–253.

patient very well and might not need to say anything or might need only to touch the patient's hand to encourage him or her to express his or her concerns more fully. Even if the researcher were directly observing the doctor–patient interaction, he would be interpreting the doctor's response for the scoring system. Would he count a smile from the doctor as active facilitation of the patient's expression or not? The main point is that the measurement tool might distort what is being measured and may turn a positive response into something negative.

There are, therefore, problems with establishing that qualitative analysis is amenable to the use of scales at all, never mind whether numbers can be used in that analysis. Even when numbers are used in a series, it is very important to indicate their direction, for example, that 1 represents 'very satisfied' and 5 'very dissatisfied', rather than the other way round. This is entirely at the discretion of the researcher and reflects how meaningless numbers are as these labels. Letters of the alphabet could just as easily be used, except that they are limited to a series of 26. The judgement of the researcher is paramount, and the attempt to disguise this by appealing to numbers is unconvincing.

The conclusion of this discussion is that the results of qualitative research cannot satisfactorily be quantified. They cannot because of the nature of the subject under consideration (i.e., subjects such as doctor or patient attitudes); because the research is context-specific (i.e., describes a particular hospital clinic or general practice); and because of the researcher's influence on the measurement process. It follows from this conclusion that we cannot use the procedures of scientific induction to generalise these results; and if they cannot be generalised, how can they be of benefit to clinicians? All research aims at increasing our understanding, but for *clinical* research to be worthwhile, it additionally needs to produce some lessons for wider clinical practice. We shall argue (in the section on Generalisability) that qualitative research without the invalid use of numbers can make a positive ethical contribution to the shaping of the doctor/patient relationship. But first (in the next section) we shall argue that the invalid use of numbers encourages doctors to view patients in a manner with unfortunate ethical implications.

The distortion of numbers: ethical implications

In the previous section we have indicated various ways in which the use of numbers distorts qualitative research. The single most important feature of this distortion from the ethical point of view we can call 'reductivism'. The term 'reductivism' is used in a variety of ways, but in the sense in which we are using it here reductivism is the process of seeing human beings and their interactions in terms of a number of discrete features. Reductivism is essential for countability; there must be an answer to the question: what are you counting? In qualitative research those features are eye contacts, or answers to questions in the form of ticks in a box. But to try to understand patients in this way, in terms of a finite number of discrete features, is to abstract from the complexity and totality of a human interaction. Blood pressure can helpfully be abstracted in this way and measured, but not a human response in its complex totality. There is something profoundly patronising, if not demeaning, in the suggestion that the complexity and profundity of human relationships can be reduced to a few factors and 'measured' with an 'assessment tool'.

There is a second ethical problem, created by the fact that the numerical interpretation of qualitative research has enormously influenced clinical practice. The desire to use numbers (because they are thought to be 'objective') rather than make a humane clinical judgement has resulted in the mass use of questionnaires, or 'assessment tools' in the hospital ward and clinic. Medical training rightly stresses the importance of listening skills. On the other hand, the reality is that rather than listen to what the patient may be saying the doctor or nurse presents the patient with a form to fill up and boxes to tick. This is done on the grounds that such a procedure provides countable results which are therefore more 'objective' than simply having a discussion with the patient.

Even in palliative care, once the paradigm of patient-centredness, the 'watch and listen' of Dame Cicely Saunders [47] has been replaced by 'assessment tools'. Indeed, there are even spirituality [48] and demoralisation [49] scales, first researched by qualitative researchers and then presented to dying patients to assess their needs by numbers. At an early stage in life one may learn to paint by numbers, but not many people want to die by numbers!

Third, it is arguable that presenting patients, who may be very sick, with forms to fill up is inhumane and creates a distance between the doctor and the patient. Indeed, even if doctors do not present patients with a questionnaire, they may still distort interviews with patients if the reductivist questions and numbers are at the back of their minds.

We are claiming, then, that quite apart from the invalid and distorting scientific implications of interpreting qualitative research in terms of scales and numbers such interpretations have at least the above three unfortunate ethical consequences.

Generalisability and qualitative research: a route to understanding

How then should qualitative research be viewed? We shall first consider the extent to which it can be viewed as a science, and then suggest the positive contribution it can make, so viewed, to ethics.

47 Saunders, C, *Watch With Me*, 2003, Sheffield: Mortal Press.

48 Speck P, Higginson I and Addington-Hall J, 'Spiritual needs in health care', *British Medical Journal*, 2004, 329, pp 123–124.

49 Kissane DW, 'The demoralization scale: a report of its development and preliminary validation', *Journal of Palliative Care*, 2004, 20, 4, p 276.

We shall not claim that the following criteria are necessary and sufficient for an activity to be classified as a science, but they are at least typical of many agreed sciences: observation, and often experimentation; hypothesis formation; reductivism (usually for the purposes of measurement); and generalisability. Qualitative research can satisfy some but not all of these characteristics of science. Thus, the possibility of experimentation is limited for the obvious ethical reasons that human subjects are involved (but see p 118ff for an unethical attempt at experimentation). But it clearly involves observations, the recording of these observations, perhaps the use of 'instruments' such as video recorders, observation of the effects produced by the phenomenon under consideration (such as the effect of the doctor on the patient), the formation of hypotheses about causation, observation over a period of time, and no doubt others. We have suggested that where qualitative research goes wrong is in its attempt to adapt itself to other aspects of science, such as measurement, with the reductivism that this entails. Thus, in order to try to generate measurement, 'patient-centredness' (for example) becomes reduced to, or defined in terms of, a few operations, such as 'making eye contact'. But, as we have seen, even reduced to a few arbitrarily selected factors qualitative research cannot satisfy the measurement criterion.

Can qualitative research satisfy the generalisability criterion? This is more important than measurement since generalisability is perhaps a necessary, if not a sufficient, condition of what counts as scientific. And it is certainly a necessary condition of qualitative research being useful to clinicians.

The qualitative researcher cannot generalise by means of the usual procedures of scientific generalisation – induction from a range of relevantly similar instances. He/she cannot do this because, as we have seen, induction, in the clinical situation, requires the researcher to ignore the many complexities of human encounters and concentrate on only a few. How then, if at all, can the qualitative researcher generalise? The answer is that the lessons of qualitative research for clinicians are derived from considering the plausibility of the particular situation in terms of their own experience, and on finding parallels which are helpful. The question for the reader of this material is, 'Are there any universal features in this situation that I recognise and can apply?' The understanding involved in qualitative research is, therefore, more akin to the understanding gained from literature and art or, perhaps, philosophy, than that gained from a numerical science. This does not mean that it is an inferior kind of understanding, but it does mean that it is different in that it is reached by a different route. It requires the active participation of the reader to identify with the situation and relate the findings to his/her own situation.

Can we therefore conclude that qualitative research is scientific? The activities of science make up a large family. Qualitative research has some of the family characteristics, but it provides generalised understanding by a different route, a route similar to that along which the humanities take us. In reaching this understanding the judgement and life experience of the researcher is all-important, and as we said in Chapter 2 and will repeat in Chapter 6 it is important for the researchers or clinicians applying the research to be developed human beings. This too is an ethical requirement, and it takes us to the second issue in this section – how qualitative research can contribute to the ethics of the doctor/patient relationship.

Consider the following example from Sartre.[50] Sartre describes a man bending down to listen at a keyhole. He believes his wife is in the room with her lover. Suddenly he hears a step behind him, and immediately his attitude changes. To begin with, he wanted to hear a conversation, but now he has become an object to someone else – an eavesdropper to be described and despised. Sartre uses the example to show how we cannot think of ourselves as separate from others. But we could also use it to show that moral emotions, such as shame, are experienced in a social context. The eavesdropper minds being caught, not for any utilitarian-type reason, but because he must now think of himself as mean and sneaky. He despises such characteristics in others and now he must despise himself. This constitutes shame.

We have used this example because it is similar to many in qualitative medical research. The route to understanding is through our identification with the situation. Through that identification we reach universal features of human emotions. There is an element of generalisation, but not by induction. The imposition of quantitative language would obstruct this understanding by distorting the findings of qualitative research and making them obscure to the reader. Even if the approach of such research is narrative and descriptive of particular situations it is still aiming at providing understanding of general features of clinical situations. In presenting its results it might, therefore, do well to follow the example of philosophy and guide judgement by using words. Qualitative researchers take pride in the fact that their approach provides new insight into clinical situations. They should not hide these insights under a numerical bushel but illuminate them with language that reflects the new kind of understanding they wish to convey. To attempt to put numbers to the research is to distort both it and the relationship between doctor and patient which it is attempting to illuminate. This distortion has ethical implications because it is encouraging the doctor to see the patient in a reductivist rather than holistic way. It discourages active listening and replaces it with box-ticking, and it involves harassing sick patients with questionnaires. But properly understood qualitative research can lead to a new kind of understanding of human beings and their emotions – a kind typical of that which derives from the humanities. The doctor we all want from the ethical point of view is not the one who scores 8.75 on a bogus scale, but one who is an understanding person.

---

50 Sartre J-P, *Being and Nothingness* (1943), Barnes Hazel E (trans and ed), 1969, London: Methuen, pp 249–253.

Conclusions

It has emerged that two areas of philosophy – logic and epistemology – which might seem remote from ethics or value judgements have ethical significance. For example, inconsistency and other failures in logic can convey false ideas with ethical significance, such as that withholding or withdrawing a treatment is equivalent to administering poison. Again, the idea that we must first define our terms may seem a morally neutral requirement. But definitions can move practice in the wrong direction under the cover of an apparent neutrality. Turning to epistemology we found that the idea that insight into patients requires numbers is quite misleading. Measuring and counting are essentially reductivist procedures and to view patients through the template of numbers is to distort human relationships, a serious moral failing. Qualitative research is best interpreted on the analogy of the humanities. Through identification with the particular situation the researcher or clinician can recognise the universal element in human emotion. This is unlike the generalisability of inductive science. It requires a moral maturity from the doctor, and it can lead to a humane understanding of the patient.

Chapter 4

Political philosophy and bioethics

From the time of Hippocrates until the 1960s medical ethics (or health-care ethics or bioethics) were seen in terms of doctors' duties to patients. These duties have traditionally been condensed into that of furthering the patient's best interests, or alternatively as those of not harming the patient (non-maleficence) and of helping the patient (beneficence). Codes of medical ethics and philosophical discussion from the 1970s increasingly added 'respect for the patient's autonomous decisions' to the duties of non-maleficence and beneficence. In Chapter 2 we have indicated reservations about these principles, and the methodology they suggest. In this chapter we shall examine other limitations they have in the political philosophy of public health.

The central point is that, whereas a system of bioethics based on best interests or non-maleficence and beneficence can easily be extended to cover many public health interventions which are intended to be 'for our own good', there are greater problems for public health ethics if autonomy is made the ethically central concept. To bring this out, we shall contrast the interventions typical of clinical medicine with those of public health medicine. It should be noted here that we are using in this chapter the definition of public health accepted by the United Kingdom from the Acheson Report:

> Public health is the science and art of preventing disease, prolonging life and promoting health through organised efforts of society.[1]

Assuming this definition we can contrast the approach of clinical medicine with that of public health medicine.

Health-care ethics and public health ethics

The clinician is typically in a one-to-one relationship with a patient who has requested an interview because of a felt problem. The clinical imperative is

---

1 *Acheson Report: Public Health in England: Report of the Committee of Inquiry into the future development of the public health function*, 1988, London: HMSO.

therefore that something must be done including the giving of advice. Public health specialists, on the other hand, do not have specific patients with whom they are in a special relationship, and have received no request from a patient. It could be said that the public health specialist responds to a collective cry from individuals in a community when some medical problem occurs which affects a large number of people in a locality. One example is the outbreak of *Eschericia coli* 0157 in Wishaw in central Scotland in 1996. But here, again, there is no continuing relationship between the specialist and the affected group of individuals and therefore no opportunity for those individuals to express their views on the public health response. The public health specialist therefore is (a) making a judgement about what it is in people's interest to have, whether they have requested it or not, and (b) dealing with populations, groups or societies rather than individuals.

The ethical consequence of these features are that public health generates problems concerned with issues such as paternalism and individual rights, which are broadly (i.e., non-party) political in their implications. It follows that for any specific intervention (legislation for clean water, a programme of immunisation, restriction on smoking in public places or whatever), the necessary precondition of implementation is that it will improve the health of the public – and this improvement must be objectively demonstrable.[2] According to this approach, effectiveness must be established by scientific means, such that all rational and competent judges can agree on the facts.[3] The most common technique for establishing effectiveness of this kind is through the discipline of epidemiology, in which clear and certain conclusions may not always be obtainable. The importance of having measurable objectives for programme management and evaluation has been recognised in some official documents. See, for example, in the United States, the Surgeon General's Report, *Healthy People*,[4] or, in England, the Report of the Department of Health, *The Health of the Nation*,[5] or Tones and Tilfors.[6]

Justice and utility in public health medicine

It follows from the above that public interventions will require to be supported by two further ethical principles: justice and utility. In this section we shall examine a number of contexts in which these principles create the ethical framework for public health policies. But first let us examine the principles.

2 Charlton B, 'Public health medicine – a different kind of ethics?' *Journal of the Royal Society of Medicine*, 1993, 86, pp 194–195.
3 Kelly MP and Charlton B, 'Health promotion: time for a new philosophy?' *British Journal of General Practice*, 1992, editorial, pp 223–224.
4 *Healthy People: National health promotion and disease prevention objectives*, 1991, Washington DC: US Government Printing Office.
5 *The Health of the Nation: a strategy for England*, 1992, London: HMSO.
6 Tones BK and Tilford S, *Health Education: Effectiveness and Efficiency*, 1994, London: Chapman and Hall.

Justice and utility: the principles

Justice sometimes means observing the rights of individuals and sometimes that autonomous patients are all equally entitled to shares in the distribution of health care. The latter emphasis is particularly important for public health. Indeed, it is arguable that justice (or equity) raises the most important of the ethical issues for public health. There are variable levels of health between countries, and within countries there are marked differences in health which can be correlated with differences in distribution of resources.[7]

In discussions of justice it is important to distinguish 'equity' and 'equality'. The distinction can best be described by looking at those factors which can influence health and health care. It is possible to divide inequalities into those which are unavoidable, and hence where questions of equity do not arise, and those which might be avoided and thus raise issues of equity. Let us look at some examples.[8] In discussing the examples, we must always remember that what is 'unavoidable' at one point in history becomes 'avoidable' at another.

First, natural or biological variations such as age, sex, race and genetic background could be considered as factors which cannot be changed and thus any inequalities related to them are unavoidable. For example, older men have a higher incidence of heart disease than younger men, a clear example of an inequality. But no one would consider this related to inequity, except to the extent that we have neglected risk factor reduction in the elderly.[9]

Second, lifestyle and behaviour, if freely chosen, can result in inequalities in health. As an example, cigarette smokers have a higher incidence of lung cancer than non-smokers. This is an inequality, but to the extent that it is created by choice, it is not inequitable. Indeed, selective uptake of health promotional initiatives, for example , by middle class groups, could even increase inequalities in health, but could not be considered as unfair, unless it could be established that health promotion is selectively targeted towards these groups.

Third, lifestyle and behaviour, if not freely chosen, and which result in poor health, are likely to be considered as avoidable by society and thus unfair. A behaviour chosen through a lack of resources, housing conditions, overcrowding, dangerous working conditions, exposure to environmental hazards, or lack of adequate public health response, would be an example of this. Disabled people often suffer unfairness (inequity) which compounds their already unequal health.

Fourth, inadequate access to health care or other public services might be inequitable if the cause were avoidable. For example, financial considerations

7 Whitehead M, *The Health Divide: Inequalities in Health in the 1980s*, 1987, London: Health Education Council.
8 Whitehead M, *The Concepts and Principles of Equity and Health*, 1990, European Regional Office: WHO.
9 Omenn GS, 'Prevention and the elderly: what are appropriate policies?' *Health Affairs*, 1990, 9, pp 80–93.

which resulted in a failure to use transport might be one such factor. Another might be lack of access to information about services due to learning or language problems, or the information not being available. This lack, or inequity, could lead to inequalities of access because of the restriction of choice and opportunity.

In summary of this discussion of the principle of justice, we can say that those examples bring out that equity is about fairness and justice, and implies that everyone should have an opportunity to attain his or her full potential for health. Inequalities exist in health and health care. Some of these are unavoidable, and thus could not be considered unfair or inequitable. Others are avoidable. It is this latter group, in which the inequalities are inequitable, to which further attention might be addressed.

In discussion of public health we must also stress the principle of utility – of maximising the benefits for the populations involved. Utility is the principle concerned with the maximising of outcomes or preferences. In the old formation it tells us to seek the greatest happiness of the greatest number.[10] As such the principle of utility says nothing about how the greatest happiness should be distributed: an aggregate of utility A might be greater than an aggregate of B, but we might still give our moral approval to the situation which produces B rather than A, on the grounds that in B the benefits are more fairly distributed. Thus, there must be a balance between the ethical forces of justice and of utility.

Justice and utility: prioritising

Some people may argue that prioritising or rationing, while it raises important policy issues, does not raise ethical issues. The assumption of this position is that ethics has to do only with the face-to-face situation. We believe this view to be inadequate. Questions of the supply and fair distribution of resources are matters of ethics, and the general ethical principles which are relevant are those of utility and justice. Ethical problems of prioritising arise in the area of health service provision. The level of provision of health services is of considerable importance particularly in relation to the balance between hospital and primary care, the use of resources to develop effective interventions, and the ability to deliver public health measures. The infrastructural organisation and management are all-important.

In recent years in Britain the government has been laying emphasis on Primary Care as the central plank of the National Health Service with talk of a 'primary care-led health service'.[11] This approach was thought to have clear

10 This slogan is often attributed to Jeremy Bentham, but it was first formulated by Hutcheson, Francis. *An Inquiry Concerning the Original of Our Ideas of Virtue or Moral Good* (1725), in RS Downie (ed), *Francis Hutcheson: Philosophical Writings*, 1994, London: Dent, p 90.
11 Bogle I and Chisholm J, 'Primary care: restoring the jewel in the crown' (editorial), *British Medical Journal*, 1996, pp 1624–1625.

advantages for a publicly funded service in that the care provided by GPs was considered to be much cheaper than hospital care. Additionally, it makes sense to provide as much care for patients locally near their own homes by doctors whom they know and who know them. But the financial aspects of this policy clearly depend on the assumption that the remuneration for GPs is less than that for hospital consultants, and that assumption may not be true. But at least Primary Care Trusts or Health Boards now have real muscle in influencing the development and scope of services provided by hospitals. The idea is that GPs know their patients and know what services they need; therefore, as the slogan goes, 'the money follows the patient'.[12]

Funding however has been slow to follow this change of emphasis. This has led to a vigorous debate about the allocation of resources between primary and secondary care. The NHS in Britain works on the basis that each person must come through his or her GP to get access to expensive secondary care resources. The assumption is that GPs are aware of the limited nature of these resources and will refer wisely and equitably. The government and health service planners recognise the crucial position of GPs as gatekeepers of NHS resources and have attempted to redress the balance of power through past and future proposals to improve the status of general practice within the NHS.[13]

Justice and utility: prevention

There is sometimes confusion between *prevention*, which is the abolition or reduction in the incidence of the disease; *avoidance*, which is keeping clear of risk factors; and *protection*, which may limit the spread of disease, say by vaccination or immunisation. For example, public health policy may encourage the prevention of malaria by swamp-clearing programmes and thus aim at the elimination of the source of the disease; or travellers may be prevented from catching the disease by avoiding certain geographical areas; or they may be protected against it by being given tablets. All these practices are loosely called 'prevention'. Of course, the categories will sometimes overlap. For instances, immunisation or vaccination programmes, which are really protection programmes, may lead to a reduction in the incidence of a disease, or even to its elimination, as in the case of smallpox. But this overlap does not always occur. The compulsory wearing of seatbelts is often regarded as a preventive measure. But it does not prevent accidents; only good driving and safer roads and vehicles do that. It gives a measure of protection against accidents.[14]

12 Stewart-Brown S, Gillam S and Jewell T, 'The problem of fund-holding' (editorial), *British Medical Journal*, 1996, pp 1311–1312.
13 A new General Medical Services (GMS) Contract for General Practitioners came into being in April 2006 considerably (and controversially) increasing potential remuneration for GPs.
14 Blaney R, 'Why prevent disease?' in *Ethical Dimensions in Health Promotion*, Doxiadis S (ed), 1987, Chichester: John Wiley.

It might seem that there is no need to provide any ethical justification for prevention: it is self-evidently a good thing. While this may be true, the general public and governments do not always act as if it were so. From the point of view of government, it seems that much more money goes in the direction of health care than of prevention, and from the point of view of the public there is often an attitude of scepticism towards many preventive measures, and even more towards what is now called 'health promotion'. Prevention as a general policy therefore requires some justification. There is an economic justification, that prevention is usually cheaper than cure; a medical justification, that some diseases are probably not completely curable so their occurrence should be prevented: and an ethical justification, that prevention avoids the pain, misery and grief of disease. It is also possible to include the economic and medical justifications in a wide sense of 'ethical justification'. As we shall see, however, this general ethical justification of prevention does not always apply to specific areas of prevention, and even when it does there are those who argue that the benefits of prevention can be outweighed in some cases by the ethical costs. Let us look at some examples.

Take the fluoridation of local water supplies. From the 1930s it was noted that there was a correlation between the levels of fluoride in the drinking water and levels of dental caries. This suggested a preventive policy of introducing fluoride where the level was low. There were objections, on the grounds of undesirable side-effects, such as Down's Syndrome and more recently cancer. But a Working Party in Britain found no evidence for such claims,[15] and other scientific groups have reached the same conclusion. The ethical objection remains, however, that adding fluoride to the water supply can count as compulsory medication, and as such it is a violation of individual rights as laid down in the UN Declaration of Human Rights. Rights, of course, are not inalienable and can be overridden when the survival of the public requires it. But it is doubtful if the prevention of dental caries can count as a justification for ignoring rights. Note that there is really no solution to this dispute. One position or the other must be overruled.[16]

The issue of vaccination for rubella raises rather different issues. The vaccine for rubella works by providing a benefit to the children of those to whom it is given. Now the vaccine can be given to girls only or to both girls and boys. If it is given to girls only, there is little effect on the transmission or eradication of the disease. A 'girls only' policy is therefore a 'protection' rather than a 'prevention' measure. If on the other hand, the vaccine is given to both girls and boys, and if the uptake is over 90%, we have a preventive measure which will eventually lead to the eradication of the disease. But, if the second policy is followed and the uptake is low, say about 60%, then we have a situation which is

15 *Report of the Working Party on fluoridation of water and cancer: a review of the epidemiological evidence*, 1985, London: HMSO.

16 Knox EG, 'Personal and public health care: conflict, congruence or accommodation?' in *Ethical Dilemmas in Health Promotion*, Doxiadis S (ed), 1987, Chichester, John Wiley.

harmful to the children of the unvaccinated young female population, for they will be much less likely to develop natural immunity. The ethical issues, then, are these. If we (the public) want the benefits of prevention then we must also put up with a degree of compulsion to ensure a high uptake. If compulsion is ethically or politically unacceptable, then the best policy, to avoid harm, is to offer protection to those at risk. Again, there is no ethically correct answer; a choice must be made. The choice is likely to be made in the end as a matter of political expediency, as distinct from a consideration of health benefits.

Justice and utility: screening

Another public health activity which falls in general terms into the category of prevention is that of screening. Screening can be defined in various ways, but a simple definition is provided by Stone and Stewart: 'Screening is a preventive activity which seeks to identify an unsuspected disease or pre-disease condition for which an effective intervention is available.'[17] Screening is currently a fashionable medical activity. The demand for it is being encouraged by governments and by certain patients' organisations.

Politically, it seems desirable because there is a belief that prevention saves money, and successive governments have therefore set up various screening programmes. A national screening programme for cervical cancer was set up in the United Kingdom in 1984, and a programme for breast cancer was established in 1988 for women aged 50–64 years. The establishment of such programmes has been enthusiastically supported by various women's groups. Indeed, such is the current demand for screening that Schikle and Chadwick in a discussion of the ethics of screening ask whether 'screeningitis' is an incurable disease.[18] If it were, no doubt there would be demand for a screening programme!

It is possible to screen for many conditions, but screening programmes must satisfy ethical criteria. First, they must satisfy the informed consent criterion for any sort of medical intervention. Second, since screening initiatives tend to be profession driven rather than individual driven, there is an additional responsibility for the professional to justify the intervention which may not have been requested. Third, some screening procedures carry health risks, and all of them are likely to be accompanied by discomfort, anxiety and inconvenience for symptomless individuals. Fourth, any screening programme carries with it the risks of the false-positive or the false-negative. Thus screening requires as much ethical justification as other medical interventions. Moreover, since screening programmes can be expensive in the aggregate, they require evaluation.

17 Stone D, and Stewart S, *Towards a Screening Strategy for Scotland*, 1994, Glasgow: Scottish Forum for Public Health Medicine.

18 Shickle D and Chadwick R, 'The ethics of screening: is "screeningitis" an incurable disease?' *Journal of Medical Ethics*, 1994, 20, pp 12–18.

Once again, therefore, the ethical principles of justice and utility must be used in the justification of screening programmes. Moreover, since governments believe, rightly or wrongly, that screening programmes and other preventive measures will save money, strong pressure can be exerted on a target population (via GPs by providing them with financial incentives) to accept screening programmes. Is this not old-fashioned paternalism?

Ethical problems of health promotion: the concept of health

The Acheson Report definition of public health makes it clear that public health medicine must not only prevent disease but promote health. The literature of the new public health, and especially health promotion, tends nowadays to have a complex view of the concept of health and to distinguish various elements within it.

The first of those is often called 'negative health', or the absence of ill-health. Ill-health itself is a complex notion comprising disease, illness, handicap, injury and other related ideas. These overlapping concepts can be linked if they are seen on the model of abnormal, unwanted or incapacitating states of a biological system. We have discussed some of the problems in the concept of disease and related ideas in the section on 'Disease' (p 71).

The second idea of 'positive health' has appeared more recently in published reports. The origins of this idea are in the definition of health found in the preamble to the Constitution of the WHO –' health is a complete state of mental and social well-being'.[19] This definition therefore claims that 'well-being' is an important ingredient in positive health. We have already discussed in the section on 'Health' (p 75) the manner in which this particular definition of health has moved health care in a new direction. As we said, this may or may not be a good thing, but it requires more justification than an arbitrary definition.

A third idea in the concept of health is that of 'fitness'. Fitness in its most obvious sense refers to the state of someone's heart and lungs. To be fit in this sense is to have a place on a scale ranging from being able to climb stairs or run for a bus without getting out of breath to being able to run a marathon or climb Mount Everest. Fitness can also be used in a related but broader sense, which we might call 'sociological' as opposed to the 'heart and lungs' sense. In the sociological sense of fitness a person is fit *for* some occupation or job. This means that people have the necessary health to enable them to perform the job or task adequately without, for example, too many days off work.

The WHO definition refers to the 'mental and social' as well as to the physical. Nevertheless, the mental and social components of health are the poor relations of the health services and do not receive adequate attention. It is

19 WHO, *Constitution*, 1946, New York: WHO.

certainly true that mental health is most often taken to be the absence of mental ill-health. The idea of positive mental health or mental well-being is an obscure one, and perhaps it is ethically dangerous if it implies that eccentricity and single-mindedness are to be discouraged and the balanced and conformist personality encouraged. Once again, more justification is required than pointing at an arbitrary definition.

The idea of 'social well-being' is, in fact, just as obscure as that of mental well-being, although at first sight it does not seem to be a difficult notion. What does it mean? In one sense 'social well-being' refers to the skills and other abilities which enable us to form friendships and relate to other people in conversation and through the many different sorts of contact which are part of ordinary social life. Sometimes these are called 'lifeskills', and the possession of them helps to create a sense of 'self-esteem' which is currently a fashionable concept in the literature of health education. Clearly, like fitness, social well-being in this sense can be graded on a scale from negative to positive. It is a property of individuals and refers to their ability to cope in a social context – hence 'social well-being' is an appropriate term.

Can we link the absence of ill-health and the presence of well-being in a single concept of health in the manner of the WHO definition? This is not a rarefied question because it affects the legitimate scope of health education. If well-being is a component in the concept of health, then clearly health education has a much wider remit than it would otherwise have.

One important factor influencing this question is that ill-health and well-being cannot be related to each other as opposite poles on a linear scale. This approach has been tried by some theorists but it is not satisfactory, for it is logically possible (and not in fact uncommon) for someone to have poor physical health but a high state of well-being – as in the case of a terminally ill patient in a hospice or specialist care unit who is supported by caring staff and loving friends – or a good state of physical health but poor well-being – as in the case of someone who has no diseases or illnesses but lacks friends, a job, interests.

The fact that health (the absence of ill-health) and well-being cannot be related on a linear scale must raise the question of whether they are in fact two components of a single concept. It can be argued that they are aspects of a single concept.[20] But it may be preferable and less confusing conceptually to think of them as two overlapping concepts rather than as a single concept with two dimensions. Thus the feeling of well-being that a person has after an invigorating swim can be fairly described as a 'glow of health', but the well-being or satisfaction that a person has after writing a chapter in a book, listening to a piece of music, or just playing an enjoyable game is less obviously related to concepts of health, and more obviously related to concepts such as 'enjoyment'

20 Downie RS, Tannahill A and Tannahill C, *Health Promotion: Models and Values*, 2nd edn, 1996, Oxford: Oxford University Press.

and 'happiness'. Again, the well-being that is created by moving someone to better housing is more obviously related to concepts of 'welfare' than to that of health. Our conclusion is that, while the concepts of health and well-being overlap, they are distinct and cannot be combined in one concept. We have already discussed the problems of attempting to define the prism-like nature of the concept of health (p 75).

But whether we think of health as a single multifaceted concept, or as a narrower concept which overlaps with related concepts such as well-being and fitness, we must still examine two charges sometimes levelled at health promotional activities – that they are unethical in that they are 'imperialistic', and that they 'commercialise' health.

Health promotion: imperialism

Those making the charge of health imperialism might argue that what in health promotion terms is 'positive health' is really just a name for a range of states which are as easily or better seen in other ways. For example, 'well-being' might be said to be just another name for happiness (as we have seen in the section on 'Health' in Chapter 3). Again, the idea of 'fitness' might be said to be a technical one, relative to specific ends, such as playing in the Premier League, but not one with an important bearing on health. Mental illness may satisfy some of the criteria for illness (although even that has been disputed),[21] but positive mental health might be said by critics to be a concept which attempts to annex the territory of the well-adjusted to that of the healthy. For example, mental illnesses, such as depressions or obsessions, are incapacitating in a manner similar to that of physical illness, but to stress positive mental health might be seen as simply making a value judgement in favour of the conventional or the well-balanced as opposed to the eccentric, as we have already noted.

In reply to this sort of objection, it is helpful to introduce the concept of health alliances.[22] There are certain activities which are indisputably health promotion, but there are many others with which health promotion can form alliances. We discuss this in detail in Chapter 7. If health and health promotion can be seen in this logically and practically flexible way, then the charge of imperialism can be avoided.

Health promotion: commercialism

The second ethical objection to health promotion is that it attempts to bypass autonomy and to sell health like a commodity. In this it might be said to resemble the advertisements for unhealthy products which it is opposing.

21 Szasz T, *The Myth of Mental Illness* (1961), New York: Harper and Row.
22 Williams G, 'Health promotion- caring concern or slick salesmanship?' *Journal of Medical Ethics*, 1984, 10, pp 191–195.

In reply to this argument we might question the premise that autonomy is something which everyone in fact possesses. People can be victims of all sorts of social processes and be lacking in power. For example, as the advertising of tobacco and alcohol becomes progressively more difficult in some countries, so the manufacturers have turned their attention to the developing world, and the huge markets which are opening up. As the countries become more affluent, so the consumption of such products increase with consequential long-term adverse health effects. Another example concerns breast milk substitutes. All health authorities are clear about the value of breast feeding for the mother and the baby. However, considerable pressure was brought to bear on mothers in developing countries to use breast milk substitutes. Not only would this be more expensive, but the health benefits of breast feeding would be lost. International action was required to deal with this issue. The WHO resolved that states ensure that there be no free or subsidised substitute, which would affect breast feeding practice. This may seem to be merely a political compromise, but it may nevertheless be an effective way of implanting an ethically defensible position.

In view of the political and commercial power of the anti-health forces in society, health must be presented in as attractive a way as possible or health education will fail totally. If health educators confine themselves strictly to the rational, critical approach to education, then it is preferable to depict health education as an element within a larger health promotion movement concerned with health advocacy, legislative change, fiscal reform, and the mobilisation of community interests, as well as education narrowly conceived.

The tension between the ethical requirement to be person-respecting in methods and the practical necessity to be effective is addressed from an interesting point of view in the literature of self-help groups. The growth of self-care groups concerned with every conceivable malady and involving both the sufferers and their relatives has been a notable development during the last decade. These movements avoid the charge of paternalism commonly still made against every branch of health care, including health education. Apart from ethical considerations, self-care movements seem to be effective within their limits, although they may benefit from a professional health educator to advise and facilitate. Advising and facilitating is indeed an important role for health education.

Public health and 'the organised efforts of society'

Public health medicine, according to the Acheson Report definition, must obtain its results 'through the organised efforts of society' (see p 91). How are we to interpret this, and what ethical issues arise from our interpretation? Is it just a metaphor to speak of 'society' bringing about health? One obvious answer to this question is that to speak of 'society' bringing about health is a roundabout way of referring to our elected political representatives. We shall therefore begin by looking at the role of the state in health care, concentrating on health legislation.

Legislation and prevention

First, a person's right to exercise autonomy may be legitimately curtailed by health legislation when he or she is suffering from certain sorts of infectious disease or mental illness such that the interests or health of others are liable to be harmed. There is no difficulty about the acceptance of this restriction in general terms. The problems arise over the more detailed application. For example, a topical question concerns the nature and extent of the restrictions which should be placed on sufferers from AIDS, or the extent of justifiable investigations or reports of those who may be HIV-positive. Again, it is controversial how far those who are mentally ill should be detained against their will, or what sort of treatment they should have if they are detained.

Pressure for legislation is generated as more becomes known about how diseases are transmitted. For example, the dangers of 'passive smoking' are now appreciated, and other sorts of environmental pollution are now known to cause or exacerbate diseases such as asthma. There is therefore a case for curbing the freedom of both individuals and corporate bodies, such as industries, in the name of the autonomy of other individuals. This issue is, of course, a source of much political debate. Some countries have banned smoking in many public places, and various 'watch-dogs' keep a close eye on the consequences of the operation of the nuclear power industry. Although there can be political debate about applications of the 'preventing harm to others' idea, the general principle is clear and acceptable.

These problems become more acute when we consider the international dimension of health. In a developed country like the United Kingdom international aspects have several implications. The first relates to communicable disease, and with the ease of transport now the possibility of transmission to different populations becomes ever easier. Movement for business, leisure, or migration of populations is occurring on a scale as never before. The great plague, cholera and influenza epidemics of the past, and AIDS, tuberculosis and malaria in the present, show just how vulnerable the world is to such infections. As we write there is a worldwide worry about avian influenza and the possible transmutation of the virus into a form deadly to human beings. There are public demands for draconian limitations on travel. But this is nothing new. The introduction of quarantine in Italy and France, in the fourteenth century, was one of the earliest attempts to control infections, and there is still ethical justification for certain sorts of boundary control for health reasons.

The need for international legislation is apparent also if we consider environmental issues, the most recent and serious of which was the radioactive release in Chernobyl. But environmental problems regularly cross international boundaries and that there is an environmental impact assessment of economic growth has been set out in a series of programmes of 'sustainable development'.

Legislation and health promotion

Has the state any justification for using fiscal policy for passing legislation to promote positive health or well-being? A strong argument for maintaining that a government does have a duty to promote positive health can be found in the preamble to the Constitution of WHO (1946), which asserts that there is a right to positive health. In ambitious terms it states:

> The enjoyment of the highest attainable standard of health is one of the fundamental rights of every human being without distinction of race, religion, political belief, economic or social condition.[23]

If this is a fundamental right, then presumably there is a correlative duty laid upon governments to implement it. In other words, acceptance of the WHO Constitution commits states to health and welfare policies. How far such policies can be implemented no doubt turns on the wealth of the country, but there can be no doubt that wealthy Western nations are committed to implementing fiscal and legislative policies to enhance positive health.

To argue that there is a duty on governments to promote health for its own sake still leaves some questions unanswered. Supposing there is such a duty, can it be implemented other than at the expense of individual autonomy?

It is easy to slip into the error or regarding all legislation on the model of the criminal law – as restrictive prohibition backed by sanction. But this is an oversimplified way of looking at some health legislation. For example, legislation may require public bodies to make provision for the disabled. This is more aptly seen as positive creation of new opportunities than as negative prohibition. There are legal requirements on factory owners to restrict unpleasant pollutants, and on car manufacturers to ensure certain safety standards. Indeed, there is an enormous range of health legislation with a positive slant. Whereas this may diminish the freedom of some groups in society, it certainly extends the freedom of the majority.

If we think of autonomy in this way, then health legislation is not *removing* our individual autonomy but rather *enhancing* it. In improving the general quality of life, legislation can add to our autonomy. This is obviously the case if we consider the example of provision for the disabled, but it is true also of anti-pollution legislation and many other types of health legislation.

Legislation and citizenship

So far in this section we have been concerned with the role of the state and health legislation. But there is much more to the 'organised efforts of society' than legislation. Let us state the five principles which the WHO (1984) sees as the basis of health promotion:

1   Health promotion involves the population as a whole in the context of its everyday life, rather than focusing on people at risk for specific diseases.

23 WHO, *Constitution*, op. cit.

2   Health promotion is directed towards action on the causes or determinants of health.
3   Health promotion combines diverse, but complementary methods or approaches, including communication, education, legislation, fiscal measures, organisational change, community development and spontaneous local activities against health hazards.
4   Health promotion aims particularly at effective and concrete public participation.
5   While health promotion is basically an activity in the health and social fields, and not a medical service, health professionals – particularly in primary health care – have an important role in nurturing and enabling promotion.[24]

How are we to interpret phrases such as 'concrete public participation'? What is the ethical importance of this approach?

One way of making sense of this idea is to think of society not in terms of individuals who make it up, but in terms of the institutions, practices, customs, political arrangements and social class relationships which give structure to the society. From this point of view, people are related to each other by the structures of their society, and indeed part of their identity is created by these social structures. We could then evaluate a society in terms of the way in which its social structures tend to produce health in the people who belong to that society. Just as we sometimes praise the 'atmosphere' in a school or hospital as one of well-being, so the social structures of an entire society might be said to make for or detract from health or well-being.

Some theorists with firm attachments to individualism might prefer to understand that what we have said refers to health determinants rather than health itself. For example, they might agree that a society with marked social class gradients and corresponding gradients in the distribution of ill-health is one with a tendency to create ill-health in individuals. Thus, in terms of this approach, if we speak of an 'unhealthy society' we are simply speaking metaphorically about the determinants, such as poor housing and diet and so on, that have helped to produce poor health states in individuals. Other thinkers might be prepared to extend language and to maintain that it is not a metaphor to characterise social relationships and structures as being themselves unhealthy. It is perhaps self-indulgent to pursue this theoretical question here, but it is certainly one way of making sense of the phrase 'the organised efforts of society', in the Acheson Report (p 91), or 'effective and concrete public participation', as the WHO principle puts it (p 103).

One context in which these phrases may have more practical meaning is that of rationing. We have already touched on this issue in terms of the debate over

---

24 *Health Promotion: A Discussion Document on the Concept and Principles*, 1984, Copenhagen: WHO.

resource allocation in primary and secondary care. There now seems to be a movement to involve the public in decisions about rationing health-care resources. For example, 'focus groups' or 'citizens' juries' can be set up to discuss priorities. Such movements have the ethical merit of returning to the citizens responsibility for and ownership of their own health. On the other hand, to the extent that there is exclusive emphasis on state delivery of health care to individuals, there is the invitation to see health as a commodity to be supplied by the state. The same is true if we think of health as a commodity bought by private health insurance. But health is not in any sense a commodity. Health and well-being are, in the end, a set of relationships among citizens and the involvement of citizens in decisions about rationing is a good example. As D Beauchamp wrote:

> Collective goods are ultimately a set of relationships among the citizens of a community, relationships in which the community as a whole participates to obtain desired benefits. These collective goods include aggregate states of welfare or well-being, including declining rates of disease and premature deaths; efforts to limit the resources society devotes to personal health services; shared and common access to a good like medical care to foster the sense of community and membership in the group itself. And finally, there are those highly important collective good, shared or common beliefs and values.[25]

It is clear that we can add a legal system to Beauchamp's list, and in particular one designed to stimulate social responsibility. Indeed, it is plausible to suggest that the increasing government intervention on drunk-driving issues has encouraged a greater social awareness about the dangers of alcohol more generally, and thus a greater sense of community and individual responsibility. In a similar way, legislation designed to assist disabled or handicapped persons can also increase a sense of community responsibility for those groups. In other words, in so far as health legislation and other governmental health policies are directed at increasing community awareness, as distinct from being directed at the good of specific individuals, it is not paternalistic.

A health alliance which has been shown to be helpful in developing community awareness is that between health promotion services and community arts. Several projects have taken place and have had favourable evaluations. For example, the Bristol Area Specialist Health Promotion Service report on these projects: photography, the visual arts and drama.[26] Again, Bromley by Bow have ongoing community arts and health projects.[27] The central message from these and similar

25 Beauchamp D, 'Lifestyle, public health and paternalism', in Doxiadis S (ed), *Ethical Dilemmas in Health Promotion*, 1987, Chichester: John Wiley.

26 Hecht R (ed), *I Talk Now*, 1996, Bristol: Specialist Health Promotion Service, Central Health Clinic, Bristol.

27 *Bromley by Bow Centre Annual Report*, 1995–96, London: Bromley by Bow.

projects is that disease and ill-health cannot be eradicated by narrow medical means; they must be tackled in a community context with the approval of the community. We discuss this further in Chapter 7. It other words, medicine needs health alliances, and the arts are a vital and ethically acceptable ally. The ancient Greeks recognised this when they made Apollo god of both medicine and the arts.

An Enemy of the People

We have discussed some of the ethical problems of public health medicine in terms of the second-order, critical discipline of political philosophy. We shall conclude this chapter with an anticipation of the approach we shall adopt in Chapter 6, and move on from the critical function of philosophy to what we have called the enhancing or supplementary function of literature.

The ethics of public health does not seem a likely subject for drama, yet it was the subject which Henrik Ibsen chose for a very compelling drama entitled *An Enemy of the People* first performed in 1883.[28] The play succeeds in making us vividly aware of the central ethical problems of public health – the problems of freedom of information, of being allowed to publicise problems of public health in a society in which anti-health forces, the forces of vested interest, conspire against the truth. It also highlights the manner in which a popularity-seeking media can manipulate public opinion for their own ends.

The central character in the play is Dr Stockman, who is the doctor in charge of the Baths. The doctor had the idea that the creation of Baths would bring tourists and some prosperity to the small town in which the Baths are situated. This has proved true and when the play opens the doctor is popular in the community both for the creation of the Baths and for his medical work among the townspeople. Unfortunately, for reasons of cost, the Baths have been located below a tannery against the doctor's advice. The water flowing into the Baths has been contaminated, and in the First Act the doctor receives conclusive scientific proof of the contamination of the water and the resultant danger to public health. He proposes to publish his report, which has been enthusiastically received by the local newspaper editor.

The Mayor of the town is the chairman of the Baths committee. He has vested interests in the Baths and tourism, argues that the doctor's scientific report is exaggerated, that the town will lose its tourist appeal, that he as the Chairman forbids the publication of the Report, and he sacks the doctor. The newspaper changes sides and will not publish the Report, and at a public meeting the Mayor and the Editor and their supporters turn the people against the doctor who is declared an enemy of the people.

Perhaps the central point for the argument of this chapter is made by the Editor of the newspaper in Act II. Dr Stockman is portrayed as in many ways a

---

28 Ibsen, H, An Enemy of the People, in *Henrik Ibsen: Plays: Two*, 1963, London: Eyre Methuen.

simple character, dedicated to scientific truth. The Editor does not dispute the scientific truth of the doctor's Report but says: 'You're a doctor and a man of science, and to you this business of the water is something to be considered in isolation. I think you don't perhaps realise how far it's tied up with a lot of other things.'[29] This is a huge ethical problem for public health medicine. The 'truth' has to be implemented in a complex social and economic situation. Some of the complexities may derive from dubious vested interests, such as tobacco industry lobbying. But at other times there can be conflict between the value of health and other values, such as individual freedom or employment. And of course political decisions are always affected by that most changeable of all factors, public opinion. And public opinion is affected by newspapers, television, popular public figures and other influences, which may themselves be affected by vested interests, such as the views of newspaper owners. Out of this then the play leaves us with two ethical problems for public health medicine. One is the priority which should be placed on the truths and values of public health, and the other is how to present these, to communicate them to a public which may be dominated by anti-health forces.

Conclusions

It is often assumed that ethical problems in medicine are the prerogative of clinical practice, and that the problems of health medicine are those of public policy and legislation. But we have tried to bring out that the policies advocated by public health medicine do indeed raise ethical issues of a basic kind involving principles of justice, utility and individual rights. Moreover, these familiar ethical concepts must be supplemented by some which are less familiar. If the collective goods which are promoted by public health medicine are to be achieved, the methods must involve the development of community identity and awareness. In other words, public health medicine, to be effective in an ethically acceptable manner, must seek health alliances with other community movements, and some of these are helpfully arts-based movements (see Chapter 7).

29 Ibid., Act II, p 144.

Chapter 5

Medical half-truths

By a 'half-truth' we mean a belief which doctors tend to have about their occupation, or about their abilities to affect their patients. The belief in question will not be entirely false, but it will not quite fit the facts or the realities of the situation as it exists, or there will be a correct diagnosis of a problem, but the method used to remedy will not be appropriate. We shall examine three such half-truths with implications for ethics; there are many more.

First, there is the deeply held belief that medicine is not only a profession but the paradigm case of a profession. Second, there is the belief that whatever is criticised in doctors, such as occasionally their attitudes to patients, can be put right by additions to or changes in medical education. Third, there is the belief that 'quality of life' is a phrase capable of clear definition (indeed of measurement), and that it is an aim (or even the primary aim) of medicine to improve it. As we have said, these half-truths are of ethical significance because of the sort of bearing they have on the way doctors perceive themselves and the scope of their job, and are perceived by their patients. To conclude this part of the book, which has been concerned with a second-order critique of medical ethics, we shall first examine the idea of a profession and how medicine as an occupation no longer fits the concept in its entirety, and then discuss an attempt by medical educators to rectify what are thought to be attitudinal failings in doctors. We shall conclude with a short discussion of the term 'quality of life' and its problems when seen as an aim of medical practice.

The idea of a profession

In order to discuss the extent to which medicine is a profession it might be thought appropriate to define a profession.[1] But the first difficulty concerns the sort of definition which would be helpful. We have already noted the considerable

---

1 We have discussed medicine as a profession from a different point of view in: Downie RS and Macnaughton J, *Clinical Judgement: Evidence in Practice*, 2000, Oxford: Oxford University Press, Chapter 3.

problems associated with definition. For example, there is a large sociological literature on the professions, but sociologists tend to identify professions in terms of criteria such as five years of training, a code of ethics, an annual conference, remuneration by fees or salary rather than wages, and so on. Now it might be possible to define a profession using such criteria, but they do not really advance our understanding of why a profession might have a valuable contribution to make to the community, or why professional decisions typically involve judgements of value. We shall therefore suggest evaluative criteria as a basis for a definition. But, as we shall see, these criteria have implications which are contentious if they are regarded as constituting the necessary and sufficient conditions of a definition.

Professions: the criteria

The first of the evaluative criteria is that a profession must be a learned occupation; it has a basis of knowledge and skills. This is perhaps the criterion which, historically, would originally distinguish a profession from other occupations; the schoolmaster, the clergyman and the doctor were the main scholars of an earlier epoch. But now many occupations have a basis in knowledge and skills and so this criterion can be no more than necessary to distinguish a profession; it certainly is not sufficient. It is clear that medicine satisfied this necessary condition. But, as John Gregory noted (p 15ff) there is more to a profession than its 'genius'.

Not only must professionals have knowledge and skills, they must know when, how, and how much to exercise the skills. For example, skilled surgeons may be able to carry out a complex operation, but they must also be able to decide whether the operation ought to be attempted. This kind of decision is of a different order; it involves judgements of moral value: What is the balance of risks and harms? Has the patient consented to the risks? What are the long-term prospects of recovery? and so on. This complex mixture of the technical and the ethical ideally requires that the surgeon be broadly educated, as well as technically skilled. We can therefore make education in humane values a second criterion for a profession.

This second criterion requires some expansion. What are the differences between being trained to have skills, and being educated in humane values? This, of course, is a large topic on its own, which we will discuss later in Chapters 6 and 9, but a few points can helpfully be made here. First, the person educated in humane values has a broad cognitive perspective and is able to see the significance of social work, teaching, medicine or the law, for example, in a total way of life. Second, the person of humane education has continual curiosity about the world, a desire to develop the skills throughout a working life, and connectedly is aware of the standards of work which must be satisfied. Here we have the familiar idea of a 'professional job', or 'a job well done'. Third, the idea of a humane education embodies the idea of ethics. It is possible to be trained to pick pockets, as in Dickens's *Oliver Twist*, but a humane education is necessarily directed to worthwhile ends. Here we have the idea of standards of behaviour, of 'being professional' in one's approach to a client or patient or student. Fourth, the broadly educated person has a flexibility of mind which enables her/him to see things in a variety of ways. How far does medicine satisfy the 'broad education' criterion, much stressed by John Gregory? (see Chapter 1).

The answer must be 'only partly'. There is an effort by some medical schools to include courses on medical ethics, but whatever their merits they tend not to be in what we are calling 'humane values'. Members of ethics committees typically suggest that if the technology is there it ought to be used, because they tend to assume that medical advances always provide 'benefits' for patients. The task of medical ethicists then becomes that of regulating the advances, as we have stressed from the start. Hence, we find that demented 90 year-olds are still treated with antibiotics for pneumonia or given PEG feeding when they cannot feed themselves, especially if relatives insist on it. Whatever is to be said about this in terms of the narrow perspective of medical ethics it lacks a balanced and broader view of the point of medicine. The ethos of 'saving lives' has become the determinant of treatment policies, but 'saving lives' is an unclear idea. If you pull a drowning child out of a canal you have saved its life. But this paradigm case of life-saving does not seem so apt in cases of the extension of life which may be accomplished by artificial means such as drugs or PEG feeding. The emotive force of 'saving a life' has been extended by persuasive definition (see p 65) to apply to much less obvious cases.

All professions offer a public service to clients, patients, students or the like. In more detail this service is offered through a special relationship. This is the third factor in our attempted definition. What is meant here by a 'relationship'? The word 'relationship' is used in two ways. It can refer to the bonds which hold two people together, or it can refer to their attitudes to each other. For example, if we see two people together, we might ask what is the relationship between them, and receive answers such as father and son, colleagues, husband and wife, teacher and pupil, doctor and patient, and so on. To characterise a relationship in this way is to ask about what we are calling the 'bonds'. But we might ask what kind of relationship do Bloggs and his son have, and be told 'Bloggs has great affection for his son, but his son has nothing but contempt for his father.' Or we might say of a husband and wife that their relationship is deteriorating, or of that between a doctor and a patient that the patient trusts the doctor and the doctor respects the patient. Answers of that kind characterise a relationship in terms of attitudes. A professional relationship requires both bond and attitude.

The bonds in a professional relationship are decided by the governing body, for example, by the GMC or the General Teaching Council. It is necessary that there should be special bonds between the professional and client because of the inequality in the relationship. In brief, the client, or student, or patient is vulnerable and needs the protection of the bond. In general, we might say that the bond takes the form of a role-relationship in which both the professional and client have rights and duties laid down by the governing body. For example, a doctor, lawyer, or accountant might need to know various intimate details about the client in order to be able to offer the service. The client must be reassured that no untoward use will be made of this information. Hence, the duties of confidentiality are imposed on the professional. Again, a teacher or tutor will need to criticise the work of a pupil or student. But the fact that they are in a role-relationship with respect to each other creates insulation against the wrong sort of emotional side-effects of criticism. Doctors are told that 'the patient is a person', and so on. Yes, but they are persons in a role-relationship when they are dealing with a professional. And the nature of the role is laid down by the professional body, and obviously reflects the values of the profession. In other words, ethics enters a profession via the professional bond.

But ethics enters also via the professional attitude. We can say that the attitude must reflect awareness of the vulnerability of the client, patient or student. Often the professional attitude is described by a term such as 'beneficence', or 'concern for best interests'. In Chaucer's *Canterbury Tales* he characterises the poor Parson as follows:

> Benigne he was, and wonder diligent,
> And in adversitee ful pacient.[2]

The pathology of beneficence is paternalism, a word from which contemporary professionals shy away. But of course in a sense the doctor does know best about your medical interests. Why otherwise do you consult the doctor? Nowadays the doctor's duty to supply information to the patient and the patient's right to give or withhold consent to the proposed treatment in the light of that information make the term 'paternalism' less appropriate. There are other sorts of problems in other professions concerning attitudes, but, whatever the details of the appropriate attitudes involved in the professional relationship in medicine, moral values are involved. Whereas professional regulation covers, to a great extent, the ethics of what we have called the professional 'bond' our claim is that it is via the humanities that professional attitudes can be affected. We shall discuss this in much more detail in our next chapter.

In the present context however we must ask how far the idea of a 'special relationship' with the two features we have described still exists in medicine. The answer is that if it is still there it is only a shadow of its former self. As far as general practice is concerned the typical practice has several doctors and assistants. Moreover, the doctors are not now involved in evening or weekend work. Hence, the same patient may be seen by several doctors, or by the practice nurse, or even be dealt with by a voice on the telephone after pressing various numbers! It is therefore difficult to speak of a relationship with a given doctor. The situation is much the same with most specialities in hospital medicine.

---

2 Chaucer G, *The Canterbury Tales* (1389), Prologue, 1957, Oxford: Oxford University Press.

There will be a senior consultant who is nominally in charge of the case, but the chances are that the patient will be seen by a range of more junior doctors, perhaps by a different one on each occasion.

But even if we allow that a 'special relationship' can exist with more than one doctor (a type of problem more familiar in other areas of life!) a question remains about the nature of that relationship. Traditionally, as we have seen, the doctor is meant to seek the best interests of the patient, as these are professionally indicated. But, on account of charges of paternalism, both doctor and patient (encouraged by governments) have been moving away from the traditional professional relationship and stressing 'patient choice'. In other words, the professional relationship is slowly being replaced by a consumerist relationship. Hence, the idea of a medical 'profession' is weakening in this aspect. Consumerism may or may not be a good thing in all respects but it is certainly quite different from professionalism as traditionally conceived. A new kind of doctor/patient relationship requires a new kind of ethics to cover it. We shall suggest at the end of this section the broad principles of such a new kind of ethics.

A fourth feature of the professions is that professional leaders have a moral duty to speak out on matters of public policy as it affects their profession. For example, judges have a duty to speak out on matters of sentencing, doctors on matters of health policy, teachers' leaders and vice-chancellors on matters of education, and architects on housing policies, planning permission, conservation and the like. Governments do not always like this. There has been a tendency for governments of both the right and the left to resist the influence of the professions, seeing that influence as a kind of threat to their own political positions. Campaigns against the professions are easy to mount with support from the media, for there have been high-profile scandals which encourage public opinion to turn against the professions and depict them as 'elitist', monopolistic, and unaccountable. But 'being accountable' generally means being subject to a government agenda, to meet targets or the like. It is good for a society if there is a measure of political pluralism, and the professions in the past were sources of values. But since governments disapprove of independent voices this function of the professions has also been weakened. One by one in the United Kingdom social work, teaching and medicine have been put under the control of politicians and bureaucrats. Even the judiciary is under threat.

If the professions are to be a reliable source of independent advice, they must be self-regulating. This is the fifth criterion which an occupation must satisfy to be a profession. Yet it is increasingly difficult for any profession to satisfy this criterion. Most professions are financially dependent on governments or large pharmaceutical companies. Naturally, if you pay the piper, you want to call the tune, and this is precisely what governments have increasingly being doing. They impose targets, curricula, policies, all with a political agenda in mind. In the United Kingdom, the GMC is nominally in charge of discipline and (for the time being) undergraduate education, but more realistically it is governments who call the tune since they pay the piper. Hence, the self-regulation of the medical profession is another illusory belief, and lack of self-regulation separates medicine from the traditional idea of a profession. Once again a change of ethics is on the way.

So far we have suggested five criteria which an occupation must satisfy if it is to count as a profession: knowledge and skills; a broad framework of values stemming from a humane education; a public service provided via a special relationship; a duty to comment on matters of public policy; professional self-regulation. The argument has been that while there may have been a historical period when medicine satisfied these criteria (see our account of Dr Gregory in Chapter 1) it no longer fully satisfies any except the first – knowledge and skills. Does that mean that we should conclude that medicine is no longer a profession?

Professions, business and other occupations

This may seem the appropriate question to ask in the light of the foregoing analysis of the present characterisitics of medicine, but it may be the wrong question. Certainly, before attempting to answer the question we should note that many other occupations are also in the position that they satisfy some but not all of the criteria. The way ahead then might be to drop the traditional idea that a small number of occupations – typically medicine, law, education and the church – constitute 'the professions', and move towards a wider notion of the professions. We can then say that a large number of occupations have what we might call 'family resemblances'.[3]

Members of a large family do not all have the same features, but they have a number of features which, as it were, overlap, and enable us to recognise someone as belonging to that family. This approach follows from the point that occupations develop over the years: some become professions, and others may cease to be such if the public no longer needs the service. For example, surgeons or dentists are now clearly in professions but it was not always so. The general point is that while it is still possible to say that medicine is a profession this claim does not distinguish medicine from a wide range of other occupations.

There is a further point however. Doctors, and perhaps members of the other traditional professions, have thought of themselves as beneficently focused on their patients, clients or students. By contrast those in most other occupations, especially the many occupations concerned with business or commerce, are thought to be directed at their own self-interest. The classic statement of the self-interested nature of business is provided by Adam Smith, Professor of Moral Philosophy at Glasgow University (1752–63). In his great work *The Wealth of Nations* he writes as follows:

> In almost every other race of animals, each individual, when it is grown up to maturity, is entirely independent, and in the natural state has occasion for the assistance of no other living creature. But man has almost constant occasion

---

3 Wittgenstein L., *Philosophical Investigations*, 1953, Oxford: Blackwell, paragraphs 65–75.

for the help of his brethren, and it is in vain for him to expect it from their benevolence only. He is more likely to prevail if he can interest their self-love in his favour, and show them that it is their own advantage to do for him what he requires of them. It is not from the benevolence of the butcher, the brewer, or the baker that we expect our dinner, but from their regard to their own self-interest. We address ourselves, not to their humanity, but to their self-love, and never talk to them of our own necessities, but of their advantages.[4]

This alleged contrast, between the beneficence of the professions and the self-interest of those in business, can have unfortunate effects. It can create a sense of moral superiority in the professions, and aggressive responses from business, such as 'We live in the real world and not in an ivory tower,' or 'We earn the wealth of a country on which the professions depend.' But how valid is the contrast implicit in Adam Smith's claim?

To answer the question we must distinguish the point at which a service is provided or an item sold in the market, and the point at which prices and fees or salary levels are fixed. It is certainly the case that professionals attempt to provide a service to fit the needs or wants of their clients. But the same (we maintain) is also true of those in business. For example, if I am buying a new computer, I will typically receive good advice about the model which best suits my needs and price-range. Certainly, there are unscrupulous salespersons persuading me to buy what is not in my interests, but equally there are unscrupulous professionals who may try to persuade me into frivolous litigation or unnecessary medical treatment.

Now the fact that I expect and most often receive good advice and choice in a free market at the point of service delivery is quite compatible with saying that at the point at which prices are fixed a business person will consider what the market will stand by way of prices. No benevolence here! But, equally, professional bodies fix their fees or salaries at a level they think the general public, or a government, will tolerate. No benevolence here either! Hence, we do not think that Adam Smith's contrast between the self-interest of a free market and the benevolence of the professions is valid. In this respect at least there is no significant moral difference between business and the professions.

It might be argued however that there remains one important difference between a transaction in the free market and a professional encounter. Suppose that I wish to buy a pair of stout shoes for walking along country lanes. I try various pairs and then my eye lights on a pair of shiny patent leather shoes and I decide to buy them. The salesperson will certainly tell me that the shiny shoes will quickly become scratched and wear out in rough lanes, and are not at all suitable for my stated purposes. But if I persist and put the money down, the shoe salesperson has no duty to refuse the sale. Having given honest information and advice, the salesperson hands the responsibility for the purchase to the

4 Smith A, *The Wealth of Nations* (1776) 1976, Oxford: Oxford University Press.

customer. That is part of the market mechanism. The question is: can that mechanism be carried over into a professional encounter?

The profession of medicine and the ethics of consumerism

Traditionally that mechanism could not be carried over into medicine. The patient was fully entitled to refuse any treatment offered, but could not insist on receiving a treatment which the doctor considered inappropriate. Yet in the name of 'patient choice' it seems to be increasingly the case that the patient is making the treatment decisions. Indeed this has been the case for some time in the United States. For example, in a survey of the literature on the issue Paris et al.,[5] as early as 1993, note that doctors will almost always continue treatment if requested by patients or relatives even if they regard it as futile. Moreover, this view was supported by many US ethicists throughout the 1990s. For example, Veatch and Spicer maintain that a physician is obliged to supply treatment even if the request 'deviated intolerably' from established standards or is in terms of the doctor's judgement 'grossly inappropriate'.[6] This view is increasingly adopted in the United Kingdom. For example, the BMA[7] and GMC[8] guidance on resuscitation seems to suggest (although they hedge their bets) that a doctor should attempt it simply because the patient requests it and regardless of its chances of success. We said that these bodies 'hedge their bets', because while advising that resuscitation should be attempted at the patient's request and regardless of its chances of success, they also state that doctors are not obliged to provide treatment which they think will not be successful.[9]

Once again the sharp distinction between the medical profession and a sales occupation seems to have weakened. It follows from this that it is only (at best) a half-truth that medicine is a profession (except in the wide and weak sense it shares with many other occupations).

The ethical consequences of this are considerable. They has a profound effect on how doctors see themselves, and how patients see themselves. The ethics of the marketplace are slowly replacing those of the old professions. This may or may not be a bad thing, but it certainly affects the ethics of the profession.

In concluding this section we shall suggest some broad ethical principles which would govern medical practice if it continues to move in a consumerist

5 Paris JJ, Schreiber MD, Statter M, Arensman R and Seigler M, 'Sounding board', *New England Journal of Medicine*, 1993, 5, pp 354–357.
6 Veatch RM and Spicer CM, 'Medically futile care: the role of the physician in setting limits', *American Journal of Law and Medicine* ,1992, 18, pp 15–36.
7 BMA, *Decisions Relating to Cardiopulmonary Resuscitation*, 2001, London: BMA, section 5.2.
8 GMC, *Withholding and Withdrawing Life-prolonging Treament: Good Practice in Decision making*, 2002, London: GMC, paragraph 89.
9 BMA, *Withholding and Withdrawing Life-prolonging Treatment*, 2001, London: BMJ Books, p 1.

direction. These principles are derived from the ethics of the marketplace. First of all, patients would require *access* to the treatments and drugs they require. Second, patients would require a *choice* of the treatments, and places of treatment, they would wish. Third, there would need to be *competition* among the suppliers of treatments, to 'drive up standards'. Fourth, patients would require *adequate information* on the treatments they might receive, and the information would need to be clearly stated and have adequate warnings about side-effects and other harms and risks. Fifth, patients should be able to obtain adequate *redress* in the event of unsatisfactory treatment or poor service. Sixth, treatments and services would be required to be *safe and subject to regulation*. Seventh, there would need to be *patient responsibility* for the treatments or services chosen after the provision of adequate information.

Now if we survey these consumerist ethical principles we can see that medicine has moved at least half-way from its traditional professional position. Some of the requirements have for long been regarded as part of good medical practice, such as the provision of information, and the regulation of safety in respect of drugs and treatments. Legal redress, and the fear of it, has become increasingly a feature in the minds of doctors and their managers. These issues can be accommodated within the traditional idea of a profession.

But the real problems are competition, choice and responsibility. Governments of the left and right in the United Kingdom are increasingly encouraging both competition, via league tables and other devices, and patient choice. It is very doubtful whether competition is a good thing in this context, but it is certainly being forced on medical practice. And it is equally unclear what in practice is meant by the rhetoric of patient choice. But to the extent that the medical profession tolerates these changes it is moving away from the traditional ethics of the profession. Finally, neither governments nor medicine seem willing or even aware of the final step towards a true consumerist ethics – responsibility. If I receive adequate information in the marketplace, and put my money down, then, as a consumer, I am responsible for my choice. Neither governments nor the public seem willing to take the final step, and accept that patients are responsible for their choices in medicine as much as in the marketplace. Doctors remain responsible even if it is the patient who has made the choice. Hence, it is only a half- truth that medicine is a profession in the traditional sense. But the fact that in some ways it retains a traditional professional ethos and in others has acquired a consumerist ethos makes medical ethics confused and complicated.

Medical education and attitudinal change

For the last 40 years or so patients have become more vocal in demanding changes in clinical practice. These looked-for changes are basically of two overlapping kinds: changes in the attitudes and manners of doctors, and changes in their ethical awareness. Medical educators have seen it as their job to try to produce new generations of doctors who are more aware of both these patient-led requirements. In this section we shall discuss one attempt by medical educators to deal with these issues. The medical educators published their findings and recommendations in a journal,[10] and we shall discuss their views as presented in the journal.

The authors address mainly the first of the challenges – how to change the manners and attitudes of doctors, or how to make them more 'empathic' – while raising concerns about the second, the challenge of ethics. How far is their article persuasive in suggesting methods which might bring about attitudinal change? We shall argue that the medical educators are facing up to a problem – how to bring about some sort of improvement in the attitudes of doctors to patients – but are mistaken in thinking that such changes can be achieved by the typical approaches of medical education. It will be remembered that in the section on the idea of a profession we suggested that the skills and knowledge of medicine, to the extent that it is a profession, ought to be based on a broad values education. To put it another way, our argument is that the knowledge and skills criterion belongs to the 'training' aspect of a profession whereas the values and attitudinal component belong to the 'education' aspect. The mistake of many medical educators is their belief that the values and attitudinal aspect can be addressed via the knowledge and skills aspect. This belief is manifest in the hyphenation of 'skills' on to other words, such as 'communication skills' or 'listening skills'. In brief, the mistake lies in the belief that you can be trained to be educated! We shall now examine one attempt to do this.

The authors of the study describe their objective as follows:

> We designed a curricular exercise intended to expose otherwise healthy second year medical students, near the end of their basic science training, to a hospitalisation experience. In this project we attempted to assess how a standardised in-patient hospital experience, for medical students, just prior to the start of clinical rotations, was experienced by student participants.[11]

The results of the study were:

> Among key themes expressed by student participants were the following: they felt a profound loss of privacy; they found the nursing staff to be caring, attentive and professional, repeatedly commenting about how much time the nurses took to talk and listen to them and take a complete history; in contrast, they were particularly upset about the distance and coldness they felt from the medical staff; they expect this experience to impact their own future practice as physicians. When asked how this experience might change

---

10 Milgrom E, Wilkes M, and Hoffman J, 'Towards more empathic medical students: a medical student hospitalization experience', *Medical Education*, 2002, 36, pp 528–533.

11 Ibid.

their attitude in the future, students' comments generally reflected a primary concern with improving the human aspects of the patient experience.[12]

The conclusions drawn were:

Student participants in a standardised in-patient hospitalisation experienced similar strong feelings about issues of privacy, and about interactions with medical and nursing staff, which they expect to have an important impact on their own professional development.[13]

And the key learning points were:

An in-patient experience for healthy medical students results in commonly shared responses about both the nature of the hospitalisation itself and the interactive behaviours of health care providers.
   Students' exposure to physicians and nursing staff had a dramatic impact on how they expect to practise in the future;
   Physician examiners, who were blind to the student status of their patients, documented physical findings consistent with the admitting diagnoses, even though their 'patients' were actually healthy medical students.[14]

The authors have correctly identified the need for attitudinal change and the question we shall address concerns the plausibility and acceptability of the method used, which was very much in the mode of medical training. The hope was that the students would become more sensitive to patients or more 'empathic'. Is this likely to be the case?

It is significant that the sorts of points the students make could have been taken from a typical textbook on medical education or the doctor–patient relationship. Others are typical patient complaints – the food, the noise, the lack of privacy. You don't actually need to go through the process of hospitalisation to learn this. Indeed, just as the examining doctors claimed to find the symptoms they were led to expect, it is plausible to say that the students reported what they were led to expect. Of course, the authors could argue that there is a gap between knowing something intellectually and experiencing it personally. True, but this gap is not filled by the experience in question, because, as the authors freely admit, the students are not actually patients; they are just pretending to be. If the aim is to develop compassion or humanity, then, it seems very doubtful if this sort of method will succeed. Indeed, if it were to become more common it would

12 Ibid.
13 Ibid.
14 Ibid.

have increasingly less impact, as hospital staff became automatically suspicious of well-educated young people claiming to have lower back pain.

What of the other patient concern – the ethical behaviour of doctors? The authors admit to some ethical worries over their method, but think that the cause of medical education justified the deception. Now there seem to us to be three aspects to the ethical issues: risk of harm to the 'patients', waste of resources, and deception. The authors are aware of the possibility of harm to the students, who were told they could refuse any treatment they did not want. This may cover the risks issue, but at the cost of removing the students even further from a genuine patient-status.

Turning to resources we can say that there is more money available for patient care in the United States than the United Kingdom, provided that you aren't poor. Indeed, one of the most significant and saddest outcomes of the episode was that a student 'patient' was turned away because he could not establish that he could pay. As far as the United Kingdom goes, it would be no exaggeration to say that if such an experiment in medical education were tried here, and caught the attention of the media, as it surely would, it would make the national headlines. There have been several recent medical scandals in the United Kingdom, and the fact that healthy young people were occupying scarce hospital beds in the name of 'empathy' would be taken to be yet another example of medical self-regard.

The third ethical issue is the intrinsic deception required. Perhaps, rarely, deception can be justified in the name of important research. But to encourage dishonest and fraudulent behaviour in young students and to attempt to justify this in the name of sensitivity and empathy indicates that it is the educators who lack humane qualities. What this article brings out is the inward-looking nature of much of medical education, its tendency to give medical students the message that they are special and exempt from the norms of acceptable social behaviour.

The authors of this article are concerned with precisely the wrong issue. Most medical students, like most bright young people, already have humane qualities such as sensitivity. The relevant question is therefore not how to create such qualities in students, but how it comes about that medical education destroys them. What is needed is for medical educators to give permission, as it were, for the encouragement and deployment of the humane qualities which students already possess. As we shall suggest in Chapter 6, optional courses (Special Study Modules or Student Selected Components in UK terminology) in the humanities may give such permission, and encourage a broader perspective on life than can be offered by the narrow world of medicine. If some students do not already possess these qualities then medical education cannot create them. Certainly, dishonesty can never be a means to developing sensitivity; indeed, such practices will simply kill off the good qualities students already possess.

Quality of life

The term 'quality of life' has become part of the English language, and is now commonly used both within health care and also in daily life. The WHO definition of the specialty of palliative care makes the achievement of the best possible quality of life for patients, and also their families, the primary aim of the specialty.[15] But despite this enthusiasm for furthering the quality of life of patients many writers note the fact that no satisfactory definition of quality of life has been produced. Judging by the volume of literature on the topic, the search for one has not been abandoned. *The Oxford Textbook of Palliative Medicine* produces the staggering information that between 1961–65 there were no entries at all in Medline under the keyword 'quality of life' but between 1996–2000 there were 12,749![16] Many of these articles are concerned with the search for a definition. Yet it is possible to explain why a helpful definition cannot be found, even in principle.

Before doing so, we must stress that the motivation behind the numerous discussions of quality of life is a worthy one. It is recognised that there is more to medicine than simply keeping a patient alive. Hence it is tempting to take the next step and say that from the ethical point of view quality of life is more important than quantity. That is a half-truth, but it is only a half-truth, since it is not possible to turn the term 'quality of life' into a technical term and attach measurement scales to it. Since this is highly relevant to our argument in this chapter we shall try to untangle some of the complexities in the term which make it impossible to define, even in principle. What is a 'quality'?[17]

What is a 'quality'?

First, a 'quality' can mean simply an attribute, a characteristic or disposition of something or someone. In this sense the term 'quality' is purely descriptive of some fact or identifiable state of affairs, and is therefore evaluatively neutral. For example, cooking apples will have certain qualities or characteristics, such as being of a certain size, cooking well and having a sharp flavour. Again, types of disease will be associated with certain characteristics, symptoms or qualities, such as breathlessness or nausea, and a psychopath will be disposed to act in certain ways or will have certain qualities. The first requirement of a quality of life judgement, then, is that it must be grounded in descriptively identifiable factual qualities.

This may seem too obvious to state, but, as we shall see, there are those who wish to base quality of life judgements simply on how the patient claims to feel. How the patient feels is certainly an important consideration, but it is not the only factor relevant to a quality of life judgement. To the extent that a quality is

15 WHO, *National Cancer Control Programmes: Policies and Managerial Guidelines*, 2nd ed. 2002, Geneva: WHO.

16 Kaasa S and Loge JH, 'Quality of life in palliative medicine – principles and practice', *Oxford Textbook of Palliative Medicine* 3rd edn, 2004, Oxford: Oxford University Press, pp 196–197.

17 There is a much more detailed discussion of the whole issue in Randall F and Downie RS, *The Philosophy of Palliative Care: Critique and Reconstruction*, 2006, Oxford: Oxford University Press.

present, some factual, or objectively identifiable, factor must be present. In the context of quality of life judgements in health care typical qualities which are factually identifiable might be nausea, breathlessness, mobility, capacity to respond to questions, and so on.

Second, when we use the term 'quality of life', as distinct from the term 'quality' on its own, we are making a judgement which *evaluates* these factual qualities. In other words, we are standing back from the factual qualities we have noted and assessing them as good or poor. The quality of life judgement is an assessment which is consequential on, or results from, the identification of the list of relevant factual qualities. To put this another way, we might say that 'quality of life' is not another item on a list which includes factual qualities such as nausea or mobility; it is rather a value judgement resulting from a total assessment of qualities on the list.

The point that quality of life judgements are value judgements about factual qualities and not in themselves factual qualities is not always appreciated. We have found that some researchers use the term 'quality of life' as if it itself were a factual quality or set of qualities. For example, in a study 'to determine the association between symptoms and depression in patients with advanced cancer'[18] Professor Mari Lloyd-Williams et al. include a table which has the following items, each of which receives a score: pain, mood, breathlessness, physical movement, general quality of life, tiredness. The point the authors have missed is that 'general quality of life' is not an item like the others. The others are descriptive or factual qualities, and 'general quality of life' ought not to be a separate item on that list; rather it is consequential on the others.

A similar error is to be found in a discussion of 'Dignity and psychotherapeutic considerations in end-of life care'. Dr Harvey Max Chochinov et al. say the following: 'A factor analysis of the dignity data set yielded six primary factors, including: (1) pain; (2) intimate dependency; (3) hopelessness/depression; (4) informal support network; (5) formal support network; and 6) quality of life.'[19] The point however is that items 1–5 are factual, descriptive, objective factors, whereas the all-things-considered quality of life judgement results from a survey of these facts (by the patient or professional) and is an *evaluation* of the quality of life as good or poor, granted the five (or more) factors to be found in the life.

The mistake of placing quality of life on the same list as the objective factors such as pain, depression, support, etc. amounts to what philosophers call a 'category mistake'.[20] For example, let us suppose a visitor to the University of Oxford goes round the colleges and at the end of the day says 'I've seen the

18 Lloyd-Williams M, Dennis M and Taylor F, 'A prospective study to determine the association between physical symptoms and depression in patients with advanced cancer', *Palliative Medicine*, 2004, 18, pp 558–563.
19 Chochinov HM et al., 'Dignity in the terminally ill: an empirical model', *Social Science and Medicine*, 2002, 18, pp 558–563.
20 Ryle G, *The Concept of Mind*, 1947, London: Hutchinson's University Library.

Colleges, but where is the University?'. That is a category mistake, for the university just is the sum total of the colleges. In a similar way, 'quality of life' judgements (logically) must be assessments resulting from the sum total of the factors surveyed.

To summarise so far, we are saying that there are two elements in quality of life judgements: there must be identifiable, factual qualities; there must be an evaluation of these identifiable factors as comprising a good or poor quality of life.

The impossibility of finding a definition

There are however other complications which arise in the making of quality of life judgements. First, the list of qualities, in the descriptive, identifiable sense, that people might value in their lives is obviously very large, and we can never be sure we have noted them all on our list. For example, people might value having friends, being at home, being able to listen to music, having a job, and so on. The list of possible items which can be placed on this list is enormously large. Second, the emphases (or evaluations) which different people might place on different items will vary. Moreover, even the same people might place a different value on different factors at different times in their lives.

It should now be clear why 'quality of life' cannot be defined in any strict sense of definition. First, since the list of identifiable qualities relevant to a quality of life assessment for a given person is very large we can never be sure we have listed them all. Second, the items which different people might consider relevant to an assessment will vary. Third, even the same person may stress different factors as relevant over a period of a month. Quality of life cannot therefore be defined, not because it is difficult to do but because it is logically impossible. Attempts to define it should simply be abandoned.

We recognise that this conclusion is controversial. In the *Oxford Textbook of Palliative Medicine*, Stein Kaasa and Jon Havard Loge note that health-related quality of life is an abstract concept, and state that:

> In order to communicate about an abstract phenomenon, one needs to agree upon a definition of the concept, how to explore the concept, and how to summarise the findings. In other words, an accurate description of a subjective phenomenon depends upon how the concept is defined, how data is collected, processed and communicated.[21]

Our position is that definition of the concept is not possible. This leads to the conclusion that data encompassing it cannot be collected, processed or communicated.

---

21 Kaasa S and Loge JH, op.cit., p 199.

Now it by no means follows from anything we have so far said that the WHO philosophy is mistaken in making its central aim the attainment for patients of an improved quality of life. For it might be said that, whereas the list of qualities which patients might value in their lives is very large, the qualities can mainly be placed under certain headings. In more detail, it would be possible to draw up a typical list of factors which many people would consider important for an overall good quality of life. For example, most people would mention being healthy, having a job, a decent income, having friends, living in a safe and pleasant environment, having some leisure, being able to make a few choices about one's life, and so on. There is absolutely no difficulty in compiling such a list and finding wide agreement about the items which should be on it. Difficulty arises only if we claim that we have an exhaustive list – for it is easy to omit an item which is crucial to the quality of life of a given person – or if we try to rank the items in any order of importance, for different people stress different items on the list, and a given person's view of the items may change with time and circumstances. Hence, while it is not possible even in principle to produce an agreed overall definition of quality of life in this broad sense, we can formulate lists of typical factors which we all might like to have in our lives. In this way the term 'quality of life' might still be a helpful one in health assessments. It is therefore a half-truth that 'quality of life' is a helpful term in medicine. But definitions are not possible and attempts to produce them can only mislead.

Conclusions

Half-truths reveal distorted perceptions and attitudes, and such distortions lead to professional delusions and unethical practice. We have tried to illustrate these claims by examining the traditional idea of medicine as a profession and suggesting how it is changing, by casting doubt on the idea that the training typical of medical 'education' can supply the humane values needed in medicine, and that medicine can solve the problems of life by improving, and measuring, our quality of life.

Part III

Medical humanities

The supplementary function of literature and the arts

Chapter 6

Literature and the ethical perspective

In Chapter 1 we distinguished between the *second-order critical* function of philosophy regarded as a medical humanity, and the *supplementary* function of literature and other arts. We have illustrated the critical function of philosophy in Chapters 1–5, and hope to have shown its relevance to the ethical issues in health care. We shall now turn to the supplementary function of the humanities and consider what they can add to traditional medical ethics. In particular, we shall argue that they can have an ethically desirable influence on medical perceptions and attitudes. We shall begin with literature, and move to the other arts in Chapter 7.

There are many aspects of literature which have an influence on ethical perceptions and attitudes in medicine, and the discussion in this chapter does not claim to be exhaustive. The various modes in which literature can affect the ethical perspective will for convenience be grouped under a number of headings and illustrated. We shall discuss transferable skills; the humanistic perspective; the ability to cope with the particular situation; self-awareness.

Transferable skills

Medical English often has one or other or both of two faults. Either it is turgid and larded with professional terms or it is in bullet points. But when it comes to presenting a case to a wider audience or a treatment to a patient then some attention to brevity and clarity and to what people might want to know is important. Perhaps such skills can be developed from courses on, say, journalism or writing. This skill might seem important but not at all connected with ethics. Yet many complaints about doctors concern the letters they write to patients. Such letters are sometimes harsh and unfeeling in tone. Yet when the writer is confronted with the complaint he/she is often genuinely surprised, having no insight into how an anxious patient might react to the letter. Some study of letter-writing – from down-to-earth referral letters to the more complex and stylistically effective letters to be found in anthologies – can open the eyes and ears of medical students and doctors to an area of ethics they may not have been aware of.

Turning now to conversation we wish to suggest that some humanities, especially literature, involve concentration on language and a study of such disciplines will develop sensitivity to what patients may be saying. It is worth noting here that doctors and others who wish to promote the employment of the humanities in medical education are currently making the idea of 'narrative' a central concept.[1] Like the use of the term 'evidence' by their scientifically minded colleagues this wide use of 'narrative' obscures as much as it illuminates. In the brief time a doctor spends with a patient in a consultation the patient might be able to relate a short anecdote about what he/she thinks has gone wrong, but there is not likely to be much time for anything that would justify the grand term 'narrative', unless perhaps in psychotherapy.

The problem with the term 'narrative' is well expressed by Christopher Jordens in a review of *Narrative Research in Health and Illness*.[2] Jordens writes:

> If ambiguity about the meaning of the term narrative has permitted the bridging of divides, the bridge is now straining. The term has become a category without boundaries and has thereby come to represent many different ways of meaning. The less clear the boundaries, the more baggage it collects. If this trend continues, the bridge may collapse. This may not be such a bad thing, however.

Anecdotes are important however in presenting the values of the patient's perspective in ways which are not open to those doctors who ignore what the patient is saying and concentrate on what their technology is recording.

In the general practice setting in particular the patients' accounts of their problem are undifferentiated and unmedicalised because they have not yet had their stories reinterpreted by a doctor. For instance, angina is not yet, 'A tight pain in my chest which I get with exertion'; it is still described in this way in this imaginary anecdote told by a patient:

> The reason I am here, doctor, is that last week I was walking to the shops with my wife and we came back with a lot of shopping and had to climb up the hill to the house because the bus broke down. As we reached the top of the hill I suddenly got this pain in my chest which made me stop and gasp for breath.

Anecdotes of this sort are often the way in which patients will explain their visit to the doctor in the first place.

1 Greenhalgh T and Hurwitz B, *Narrative Research in Health and Illness*, 2005, London: BMJ Books.
2 Jordens C, 'Narrative research in health and illness' (Review), *British Medical Journal*, 2005, 330, p 1336.

Anecdotes are also used by patients to illustrate how the particular symptoms are affecting their lives at that time. This is an exchange one of the authors (JM) had with a patient who is particularly keen on the game of bowls:

JM: How are the knees just now? Are the new painkillers working better?
Patient: Oh no, it's just as bad, doctor, and with me Lady President of the bowling green this season too.
JM: How are you getting on with the bowling?
Patient: Oh, I'm not able to play just now. The last time I had a match I tried to deliver a bowl and I couldn't get up again! Some of the men had to lift me up off the green. It gave everyone a good laugh but I haven't been able to play since.

This kind of patient anecdote is important because it reflects the individual's experience of the problem and gives the doctor a clear idea of how function is affected. For the patient, mild osteoarthritis of the knees was having a major impact on her lifestyle and merited physiotherapy and an orthopaedic surgeon's opinion. For another elderly woman, whose lifestyle was not so active, the condition might not have promoted any action. The anecdote reminds us that what the patient is interested in is his or her ability to function, not the severity or otherwise of the pathology. Doctors will often say reassuringly to their patients, 'You'll be glad to hear that the test result is normal', only to be greeted with, 'So why am I having these problems?'. Patients want to be restored to normal function or at least to have an explanation for why they cannot function normally.

Patients' illustrative anecdotes can also be revealing of their understanding or misunderstanding of a suspected illness. A patient who had a urostomy scar that had developed herniation commented:

But my Uncle James has his hernias operated on down here [indicating her groin area]. I thought it was only men who had hernias. Mind you my sister had one up here inside [indicating the epigastric area] and she had problems eating with it.

This series of anecdotes reveals the patient's (reasonable) confusion over the idea of a hernia and how it can exist in several different places. Paying attention to patient anecdote allows doctors the chance to clarify areas of misunderstanding and become aware of how the patient perceives his or her illness and his or her own ability to do something about it.

Even the way in which a patient orders events in her story can be highly significant. Compare two presentations of breast cancer:

'About a month ago I fell against the banisters and it was just after that that I felt the lump.'
'I don't usually examine myself but about a month ago I fell and hurt my chest and when I was rubbing on a pain reliever I felt the lump.'

The first patient clearly feels that there is some connection between her injury and the development of the cancer, whereas the second sees the injury as fortuitous, as it allowed her the opportunity of discovering the lump earlier. If the doctor ignores the significance of these different kinds of anecdote, the patient can be left confused and disorientated with many questions left unanswered. Alertness to the patient's story and the implications of the language used in telling it allows the doctor access to a deeper understanding of the patient beyond the purely scientific and pathological,[3] and for that reason it is every bit as relevant to diagnosis and treatment as scientific evidence. And being aware of what is important to patients is a fact with ethical significance, because not only does it assist with diagnosis but it also helps patients to feel that they are being taken seriously.

But doctors who wish to learn from the humanities might do well to become aware of the *range* of conceptual tools which are available – from hermeneutics, rhetoric, linguistics, and so on – rather than march behind generalised slogans such as 'the patient's narrative'. There are many other concepts which might more precisely direct the doctor's attention to the nature and implications of the language used by the patient.[4]

Perhaps it might be helpful by way of example to mention two, from literary interpretation, which can be helpful in a medical context: 'voice' and 'iteration'. 'Voice' can be explained initially in simple grammatical terms. It is the difference between an account of what *I* feel/think/experience and what *he/she* feels/thinks/experiences. But the voices become intermingled when the patient says: 'I had a touch of pain last week and I wouldn't have bothered about it, but my husband – he's a great worrier – said, "Jean, you must go to the doctor." So here I am.' The wife is here putting the blame on the husband, and this is of significance. It means that she is worried but does not wish to admit to the worries. Some practice in using this kind of distinction in works of literature will enable a medical student or doctor to develop sensitivity to certain types of nuance within a patient's account of his or her problems.

Another helpful concept is that of iteration. If a problem is especially worrying to us we tend to return to it in different ways. This is a device used to great effect in poetry. For example, in the following short poem by John Davies of Hereford (1565–1618) the lines themselves are not striking – banal even – but the iteration makes them together very effective in conveying the state of mind of the poet.

> Death has deprived me of my dearest friend,
> My dearest friend is dead and laid in grave,
> In grave he rests until the world shall end,
> The world shall end as end must all things have.

3 Macnaughton J, 'Anecdotes in clinical practice', in Greenhalgh T and Hurwitz B (eds), *Narrative Based Medicine*,1998, London: BMJ Books.

4 See, for example, Culler J, *Literary Theory*, 1997, Oxford: Oxford University Press.

All things must have an end that nature wrought,
That nature wrought must unto dust be brought.[5]

Sensitivity to a certain sort of repetition is a quality which a doctor might find worth developing, because it may indicate the patient's values.

Nevertheless, the term 'narrative' does have the merit of identifying a general type of explanation of behaviour which can be as revealing of a medical condition as an X-ray. It depicts a slice of life-story, a way of understanding patients through their own language rather than through that of science. Skills of this kind can be developed through reading and writing narrative. Indeed, it cannot be overemphasised at the moment that the evidence from randomised clinical trials is only one sort of evidence relevant to clinical judgement. A biographer, say, or a detective, will look for a different sort of evidence: one related to *specific* incidents or events. Their sort of evidence may be logically closer to the kind which influences a clinician, who is dealing with the particular patient, than the evidence of trials, which is generalised. In general, science works mainly with inductive evidence, but the arts can introduce doctors to a range of other ways of thinking which are equally relevant to the practice of medicine. Familiarity with these alternative[6] sources of evidence comes from creative writing and reading. We have already suggested that the kind of understanding which comes from literature is more relevant to the interpretation of qualitative research than is a numerical approach (p 87ff).

Literature also develops the ability to see connections between apparently disparate situations. For example, EM Forster's novel *Howard's End* stated its overriding theme before the book starts: 'Only connect...'[7]: and the story illustrates the tragic consequences when the characters fail to do this. The ability to see connections is one which can be developed by creative writing. For example, a good plot will be one in which clues are given in such a way that, as the story develops, the reader is led to feel the inevitability of the outcome. For example, in the first scene of Shakespeare's *King Lear* we can already form our ideas about all the characters, and as the drama unfolds we feel the inevitability of the tragic outcome.

Alertness to the connections between apparently disparate events or to the significance of apparently trivial incidents can be important in diagnosis. For example, a patient may present with flu-like symptoms, and casually mention that he is just back from holiday in Africa. The doctor who can 'connect' might wish to consider the possibility of cerebral malaria. Those who take literature

5 Grossart AB (ed), *The Complete Poems of John Davis of Hereford*, 1873, Oxford: Oxford University Press.

6 Downie RS and Macnaugton J, *Clinical Judgement: Evidence in Practice*, 2000, Oxford: Oxford University Press.

7 Forster EM, *Howard's End*, 1946, Harmondsworth: Penguin Books, p 1.

seriously thereby develop a sensitivity to the unexpected connection. Sensitivity of this kind can transfer to the process of medical diagnosis.

The humanistic perspective

There are many different ways of seeing human beings of which the scientific is only one and there are many different ways of seeing society of which a Western liberal way is only one. For example, both authors were involved in teaching a special study module (SSM) on Plato's *Republic*.[8] It so happened that the medical students had just finished their 'Family Project', a project which presupposed the importance of the family unit. They were then faced with Plato's arguments against the family. It was salutary for the students to appreciate that not everyone thinks that the family and family values are good and to be obliged to make explicit and defend the values which their project was presupposing.

The development of broad perspectives may be especially important in medicine because, like the military and the police, medicine has its own ethos and bonding is encouraged. There is therefore a tendency to develop narrow perspectives and to close ranks. Let us take the example of the teaching of medical ethics.

The teaching of medical ethics has tended to fall into the hands of philosophers. But, as we have pointed out in Chapter 2, philosophers are interested in the critical investigation of assumptions and arguments. Such investigations have limited appeal to doctors because of their abstract and generalised nature. On the other hand, literature or film can make a much more powerful impact on moral awareness because of its immediacy. Like medicine itself literature deals with the details of cases. Indeed, there is a danger that philosophy actually blunts moral awareness because students become caught up with terms such as 'deontology' or 'patient autonomy' or with the technicalities or moral argument which blind them to the reality of the situations they will be dealing with.

To illustrate the points we are making here we shall quote a poem by Dr AA McConnell, a consultant pathologist. The poem, entitled 'Roswell, Hanger 84', requires an introduction, which Dr McConnell provides:

> The Channel 4 television programme, *The Roswell Incident*, first broadcast in 1995, describes the crash landing of an alien spacecraft in the desert of New Mexico, near the Roswell air force base in July 1947. Eye witnesses claim to have seen the wreckage of such a craft, together with living but injured aliens, and stated that the wreckage and a number of corpses were stored in

8 Downie RS and Macnaughton J, 'Should medical students read Plato?' *The Medical Journal of Australia*, 1999, 170, 3, pp 125–127.

hanger 84 (hence the title) at the base. The television programme showed a post-mortem examination being carried out on one of the corpses. The question of the relationship between humans and intelligent aliens is one which may have to be faced sooner rather than later, and perhaps it is now time seriously to consider the ethics of the relationship between all life-forms.[9]

Roswell, Hanger 84

For the animals every day is Treblinka,
And that includes the *Homo Erectus;*
We no longer say *Sapiens.*
We had no choice;
Our world was too small;
Our first ships brought ambassadors of friendship.
They were killed and dissected.
Then our secret studies showed
That these animals were untrainable;
Too aggressive, too stupid, too selfish.
What else could we do but eat them,
And thus save the universe.
That last was a jest –
You see, we are civilised with a sophisticated humour;
And that was the meat of it –
The marrow in the long bones was irresistible.
We tried conversation, humane breeding,
But they would not reproduce in the factory farms.
Now the numbers are below sustainable limits.
At least we still have the intelligent whales
With their beautiful songs and thoughts in the waters,
Their music, their ancient sagas of sorrow.
Their flesh is, however, not so succulent,
And it is bad for our circulatory system.
By the way, any concern about Human CJD
Infecting us is just nonsensical;
After all, you will have seen the Commissar
Feeding his daughter a human-burger.

AA McConnell

What contribution can a poem such as Dr McConnell's make to the development of the ethical capacity in medical students and doctors?

---

9 McConnell AA, 'Roswell, Hanger 84', *Journal of Medical Ethics*, 1999, 2, p 528.

The first thing the poem offers is the encouragement to see human beings in an unusual perspective. Many philosophers are given to congratulating the human race on having a 'higher moral status' than the rest of creation. Having plucked this judgement from the air they proceed to draw from it conclusions such as: it is quite all right ethically to cut up any animal, from chimpanzees to pigs, if it will save a human life by providing organs for transplant. The poem encourages us to realise that human beings are 'untrainable...too aggressive, too stupid, too selfish', so that all that can be done is eat them, risking the infecting of the higher species of alien with 'Human CJD'! The adoption of a broad perspective of the kind presented in the poem is an important necessary condition for the development of ethical awareness, perhaps especially so in doctors who have a tendency to be narrowly focused. The adjectives 'medical' or 'health care' or 'bio' as qualifiers of the term 'ethics' indicate that we are dealing with an approach which is narrow – ethics from the health-care point of view. The ethical perspectives offered by literature are much wider, and in them doctors, nurses or other human beings, are not always the heroes.

Second, this poem and similar literature can offer the specifics of a particular incident. In our experience of teaching medical and nursing ethics over a period of years, students and their elders will listen politely to the outline of ethical theories, but they become interested only when we get on to actual case studies, at which point the ethical theories, or the 'four principles', are forgotten. This is no doubt why the case study method is popular in the discussion of first-order medical ethics, and we have discussed this in our account of casuistry (p 45ff). But literature can also offer the circumstantial detail of medical cases, but in a wider non-medical perspective. It can be used to supplement rather than supplant these first-order medical cases.

Third, literature can offer a stimulus to the moral imagination, to what we might call 'consciousness-raising'. There is a marked tendency, picked up by the media, to see medical ethics in terms of what are termed 'dilemmas'. But not all problems are 'dilemmas'. We have a problem when we don't know what to do or to think; we have a dilemma when we are already clear that there are two courses which we can take and we cannot decide which is the better. But even if we leave that distinction aside, the ethical failing of many of us, perhaps especially of doctors, is not the inability to solve an ethical problem, but the total lack of awareness that there is a problem at all! This is the classic case of moral insensitivity, and it is precisely this which is a common complaint against doctors. No application of principles is at all relevant here, since the fault lies in a failure of imagination or awareness. If this failure can be prevented at all (and we are not optimistic) it is by the stimulation to the imagination which comes from literature. Literature, perhaps especially poetry, can do this in various ways, but the impact of its imagery and language can affect the imagination with a force which the plainer language of philosophy can never use (and should not attempt to).

Defenders of philosophical medical ethics might say here that what philosophy can offer is assistance in the development of analytical skills. No doubt, but it is a common illusion among philosophers that they have a monopoly of analytical skills. The analysis of a poem is a highly skilled and complex matter, especially since poems are resonant with irony and ambiguity. Indeed, perhaps the diagnosis of a patient's illness and the analysis of an ethical problem have this in common: each is more like the interpretation of a difficult text than like either the scientific analysis of urine or the logical analysis of an argument.[10]

What about the justification of a moral decision in medicine? Literature cannot offer a transferable skill here, but, as we have seen (p 44), neither can philosophical theory. Indeed, the truth is that the latter is simply spurious in the context of justification, because it is in the wrong logical category to serve as the justification of a first-order moral judgement. Here we differ from Professor Gillon.[11] For example, 'We should stop the treatment' might represent a combined technical and moral decision, and 'The patient is no longer responding to it' might be offered as its justification. There is no need for a doctor to link that justification to any philosophical theory (although consenting philosophers in private might enjoy discussing universalisability or the three sorts of utilitarianism which might be relevant).

There are various historical reasons why the teaching of medical ethics has fallen into the hands of philosophers. Stephen Toulmin has argued that medicine has saved the life of ethics, in the sense of 'moral philosophy'.[12] Perhaps. Our question here is: what does philosophical medical ethics do to the first-order ethical sensitivity of doctors and nurses? Our answer is that it may kill it! If, for example, students are invited to read a case and decide what (a) a deontologist and (b) a utilitarian would say, they may feel encouraged to think that philosophical theories are a substitute for the moral sense they bring with them to their experience. Philosophy is certainly one kind of expertise, but it is not a kind which has direct bearing on first-order moral decision making, as we stressed in Chapter 2.

The conclusion which we draw from this comparison of philosophy and literature as possible vehicles for teaching first-order medical ethics is that perhaps neither will make much practical difference, but at least literature does not attempt to substitute abstract principle and foundationalist theory for lived experience. Note that we are not rejecting medical ethics, where that is understood simply as first-order discussion of the morality of various medical practices. Medical ethics just is ordinary morality with a medical content and does not need special principles or a special kind of theoretical justification. This is the point behind our

---

10 Montgomery HK, *Doctors' Stories: The Narrative Structure of Medical Knowledge*, 1991, Princeton: Princeton University Press.
11 Gillon R, 'Imagination, literature, medical ethics and medical practice', *Journal of Medical Ethics*, 1997, 23, pp 3–4.
12 Toulmin S, 'How medicine saved the lie of ethics', in DeMarco DJ and Fox RM (eds), *New Directions in Ethics*, 1986, London: Routledge and Kegan Paul, pp 265–281.

recommendation of casuistry as a method of analysing and reaching decisions on first-order problems in medical ethics. And of course, as we have said in Chapter 2, first-order discourse is a legitimate subject matter for second-order philosophical theorising, just as any sort of discourse might be. Our point is that second-order philosophising is no help in first-order decision making, whereas a study of literature, sometimes, and for some students, just might be.

Let us turn briefly to another way of looking at the value of the humanities for medical education, as that affects ethical awareness. If we may presume to speak for the general public, we want our doctors to be competent and wise. The competence comes from the scientific technicalities of medical training. The wisdom includes ethical sensitivity but is much wider than that, and it mainly comes from being broadly educated. Here, as we hinted at the start, literature and other humanities may have parts to play. The humanities are not just instrumental in creating the educated doctor; along with an understanding of the sciences they constitute what it means to be 'educated' as distinct from simply 'trained'.[13] We discussed the distinction between being trained and being educated in the section on Professions in Chapter 5 and will raise it again in Chapter 9.

Self-awareness

One criticism of doctors is that they are not always aware of how they are coming across to patients; and one problem of some doctors is emotional burn-out, which is not only self-destructive but also has a bad effect on patients. What we call a person's inner life is the inside story of his/her own history, the way living in the world makes him/her feel. This kind of experience is usually only vaguely known, because most of its components are nameless, and it is hard to form an idea of anything which has no name. This easily leads to the conclusion that feeling is entirely formless, that it has causes which may be determined, and effects which must be dealt with (sometimes with drugs) but that it itself is irrational, a disturbance of the organism with no structure of its own. Yet subjective experience has a structure which can be reflected on and symbolically expressed. It cannot be expressed through the discursive – everyday or scientific – use of language but it can be known through the arts.

Works of art are expressive forms and what they express is the nature of human feeling. The arts make our inner subjective life visible, audible or in some other way perceivable, through symbolic form.[14] What is artistically good is what articulates and presents feeling to our understanding. Note that while an artist expresses feeling it is not as a baby might. The artist objectifies subjective life. What the artist expresses is not his own feelings but what he knows about feeling. A work of art expresses a conception of life, emotion and inward reality.

13 Downie RS and Macnaughton J, 2000, op. cit., pp 161–166.
14 Langer SK, *Feeling and Form*, 1953, London: Routledge and Kegan Paul.

That is why the arts can help to create the self-understanding which is important for any doctor dealing with vulnerable human beings.

Joint investigation

One indirect outcome of the discussion of literature has direct relevance to the ethical behaviour of doctors. Patients nowadays frequently arrive with their own ideas of what is 'wrong' with them, and how they should be treated. If the doctor simply caves in to the patient's demands for specific treatments regardless of how appropriate they might be medicine has ceased to be a profession and consumerism has replaced it. This is as bad for the patient as old-fashioned paternalism – 'This is what is good for you.' Nowadays a more acceptable process for obtaining the patient's informed consent and compliance might be called 'joint investigation'. In this process the patient's suggestions and the doctor's suggestions may each be modified in mutual consultation. Each party may come to appreciate the view point of the other and a positive consensus may be reached. What is of ethical significance here is the process by which consensus and then consent has been reached.

But this is precisely what happens in a good literature seminar. Thus, it is arguable that for some subjects the outcomes in terms of new knowledge or skills are less important than the process by which these outcomes are approached. In the humanities, or some of them, it is possible for the student to challenge the point of view of the teacher to an extent that would not be possible in a subject such as biochemistry. This is not the same as learning to work in a team (which is important but is learned elsewhere). The study of the humanities can involve a joint exploration in which students can put forward points of view which can then be modified in the light of what their peers say. The result might be that all members of the study group, including the teacher or facilitator, reach a more considered understanding than they had before. The point here is the nature of what is learned in the process of discussion rather than the outcome. Process-led approaches to higher education have been proposed by Laurillard.[15]

Practice in this ethically important skill is something that doctors can acquire in the discussion of literature. Just as consensus in a literary discussion can leave all the participants with a deeper understanding of the work, so joint investigation by patient and doctor of possible treatments can leave both satisfied that the best regime has been drawn up.

Coping with the particular situation

Doctors must learn to cope with particular situations, or individual cases, where ethical rules and guidelines do not apply, or rather (as we stressed in the

---

15 Laurillard D, *Rethinking Teaching*, 1993, London: Routledge.

discussion of casuistry) where several apply. In this context it is helpful to refer to Plato's discussion of Book X of the *Republic* of an 'ancient quarrel' between philosophers on the one hand and poets and dramatists on the other.[16] The quarrel concerns the qualifications of each to make recommendations about the nature of the good life. Plato has no doubt that poets and dramatists are trying to do the same sort of thing as the philosophers (otherwise there would be no quarrel) but he holds that they lack proper understanding for the job. Plato's view is that real understanding comes from having insight into the blueprints, the timeless patterns, which make things as they are. In our day the task of discovering such patterns has been taken up by scientists and of course doctors are keen to follow the lead of scientists.

Now Plato's arguments against the humanities as a source of knowledge or understanding are limited because they depend on his assumption that the arts and humanities are essentially imitative, an assumption which would not nowadays be accepted. But even those who do not make that assumption may agree with Plato that the arts are not a source of real understanding. In terms of this point of view the arts are to be seen as decorative or entertaining or expressive of emotion. But this position can be challenged. It can be maintained that the arts and humanities can provide a distinctive sort of understanding, an understanding of the particular situation, and the qualitative distinctions involved. Let us examine this sort of understanding.

Literature, drama, and film are concerned above all with qualitative distinctions. There is no one measure or scale in terms of which the interaction of the characters can be measured. One event or action is not just a different quantity of another; rather, novels, plays and films are concerned with the qualitative richness of human interaction and the possibilities for tragedy involved. Moreover, literature shows us that in order to understand any particular action or character it is necessary to see the interrelatedness of them all ('only connect'). This kind of understanding is quite different from the understanding generated by science, which enables us to understand by demonstrating the patterns or laws which cover individual events or changes. Social science tries to do the same, perhaps less certainly, for human actions. But such understanding is achieved only if we abstract from the complexity of human motivation and interaction. For example 'rational economic man' is not any man of flesh and blood but an abstraction. But he is an explanatory concept in economics, just as 'the role of the patient' and its associated behaviours is thought to be explanatory in medical sociology.

But although this may help to explain the behaviour of Hamish MacTavish, if he is considered in general terms as a patient who has just been admitted to hospital, it may also mislead since it is abstracted from the complex motivation and interrelatedness of this specific individual. It is in literature or drama or film

16 Plato, *Republic*, Jowett B (trans), 1970, London: Sphere Books, Book X, 607b.

that we find this distinctive sort of understanding pre-eminently illustrated. It is a genuine kind of understanding, but quite distinct from that provided by science or social science. Through imaginative identification with the characters in a story or play we can develop the capacity for insights into the human condition with which medicine is concerned.

These issues are of such importance for the understanding of ethical issues that we shall develop them in an extended contrast. We shall contrast scientific/medical views on madness with a literary approach. What will emerge is a contrast between explanations of the typical, or the general, what is mainly correct, and explanations of the particular case. The ethical importance of this is that doctors must deal with particular cases whereas their scientific background inclines them towards the general.

We are not suggesting that one type of explanation is superior to the other, for each has merits for different purposes. One of the merits of the humanistic explanation is the insight it provides into the ethical considerations. The example we shall take is the explanation of madness. Let us first consider the approach of medical science.

Scientific understanding and madness: an extended example

Let us first return to Plato's views on creative writers and the limitations of their attempts to understand the world. As we said, Plato's view is that real understanding comes from having insight into the blue prints, the timeless patterns, which make things as they are. In our day the task of discovering such patterns has been taken over by the scientists. We might say that scientists are attempting to trace order, or repeatable patterns, in the apparent randomness of what we observe. These patterns can be anything from the orbits of the planets to the typical development of a tumour. We could put it another way by saying that one way in which the sciences provide understanding is by demonstrating that events, and indeed pieces of organic and non-organic matter, are not endlessly different or individual but can be classified into types. The beginnings of scientific classification can be found in Aristotle, who distinguished the types into 'genera' and 'species'.[17] For Aristotle, to understand is to be able to classify, to be able to show that there is order in the apparently random; and the better the scientist the more refined the systems of classification. Whereas the terminology has a changed a little (say, in botany) Aristotle's approach to the scientific understanding of the world is still accepted, especially in medicine.

The same kind of account can be given of the behavioural sciences. They attempt to provide understanding by tracing patterns in human behaviour.

17 Aristotle, *Metaphysics*, in *The Basic Works of Aristotle*, Richard McKeon (ed), 1941, New York: Random House, pp 1037–1039.

There has been less success here because of the complexity of human behaviour, and the ethical and practical problems which arise through any attempt to experiment on human behaviour. Nevertheless, the principle is the same: the behavioural sciences, like the natural sciences, attempt to provide understanding through tracing repeatable patterns, the types of behaviour shown by the manic-depressive or indeed by a normal person who is dying.

There is a second, although connected, way in which the sciences try to give us understanding of the world, and that is through discovering the underlying causality of the patterns. For example, an early botanist might have observed that insectivorous plants, such as butterwort, typically grow in boggy terrains. The more modern biochemically minded botanist could explain the pattern by establishing that a boggy terrain is deficient in nitrogen and that the plant obtains nitrogen by ingesting insects. Thus the pattern is explained in terms of an underlying causality. Once again the same is true of behaviour patterns. An early scientist, such as Hippocrates, noted the behaviour patterns which are typical of epilepsy, say, and a modern scientist would try to explain such patterns in terms of the underlying causality of the brain.

These two characteristics of scientific explanation are to be found also in scientific accounts of madness. For example, a psychiatrist will record the behaviour patterns which are typical of certain sorts of neurosis or psychosis. Perhaps more accurately he will note certain abnormal behaviour patterns and name these in terms of the classificatory language of psychiatry. Thus, the manic-depressive or the schizophrenic will typically exhibit certain behaviour patterns, and a patient displaying some or all of these will be appropriately classified. Some scientific understanding of madness, then, is created when the psychiatrist can identify and label the behaviour pattern which the patient is exhibiting. But the psychiatrist in research mode will not be content with classification, but will seek the underlying causality of such patterns. Is there a biochemical imbalance? Is there some decay of brain cells? Have there been disturbing events in childhood?

It is worth nothing that although the modern psychiatrist is much more sophisticated than Plato in his explanations of madness the type of understanding he attempts to provide is no different in principle from that which Plato attempts to provide. Plato sees the behaviour of a person who possesses mental health as balanced. The different elements of the mind – desires, emotions and reason – are in harmony, and this harmony stems from an understanding harmony in the elements of the body. Madness, for Plato, occurs when the normal equilibrium is disturbed, and in particular when reason is no longer in charge. He is a little afraid that this is what happens not only to the straightforwardly mad but also to poets and lovers. Perhaps he is right.

A rather similar account of mental health and mental illness is given by Freud.

> The mental apparatus is composed of an 'id' which is the repository of
> the instinctual elements, of an 'ego' which is the most superficial position

of the id and one which has been modified by the influences of the external word, and of a 'superego' which develops out of the ego and represents the inhibitions of instinct which are characteristic of man.[18]

Freud is here offering a tri-partite view of the psyche rather similar to that of Plato. Moreover, he goes on, again in a manner similar to Plato, to regard mental health as harmony between the parts of the soul, and mental illness as unresolved conflict between them.

There are many similar contemporary accounts of mental health and mental illness, sometimes using a word like 'equilibrium' as a scientific-sounding equivalent of Plato's 'harmony'. The different types of disequilibrium can be classified as the different types of mental illness. What all these accounts have in common is an attempt to generalise, to say something which is true of all species of mental illness. This kind of project is characteristic of both the scientist and the philosopher. It is the attempt to find a pattern, or a blue print, of mental illness or of madness, and then to find the causal structure underlying the pattern.

There is a third feature of the scientific approach which we might term 'reductivism'. The term is used in a variety of ways, but what we have in mind here is the tendency to treat the phenomenon to be explained in isolation from its total context. The origins of this tendency can be seen in early modern physics where the laws of moving bodies, for example, are investigated and established in isolation from other factors such as air resistance. To the extent that the behavioural sciences modelled themselves on the natural sciences this tendency is also found in them. This reductivist tendency is encouraged because reductivism makes it easier to assign numbers to the phenomena being explained, and numbers give the appearance (often deceptive) of objectivity and rigour.

A fourth characteristic of scientific understanding concerns the scientific attitude. This characteristic can best be identified if we take an example. Suppose a psychiatrist is interviewing a patient and the patient becomes angry and abusive. The response of the psychiatrist will be detached in the sense that she will not take personally anything said, but rather will see the anger as the result of causal forces the patient cannot control; the anger will be seen as a symptom.

Suppose now that the same psychiatrist later in the day encounters anger from the Chief Executive of the hospital trust. Let us say that she has parked her car in the Chief Executive's space. In this case she will respond differently, perhaps with indignation 'There was no other space and I was called in urgently to see a case', or perhaps with embarrassment, 'I'm sorry I just didn't notice that

18 Freud S, *The Standard Edition of the Complete Psychological Works of Sigmund Freud*, 1973–74, James Strachey (ed), London: Macmillan, vol. 20, p 201.

it was exclusively your space'. But however the psychiatrist responds, the general nature of the response will be essentially different from that which she offers to the patient. Some philosophers have contrasted the 'objective' attitude, when we respond to deeds and words as if to the effects of causes, with the 'reactive' attitude, when we assume that deeds and words have a human meaning and are to be taken at their face value as parts or ordinary human interaction.[19] We might say that the distinction is between the scientifically or technically or professionally detached, where the interest terminates in the phenomenon in question, and the humane where there is a deeper resonance involving human feelings.

There are well-known lines in Wordsworth's poem *Peter Bell* which illustrate the point here:

> 'A primrose by a river's brim
> A yellow primrose was to him
> It was nothing more'.

or more tellingly in the parody:

> 'A primrose by a river's brim
> Dicotyledon was to him,
> It was nothing more'.[20]

A fifth feature of the scientific approach to understanding, like the fourth, characterises the professional scientific attitude; it concerns the absence of any value judgements which the psychiatrist might make on the patient. The psychiatrist is concerned only with the fact that the behaviour pattern or the thoughts and words of the patient are either socially damaging or may lead to self-destruction. The thoughts, words, or deeds of the patient are abnormal in the sense that they deviate from what is the social norm of the society at the time, or they prevent the patient from doing what he/she might want to do, or what a 'normal' person of that society might want to do. This fifth aspect of the scientific approach to understanding we might think of as the 'non-judgemental' approach and it means something like 'neutral with respect to values'.

So far we have suggested that the scientific understanding of madness has five (perhaps overlapping) characteristics: it requires the discovery of patterns, underlying causality and it is reductivist; and it requires professional detachment and value neutrality. If that were the only mode of understanding then we would

---

19 Macmurray J, *Persons in Relation*, vol. 2 of *The Form of the Personal, 1961*, London: Faber and Faber, pp 28–31; Strawson P, 'Freedom and resentment', in *Freedom and Resentment and Other Essays*,1961, London: Methuen pp 1–26.

20 Wordsworth W, Peter Bell, *Poetical Works*, Ernest de Selincourt (ed), 1981, Oxford: Oxford University Press, pp 188–198.

need to agree with Plato, that the arts cannot give us real understanding of madness, or indeed of anything else. For literary writing lacks the five features we have identified. But we shall try to show that there are other modes of understanding which a creative writer can offer, and that these are relevant to the understanding of madness.

Literary understanding and madness

How can we understand something if not by discovering the kind of pattern into which it fits? One possible way is in terms of a type of formation other than a pattern, namely, a sequence. Patterns are a-temporal and, as it were, they structure space. An example is the double helix which is the pattern of the DNA molecule. But events and human actions follow each other in time. This gives us a sequence, and a sequence structures time. This suggests another type of understanding: we can be shown how a person's action might fit into the unique sequence which is their life. For example, we might ask why Mr A, who lives next door and is known to dislike gardening, has spent all weekend working in his garden, and we might come to understand when we are told that he is putting his house on the market and thinks it will sell better with a tidy garden.

The first point is that we can now see the action in the sequence of events and actions which constitute Mr A's life. Second, there are explicit and implicit references to individual and social purposes and values, such as selling houses and keeping gardens tidy. These are familiar to us and for that reason the relating of Mr A's actions to them helps our understanding. Third, because such purposes and values are ones which those who are in a certain social context can share, and with which they can have a sympathetic identification, understanding is deepened. Fourth, the story of Mr A implies a variety of standpoints. There are hints of curious neighbours, perhaps disapproving of the untidy garden, of speculation about Mr A's motivation and so on. Our understanding involves a complex mixture of individual purposes, social norms and contrasted viewpoints. In a word, it is holistic.

The points are better illustrated by stories on a grander scale, such as those offered by a biographer or a historian or a novelist. The kind of understanding created by such literary works has become fashionable at the moment in medical circles, and more widely. As we have already discussed it is sometimes called 'narrative' understanding because it is the sort of understanding which we can obtain from a story. We have already noted (p 128ff) that, perhaps in reaction to the current emphasis on 'evidence-based medicine', there has been a new awareness that patients' stories about themselves, their anecdotes, can be relevant to their diagnosis and treatment. Indeed, it can be maintained that it is in terms of our stories about ourselves, and also our emotions and future projects, that our very identity as persons exists. The identity of a person, it might be argued, is more like that of a drama than like that of a material object. To maintain this is really to maintain two points: that we have a serial identity and that we have an individual identity. Just as the play *Hamlet* has a serial identity through time, and a different one from *Macbeth*, so we all have our own unique identities unfolding through time.

This account suggests that we have identified an important kind of understanding which cannot be provided by the sciences but can be provided by the arts. Moreover, understanding can be assisted if our emotions are engaged and we can identify with someone's situation and are enabled to appreciate his or her values, and how these values might derive from or contrast with those prevailing in his or her culture. To develop these abstract points we shall now take some examples of the ways in which great writers have used this method of giving us understanding of a particular sort of madness.

The first example is that of Septimus Warren Smith in Virginia Woolf's novel *Mrs Dalloway*.[21] Septimus is introduced to us in the middle of other events. Mrs Dalloway has been buying sweet peas in Oxford Street for her party when a large car with blinds on the windows draws into the pavement. Passers-by stop and speculate about the important passengers in the car. In the middle of this inconsequential scene Septimus Warren Smith is introduced because he too is unable to pass because everything and everybody has stopped. We are given a description of Septimus: '... aged about thirty, pale-faced, beak-nosed, wearing brown shoes, and a shabby overcoat, with hazel eyes which had that look of apprehension in them which makes complete strangers apprehensive too'.[22]

The description is significant but is tucked in amidst a scene resembling an Impressionist painting: old ladies on tops of buses with black, red and green parasols against the heat, Mrs Dalloway with her arms full of sweet peas. But this charming description is disturbed again when the theme of the apprehension in Septimus's eyes is developed and he is depicted as seeing the bright colours becoming flames and as feeling responsible for blocking the way. He feels rooted to the pavement and everyone is looking at him. We feel something is badly wrong here, and sympathise with his Italian wife, Lucrezia, when she moves him on. With a nice touch we see the complexity of her feelings: she is worried and embarrassed by his behaviour, but cannot help looking at the car too and speculating about its occupants. The scene introducing Septimus and his problems then merges with the bustling activity of Oxford Street, further speculation about the occupants of the car, perhaps the Queen, and an aeroplane overhead trailing a smoke advertisement for toffee. The first step in assisting us in our understanding of Septimus has been taken in that our interest and our sympathies have been engaged and the problems of Septimus have been placed in the value-framework of a total social context.

Septimus appears again a little later when he and Lucrezia have reached Regent's Park, and she draws his attention to the aeroplane. This gives the author

21 Woolf V, *Mrs Dalloway* (1925) 1981, London: Granada.
22 Ibid., p 14.

a context for telling us that Septimus has already been attending a doctor, for Dr Holmes has recommended to Lucrezia that Septimus be encouraged to take an interest in things outside himself. But he stares fixedly at the smoke trail and is not diverted by it. Lucrezia is embarrassed and walks off a little by herself, and via her thoughts we learn that Septimus has threatened to kill himself. But despite the views of Dr Holmes he is not a coward because he fought bravely in the war. In this passage we are told a bit more of the story of Septimus, but also we feel the isolation of Lucrezia. She cannot understand his behaviour, and she can tell no one about her worries. Her isolation is made worse because she is in an alien country.

In a subsequent episode we learn of the young Septimus in love with Miss Isabella Pole who lectured on Shakespeare, and of his boss who approved of his work in the auctioneer's but wanted to make a man of him. Septimus volunteered, and with understated bitterness Virginia Woolf tells us that in the trenches in France manliness developed. Septimus was promoted and became very friendly with his officer, Evans. Then we learn that Evans was killed, and that Septimus felt very little about it at the time. But he began to have moments of fear, and found a refuge in the company of the daughters of the innkeeper in Milan where he was billeted. After the war he is welcomed back to his firm as a hero. But then in assorted contexts we are led to see the seriousness of his problems: sexual problems, loathing of other human beings and self-loathing. Finally, he is persuaded to see Dr Holmes, who is described in a very unattractive manner, perhaps reflecting Virginia Woolf's own experiences of doctors. The scene ends in a very worrying way because Septimus is now hearing Evans speaking, and Dr Holmes recommends a Harley Street specialist, Sir William Bradshaw. Our understanding has deepened because we have learned more of the biography of Septimus and the history of his time. It is also worth noting that this kind of understanding can proceed in tandem with scientific explanation, for there are at least hints of classification and causality of this type of madness.

Sir William Bradshaw prescribes that Septimus should be taken to a home. Interestingly enough, Sir William's view of mental health and illness is precisely the one we have seen in Plato – harmony or equilibrium – which he calls 'proportion':

> Worshipping proportion, Sir William not only prospered himself but made England prosper, secluded her lunatics, forbade childbirth, penalized despair, made it impossible for the unfit to propagate their views until they, too, shared his sense of proportion – his, if they were men, Lady Bradshaw's if they were women...[23]

In the long final scene there is a faint ray of light in the gathering darkness. Septimus briefly seems more like himself and jokes and helps design a hat for

23 Ibid., p 15.

Lucrezia. She is on his side. But then she tells him he must go to Bradshaw's home, 'must' because he threatened to kill himself. When Holmes finally arrives to take him away Lucrezia tries to block Holmes' approach but he forces himself in. Septimus is poised on the window sill and throws himself onto the railings.

Now of course we have been obliged to omit many of the details of this account of developing madness, but perhaps we have provided enough to enable us to make some general comments. First, by means of a story which gradually unfolds, we come to understand something of the condition which Septimus has got into. That story is part of a complex tapestry of events in the novel. Moreover, we can see the problem from several points of view. From that of Septimus we understand how he has come to feel a hatred for human beings because of the events he was part of in the war, and we see that he had developed a hatred of himself because he feels responsible for the events and especially for the death of his friend Evans. This story is set against other trivial incidents in London which have the effect of sharpening the poignancy of the unfolding story. But we also see the case from the point of view of others and especially from that of Lucrezia, who fills in details of the story of Septimus and provides a set of reactions.

The case of Septimus then is a good account of the sequential understanding which we can acquire from a quasi-biography with its assorted value standpoints and social context. There is no attempt to generalise, or to fit the case of Septimus into that of other shell-shock cases. It may be a typical case, but our understanding is of the specific case of Septimus because it is with that case that we are identified.

We should note too that the author does not ignore hints about the causality of the madness. Obviously the events of the war are shown to be the major factors, but also we learn that Septimus has a sensitive nature, that he feels guilty about Evans, and that he feels guilty about marrying Lucrezia, whom he did not love. Nothing much is made of these causal factors because the stress is on a different kind of understanding via the total narrative.

Turning now to the attitude we are encouraged to adopt to Septimus and the events in his life we find that instead of the attitude of scientific detachment other aids to understanding are used. We the readers are not detached from the story of Septimus but enter into his situation. We are made to feel his horror of the shells and the death of his friend; we can share his loathing of the human race; like him we can fear and detest Holmes and Bradshaw. But we are also brought to share the feelings and the point of view of Lucrezia. In a word, we are involved in the unfolding story.

Value judgements also are everywhere implicit in the story, and they also assist our understanding of the growing madness. But the value judgements are complex. The war, the main causal factor in the madness, is certainly deplored – 'school boys with gunpowder'.[24] It should be noted that the condemnation of the

24 Woolf V, *Mrs Dalloway* (1925) 1981, London: Granada, p 86.

war in that bitter phrase brings out a huge amount about the English society which created that war – the misplaced (public) school boy attitudes, the patriotism, the lack of grasp about what would be involved, and so on. The upper class social attitudes of the time are also deplored when they masquerade as medical knowledge – outside interests, cricket, not too much Shakespeare, a sense of proportion and so on. The value judgements are always subtle and subtly expressed. From one point of view Clarissa Dalloway is a silly rich woman, but yet we can understand the value of her life, and we note that she comes to condemn Sir William Bradshaw.

The attitude which we are encouraged to adopt towards Sir William Bradshaw can be detected in other novels of madness. For example, in Wilkie Collin's novel *The Woman in White*[25] we are shown the powerlessness of the individual against 'expert' medical opinion. The tensions produced by this tapestry of varied values is an aid to our understanding of specific cases, such as that of Septimus.

But our understanding does not terminate with the case of Septimus. By means of that story of developing madness we come to understand a total social context. It points beyond itself and becomes a symbol of something much deeper. It enriches our human perceptions of ourselves and of a historical period. Even more than that it reaches what is universal in the human condition through the exploration of the particular case. To stress this kind of understanding is not at all to denigrate the attempts of psychiatrists and others to understand the phenomena of madness and shell-shock in particular; no doubt numerical generalisations of types of cases have their important place. But we wish to make a plea for the kind of understanding which comes from literature, an understanding in which the reader can move from a total involvement with an individual case in its full context to something universal.

Shakespeare is another writer who gives us insight into different types of madness, interestingly before scientific accounts existed. Moreover, he distinguishes madness of different kinds brought on by a variety of circumstances in *Macbeth, Hamlet* and *King Lear*. We shall take just one example.

In *King Lear* we find a very complex study of madness, involving Lear himself, the simulated madness of Edgar, and the commentary of the Fool.[26] The different sorts of madness are judged against a running discussion of what it is 'natural' to do, and what it is reasonable to do. We are warned that the seeds of madness have always been there in Lear. Regan reminds Goneril: 'Tis the infirmity of his age: yet he hath ever but slenderly known himself' (Act I, Scene I). The events of the play exacerbate this condition. At the start we have a display of embarrassing senility – behaviour which, while it is not mad, is certainly perceived as contrary to natural reason and sentiment. Lear is depicted as having

25 Collins W, *The Woman in White*, Matthew Sweet (ed),1999, Harmondsworth: Penguin.
26 Shakespeare W, *King Lear*, Hunter, GK (ed), 1972, Harmondsworth: Penguin.

a traditional hierarchical outlook of which his behaviour represents the pathology. Goneril and Regan, on the other hand, come from another way of looking at what is reasonable; for them the reasonable is the pursuit of rational self-interest and the only sentiment they recognise as having a claim is the satisfaction of the desires of the self. The tragedy of the play is the collision of these two ways of looking at the world, and Lear's madness is the outcome of that collision. He cannot understand how what he considers to be the natural sentiments of love for a parent and deference to authority can be so ignored by his own daughters. But with his madness comes insight. He sees the harsher side of the world order he represents and, spurred on by the Fool, he comes to see his own failings, and those of all of us.

Conclusions

We have tried to bring out in this chapter the insights into medical ethics which can result from the widely varied perceptions of life and contrasting attitudes to be found in literature. These insights are not of course a substitute for regulation. But regulations deal with the broad issues whereas literature can open our eyes to the ethical importance of the particular situation.

Chapter 7

Arts in health

In Chapter 1 we noted that the term 'medical humanities' is sometimes used widely to cover three distinct movements: the use of the arts and humanities as therapies, the arts in health, and the use of the arts and humanities subjects in the education of doctors or nurses including the ethical side to medical education. We do not propose to discuss the first movement, which has its own philosophy of therapy, and we have so far been mainly concerned with the third – the uses of the humanities in medical education and especially ethical education. In this chapter we will say something about the second category, which is often called the 'arts in health' movement.*

At the risk of being repetitive we shall stress the difference between the arts as therapy and the arts in health. The art therapies include music, theatre, art and dance. The practitioners involved in these therapies are artists but are also trained therapists and recognised as Professionals Allied to Medicine (PAMs). As such they have their own professional bodies and codes of conduct. The second category is that of the arts in health-care contexts – including hospitals, general practices, mental health institutions – but also in the wider community. Activities in the 'arts in health' category are to be distinguished from those of the art therapies in two respects. First, the practitioners in the arts in health movement are artists without additional training as therapists. They may have a number of reasons, including professional and personal, for choosing to work in these contexts, but they do not see themselves as therapists. Second, these artists often work in contexts that are not normally recognised as delivering health care, such as schools, libraries, community halls and other public spaces such as parks, public transport or town squares. This chapter will focus on the 'arts in health' movement and will not discuss the formal art therapies.

The arts in health field is a potential minefield of ethical problems as the artists are unregulated and self-selecting for the work that they do amongst often very vulnerable people. Moreover, the picture becomes more complicated when we

---

* This chapter draws mainly on research work done on arts in health projects at the Centre for Arts and Humanities in Health and Medicine (CAHHM), University of Durham.

remember that artists themselves have professional needs such as proper involvement in the way in which their work is handled or displayed (i.e., for curation) which may be problematic in a health-care environment. In addition, there are philosophical questions arising about the purpose of art in such contexts if it is thought by managers to be purely an instrumental means to health, or purely a hospital decoration. Many artists want their work to be challenging or disturbing, and this can cause problems in a health-care context. Thus the field of arts in health raises questions of both philosophical and ethical interest.

Before discussing these issues we will describe a range of projects that exemplify typical activities in the field. We will then go on to discuss ethical issues which arise as follows: first, from the involvement of the artist in these projects; second, from the involvement of the participants; and third, from the role of the context in which the project is taking place.

Some projects

The following projects have been chosen to show the range of contexts that play host to arts in health projects. These examples are not meant to be comprehensive but will provide reference points for later discussion.

Music for health

This project was part of a three-year initiative funded by the Health Action Zone in Tyne and Wear in the North East of England. The wider project was called 'Common Knowledge' and it aimed to improve health in this part of the country by encouraging individuals from different service sectors (arts, education, health, social care) to get together and set up arts in health projects in the region.[1] The 'Music for Health' project was the result of collaboration between a cabaret singer, a cellist, a GP and a nurse practitioner. The performers visited a doctor's surgery, a residential care home and hospital in-patient and out-patient departments. Some of the visits took the form of set performances, where the patients would sit round to listen to a pre-arranged programme, but as the initiative developed the performers felt that their audience wished something more tailored to their specific preferences, so they started to respond to requests from individuals and performed at the bedside. On one occasion, for example, the musicians performed music for a patient who was celebrating her wedding anniversary with her visiting husband. The musicians also visited an intensive care unit (ICU) in response to requests from staff who felt that ICUs were often omitted from arts projects because these units were seen as inappropriate places for such projects. Again, the group performed requests for patients but also for relatives and staff who felt their

---

1   Smith T, *An Evaluation of Sorts: Learning from Common Knowledge*, 2003, Report published by CAHHM, University of Durham (available from www.dur.ac.uk/cahhm).

presence and the music helped reduce stress levels in the unit by providing distraction. Having come into being supported by Common Knowledge, the Music for Health then developed its own funding momentum as a result of its success and continues its work at least three years beyond the end of that initial support.

James Cook University Hospital healing arts

The first example was of a project that was conceived and run on the initiative of two performers offering their services to a hospital context on the basis of short-term funding from a wider pilot project. This second example is also hospital-based but very different in character. The James Cook University Hospital (JCUH) is a new hospital built on funding from the government's Private Finance Initiative. The chief executive of the NHS trust in charge of the building believed that their commitment to 'patient-centred care' would be improved by high quality architectural design and the integration of public art – commissioned and created regionally – into the health-care environment.[2] The development of JCUH, therefore, paid special attention to building design, colour schemes, materials, lighting, space and acoustics. The design features and colour schemes were intended to individualise departments within the hospital to help create a sense of intimacy within this huge hospital of over 1,000 in-patient beds. In addition, £250,000 from the building budget was ring-fenced for the purpose of commissioning artwork for the hospital. The Trust set up a 'Healing Arts' Committee to seek further funding for art works and also to fund artists residencies to create works appropriate to this hospital environment. The Trust introduced to the building a theme of Captain James Cook and his voyages, and some of the commissioned artwork reflected the chosen theme. The theme was intended to link the hospital with the local area and to give the hospital a sense of coherence as a single building.

This project involved a number of artists working in the hospital in different ways: some on commissions, some on artists' residencies and some in performance. There is an ongoing programme associated with the 'Healing Arts' project at the hospital but the main thrust of it was during the building phase. The commissioned works remain *in situ* and this project helps to raise questions about the continuing display and maintenance (curation) of the works as time goes on. For example, what is the responsibility of NHS Trusts for publicising commissioned artworks on behalf of artists, in the way they might expect from a gallery?

Wrekenton lanterns

Wrekenton lanterns is a community-based project which takes place in a primary school in Wrekenton, a borough of Gateshead which at the time of

---

2 Macnaughton J et al., *Designing for Health: Architecture, Art and Design at the James Cook University Hospital*, 2005, NHS Estates and University of Durham.

setting up the project in 1994 had the highest morbidity rate from coronary heart disease in England.[3] The area also has higher than average unemployment rates and is one of the most deprived areas in England. The project came about as a result of collaboration between an arts worker with Gateshead Arts and Libraries Department (the local arts support organisation), an artist, local health promotion workers and a primary school. The aim was to encourage children to think about healthy lifestyles at an early and impressionable age. Because of the high levels of heart disease in the area the artists decided to focus on the theme of 'Healthy Hearts', so while the children were engaged in art workshops creating paper lanterns on this theme the artists, teachers and health promotion staff would discuss lifestyle issues – such as good diet, exercise and not taking up smoking – that would help keep their hearts healthy. The workshops were run in the school over a two-week period which culminated in the 'Happy Hearts Parade' when the children had their lanterns lit and paraded round the district with them accompanied by music and song.

Although the project is aimed at primary school children it involved adults as well. Mothers and some fathers and grandparents became involved in the workshops as helpers and they would also accompany their children on the parade. The final event also involved the whole community who would come out onto their doorsteps to watch the parade. The project is a good example of how aiming health promotion messages at the young can have a knock-on effect on the whole family. It is also a practical example of a project that illustrates the Acheson Report's definition of pubic health: 'the promotion of health through the organised efforts of society' (see p 91 in Chapter 4). The messages did not necessarily have the desired instrumental effect, however, as many young mothers could be observed lighting up their cigarettes as the parades came to an end. On the other hand, several volunteer mothers on the event have established home-made vegetable soup as a staple of the family diet as a result of lunches at the workshop.

This project is an example of a small-scale (annual funding around £8K) annual project in a community setting. It happened only for two weeks every year but became recognised as an important event in the Wrekenton calendar with enthusiastic engagement from the individuals and wider community involved. However, the local authority who provided most of the funding for this event lost interest after personnel changes, and, after over 10 years, the event has lapsed.

Looking Well in Bentham

This project grew out of a community consultation exercise in High Bentham in 1995 which revealed high levels of depression, loneliness and isolation amongst people of all ages, particularly women, within the farming community of this small

---

3 Everitt A and Hamilton R, Arts, *Health and Community: A Study of Five Arts in Community Health Projects*, 2003, University of Durham.

market town. The consultation exercise also revealed a lack of opportunities for children to undertake physical activity. Acknowledging that social exclusion within this community was leading to a cycle of declining health, the Looking Well was established in 1997 by Pioneer Projects (Celebratory Arts) Ltd, a charity run by artists who live in the local area. The aim of this project is to enhance the health and well-being of individuals of all ages in the local community and to improve their social and physical environment through engagement in creativity and the arts.[4] The project is run on a shoestring through a rented shop in Bentham High Street. The shop is furnished mainly by a long table at which participants in the various groups make their art and by a scattering of easy chairs around a wood-burning stove. Conversations about difficult issues like depression, stress and loneliness take place more easily while the participants' eyes are focussed on a creative activity and not on each other. The art work is geared towards the health promotion needs of the community and is displayed and distributed in local health centres and around the town. There are also opportunities for parents to engage in creative play activities with their children at the regular 'Mucky Buckets' sessions and the centre runs a weekly after school club for primary school children. Individuals can access the centre via their GP or other local health workers and they can self refer. Currently, around one third of the local population of Bentham (3,000) has accessed its services. It has received funding from local authority sources but also generates income through donations and selling its art work. It has also been granted Healthy Living Centre status with funding from the New Opportunities Fund. Its income is, therefore, ongoing although not secure and it has grown from being almost entirely voluntary to having a full-time director and five part-time paid staff.

These four projects illustrate the variety of work that is going on in arts in health in different contexts and with different aims. They can be seen as following from the definition of public health medicine which we discussed in Chapter 4. That definition spoke of improving community health through the 'organised efforts of society', and the projects include organised efforts with a good health aim. They show that there is no set pattern to the work and that the form of it depends largely on the impetus and interests of the individual artist or a significant 'champion', such as the chief executive of the NHS trust in the JCUH example. The artists, therefore, do more than just provide the creative input into the project; they are often the originators, planners, fund raisers and evaluators of their work. The next section will examine the ethical implications for artists engaged in this work and the implications for the contexts in which they work on such engagement.

The artists

The artists involved in arts in health work are not trained therapists. They could chose to go down that route by taking professional qualifications in one of the

---

4 Everitt and Hamilton, op. cit.

art therapies, but these artists wish to remain as professional artists and are usually self-employed generating income via a number of sources which may include selling their own work. Their motivation to get involved in arts in health work includes a desire to help people with health problems get better or to use their skills to enhance people's enjoyment of life, but they also insist that the work inspires them in their creativity in some way, or else they would not get involved. In a study we carried out to evaluate the arts programme at the JCUH one of the artists spoke about what went through her mind while creating a large glass sculpture:

> The therapy I suppose is partly about distraction, but I also feel there's an uplifting effect. The way that it works with the light seems to have some effect on how people feel.[5]

Of course, artists have to earn their living and arts in health projects are one way of doing this giving them time and ideas for their own work. One example of how this works is the South Tyneside Artists Studio which is based in an old synagogue. The upper floor of the buildings is divided into five small artists studios while the lower floor provides space for the artists and other studio members with mental health needs to engage in work together. The artists thus barter their time and skills for the use of the studio spaces.[6]

Problems for the artist as therapist

Artists working in a formal health-care context are in an anomalous position. Most therapeutic relationships are governed by some form of regulation either by virtue of the training of the health-care professional or because of the institutional requirements of the therapeutic environment. The existence of such regulations minimises ethical problems. By contrast, the piecemeal nature of arts in health projects and the fact that there is no formal training for artists to prepare them for working in these contexts can give rise to ethical problems. Artists working within NHS contexts may find it difficult to understand the organisation of a ward setting, for example, and it may take time to appreciate precisely what can be achieved with patients who may be called away at times for treatment or tests. It may also be difficult to appreciate the requirements of patients with particular conditions and take time to understand what such patients might like or be able to do. One of the initiatives associated with the JCUH Healing Arts project was the creation of an electronic interactive scene in the hospital's unit for children with severe learning difficulties. The project involved a dancer and a digital media artist who worked together with the educational and nursing staff on the unit to design the interactive screen which

5 Macnaughton et al., op. cit.
6 Everitt and Hamilton, op. cit.

would help the children understand the notion of intentional movement. It took about a year of discussion meetings before the artists and the teachers were able to agree on what software for the screen should be designed because the artists found it difficult to comprehend just how simple some of the interactions would need to be for the most severely disabled children.[7]

Clearly, artists will come into contact with vulnerable people doing this work and there is potential for abuse from both sides. Patients may be at risk from breeches of confidentiality if artists do not feel themselves to be bound by a professional code of ethics. Artists can find themselves engaged in quite intimate conversations about patients' and participants' problems during the course of their work in the close and friendly space created within these projects. It can be difficult to preserve confidential information in such situations but, in addition, artists may find it difficult to deal with some of the information they are being given. During the course of one of the Wrekenton Lanterns workshops a child confided sexual abuse to one of the volunteer artists. The artist did not feel she had the skills to deal with this information and was unable to continue with that year's event. In this situation, and as the child was under the care of the school at the time that this information was given, the artist felt obliged to reveal what she had been told to the child's teacher. In a hospital context, even when dealing with adults, artists may feel that they need to share any potentially important information about patients with their health professionals, but there are no clear ethical guidelines here.

In the absence of a clear professional relationship, the duties of the artist engaged in this work depend on how patients and clients view the relationship with the artist and what they expect to get out of it. There are important distinctions between the doctor–patient and the artist–patient relationships. When the patient is vulnerable, either through illness or low social status, there is a power differential between doctor and patient. The doctor has not only knowledge and skills but has the confidence of high social status and is well able to take charge of a consultation. Even when the patient is less vulnerable and of equal social status patients are in a supplicant role to the doctor seeking answers in the form of diagnosis, referral or medication that only the doctor can provide. Moreover, the relationship between doctor and patient is governed by certain professional rules, including ethical rules, which mean that the encounter cannot be spontaneous and relaxed such as that between friends. For example, the doctor must make a record of the consultation and of any action taken; or may need to seek written consent for any procedures he is planning and make sure the patient receives a copy of such consent.

A contrasting kind of encounter is possible between artist and patient/client in arts in health. Certainly, the artist has specialised knowledge and skills to offer

7 Greenland P, Macnaughton J and White M, *The World, Their World: Evaluation Report on the Cleveland Unit's Digital Arts Project*, 2004, University of Durham.

and the artist may offer these skills as art tutor or as therapist or, more commonly, as both at once. It is not possible, therefore, to say that the artist–patient relationship is characterised by equality. But, whereas doctors are perceived to work on the patients through diagnosis and treatment, the artist's role is often to work through the patients or clients to enable them to recognise their own abilities and skills. If the patients ask the artists for advice about their work, the artists (as tutor and therapist) are likely to try to encourage the patients to come up with an answer themselves. It is possible to go further and suggest that in some cases the artist–patient relationship is characterised by mutual benefit. Artists can share their skills with patients, providing them with the opportunity for distraction and to explore their own creativity, but at the same time the artist is gaining potential subject matter for his or her own art. An expression often used to characterise the atmosphere created around an arts in health activity is 'congenial space'.[8] This term accurately describes what it feels like to be gathered around a table with others intent upon a piece of creative work jointly or separately. In these circumstances, when eyes are focussed upon the work rather than on each other, it can be easier to speak more freely about symptoms, feelings and concerns.

Congenial space has been described as 'homely', an epithet greatly valued by patients in a hospital context.[9] Patients and clients feel that in this space they are in some way separated from professional care and – especially in the case of those with mental health problems – scrutiny. There are no rules and guidelines that govern the artist–patient relationship: no written record is kept, although resultant artwork may demonstrate whether the project has been successful or not. The artist in arts in health work, therefore, has come to occupy a position somewhere between health professional and friend, and this seems to be a position that is valued by patients who feel increasingly distanced from health professionals and social workers by virtue of the rules and regulations governing their relationships with them.

Medical education and Continuing Professional Development (CPD) require the enhancement of knowledge, skills and attitudes. The attitudinal component was thought to be developed by medical ethics. But, as we have stressed throughout, medical ethics has become very much a matter of rules and regulations. However important (and we are not denying their importance), rules and regulations are poor vehicles for developing attitudes in an ethically desirable manner. But ethically desirable lessons can be learned from the relationship of artist and patient. Doctors and nurses characteristically view patients as problems to be solved. But artists view patients in two ways: as people with potential for creativity, and as stimulants to their own creative work. This feeling of being positively regarded is one explanation of why arts in health projects can be successful at raising the expectations and self-worth of patients.

8 Everitt and Hamilton, op. cit., p 46.
9 Macnaughton et al., op.cit.

Granted that this is the case, it is potentially detrimental to the relationship between artist and patient to impose regulations upon it and to require that artists undertake training – statutory or otherwise – to prepare them for the role. Nevertheless, most artists recognise that they have responsibilities to the patients and to themselves and they will try to establish formal ground rules with the groups they work with. These ground rules will include confidentiality and boundaries about what can be raised within the group and what is not appropriate to be discussed. This is often not easy. Artists who opt to work in this area are often people with charismatic characters whose personalities are a key factor in the success of the projects.[10] In these circumstances it can be difficult to recognise the limits of one's responsibility for vulnerable people. One artist working at the Tyneside Artist Studio described the problems that arose when she gave her phone number to someone whom she felt needed extra support:

> I was getting phone calls at 12 midnight, 1 o'clock in the morning, and I realised that what I'm here for is to facilitate that work going on in the project so that people can come in between 10 and 5 and make art work. I don't have professional skills to support people in anything that doesn't involve their artistic work. I'm not a counsellor and I'm not their friend either. I'll be really friendly in the Studio but I'm not a friend. It makes it easy on me to know that we've [now] got a rule in place that said we won't support people outside of the project because then I can say to people I can't actually do that. But in here between 10 and 5 we're 110% here for people, but I think we've got to realise that we're here for people in terms of what the project can do for them.[11]

Where arts in health projects are carried out in hospital wards or health centres, it is important for the artists to work collaboratively with the health professionals who should be aware that problems may arise and be prepared to deal with them. In contexts, such as the South Tyneside Artists Studio or the Looking Well, where health professionals are not directly involved, artists will often undertake voluntary supervision. In the case of one artist (working with the Wrekenton Lanterns project) the supervisor is a psychotherapist whom she sees once a month. The purpose of the sessions is to provide an external view on the work she is doing to provide a check and balance on her involvement with the participants in the project but also to allow her time to reflect on the creative opportunities the project provides for her as an artist.

The balance for artists in the work is always between their roles as therapists and as artists. Because of the needs of the often vulnerable participants in these

10 Everitt and Hamilton, op. cit., p 55.
11 Ibid.

projects, and the personalities of the artists involved, they can find that the care-giving role predominates and they can begin to slip into involvement in areas beyond their expertise and also to lose sight of their needs as artists. We shall now look at the ethical problems created by these needs.

Problems for the artists as artists

Although the artists engaged in arts in health work consider that their major role is that of creative artist, those involved in employing them within the health-care context do not often give consideration to the practical needs of that role. This was particularly clear for the artists involved in the Healing Arts project at JCUH who suffered from the consequences of building delays and changes of plan. Much is made in health-care ethics of the power of doctors, but the power of the managers who control the flow of money also raises ethical problems. It is easy for salaried NHS managers to forget the needs of self-employed artists. One artist commented on her commission:

> It was a very long drawn out process involving a lot of planing and a lot of changes. You can lose the thread a bit.... If I was being very hard nosed about it, it actually was a terrible financial disaster for me in some ways because it lasted such a long time, yet it was such a big project I couldn't take on anything else.[12]

A further problem for artists is the fact that their work is rarely credited to them when it is featured in NHS publications and publicity. This anonymity has both practical and artistic implications. Artists rely on the fact that their work is seen to attract further commissions, but this is difficult if the viewer does not know who the artist is. If their work is used merely as a symbol to identify the hospital this can devalue its artistic merit. One artist involved in the JCUH project objected to the use of his work as such a symbol:

> Well I did feel a bit equivocal about this pictogram. ...because I'm not a designer, you know, and that's very much a piece of graphic design really rather than a piece of artistic invention.[13]

If hospitals or general practices are making use of what artists can offer they need to recognise that they have a duty to attend to the needs of the artists as professionals artists as well as to monitor their performance as care workers. This involves adequate curation of the works commissioned or produced during

12 Macnaughton et al., p 193.
13 Macnaughton J, 'Art in hospital spaces: the role of hospitals in an aestheticized society', *International Journal of Cultural Policy*, 2007 , 13, i (in press).

a residency. Works should be appropriately labelled with the title and name of the artist, just as they would be in a gallery, and if the work is used in any written materials about the hospital there should again be recognition of the artist's contribution. It may be too much to expect that a hospital with a major arts programme should have a professional arts organiser who would have responsibility for curating the works on display but, as a number of hospitals are beginning to take on the appearance of art galleries, perhaps this is a step some of the larger trusts should be considering. In addition, artists need to be taken into account when building delays affect the timing of the delivery of commissions or residency work.

These practical concerns have important implications for the working lives of artists involved in arts in health work but there are also problems that arise for artists aesthetically and artistically in producing work or doing work within health-care contexts. Artists working in these contexts recognise that they have a responsibility to the users of the space to produce something that will soothe or calm them. As a sculptor working for JCUH commented:

> People who are going to a hospital might never set foot out again you know, so what went through my mind was what one should be aspiring to do in a sculpture that goes outside a hospital. Are you attempting to calm people?[14]

The Chief Executive also felt that the art had to be 'the nicer end of art, not intruding on or jarring on the nerves but actually adding to a feeling of tranquillity and calming'. These comments suggest that art in the hospital context has a function – to comfort and soothe. This aim was in fact an explicit one for the 'Healing Arts' at JCUH as was the intention that the art should assist in 'inspir[ing] confidence in the service thus improving patients' physical and psychological well being'.[15]

The idea that their art would have to be 'at the nicer end' and serve a kind of propaganda role for the NHS Trust is potentially challenging for artists aesthetically and morally. On the one hand the artists at JCUH clearly felt that they had a responsibility to respond to the needs of these particular viewers but on the other hand they had to maintain a certain amount of artistic and creative freedom. Artists working in this context may feel a certain tension between being called upon to act as mere decorators and being 'artists', true to their own means of expression.

Wolfgang Welsch expresses this point in his critique of the notion of the 'aestheticization' of society. Welsch suggests that public spaces, such as city squares, shopping malls, airports and (we would also say) hospitals are becoming increasingly 'aestheticized' or decorated with high quality materials in

14 Macnaughton et al., p 168.
15 Macnaughton et al., 2007.

pleasing colours with attractive design features. In this context, he says, art in public spaces is in danger of becoming superfluous. If public spaces are already beautifully designed and decorated then art – in its role as providing further 'aesthetic beautification' – will be redundant.[16] If art has to have any meaning within these aestheticised spaces it should

> set itself against beauteous aestheticization instead of adapting itself to it. Art should not impact accommodatingly as an article, but rather strike like a meteor.[17]

Welsch goes on to say that 'strangeness, disruption, interruption...[are] mandatory categories for art in public space today'.

We are used to the idea of the artist as challenging conventional ideas and to the idea of art as disruptive, even shocking – think of the work of Damien Hirst, Tracy Emin or Gilbert and George. But there are many theories about the place of art in society from Kant's idea that our responses to art should be entirely disinterested and distinct from what art might do for us to Dewey's notion that art is 'the expression of the life of the community'.[18] This idea, expressed in his book, *Art as Experience*, resonates with what the artists at JCUH were trying to do in interpreting the James Cook theme for their own art form within the constraints of what was required for a hospital. Far from constraining them, the artists seemed inspired by the theme and excited by the challenge of interpreting Cook and his travels for the Middlesbrough community which was already familiar with the stories.

In summary, then, the artists involved in arts in health work face ethical challenges by virtue of their multiple roles as untrained therapists and as artists who are at the same time aware of their practical economic needs as self-employed artists and of their responsibilities to themselves as creative artists. Similar themes will arise as we now move on to consider the role of participants in arts in health projects.

The participants

The ethical issues that arise for participants in these projects can be considered in terms of the type of relationship that may exist between the artist and participant: the relationship may be that of therapist and patient or artist/teacher and student. Both these relationships may exist at one and the same time and, indeed, the role of artist/teacher in which the artist is encouraging the participants to engage in creative activity themselves may be regarded as an

16 Welsch W, *Undoing Aesthetics*, 1997, London, Sage.
17 Ibid., p 121.
18 Dewey J, *Art as Experience*, 1958, New York, Capricorn Books.

integral part of the therapeutic role. This confusion/overlap is reflected in the fact that few arts in health projects actually state that they intend to improve health in their target group.[19] A review of arts in health literature found aims of arts in health project variously stated as:

- Raising awareness of health issues and encouraging people to take responsibility for their health;
- Personal development;
- Aesthetic improvement of buildings and environments;
- Acquisition of art and craft skills;
- Social activity and participation;
- Health needs assessment;
- Communication between consumers and the health and social care agencies;
- Cross-sector partnership working.[20]

Thus the aims of projects can be very wide and various and some projects will address several of these aims at once. It is, however, useful to consider the relationships separately as this will help us to identify the kinds of problems that may arise.

Problems for the participant as 'patient'

In this unregulated context with the artist as an untrained 'therapist' the quality of the care received by the participant in the project is highly dependent on the personality of the artist. Participants are, therefore, potentially vulnerable if artists are unaware of how to respond to their needs and do not have back up. As we have seen in the example from South Tyneside Artists' Studio (p 157), there is a danger of over-dependent relationships developing in a context where there are no recognisable or accepted professional boundaries. Further, arts in health projects tend to be funded on short-term one-off budgets and may lapse leaving participants bereft. When expectations have been encouraged and fulfilled vulnerable participants can be left in a worse state if a project comes to an end.

However, participants recognise that the environment of an arts in health project is a very different thing from a professional environment and that the relationships within it are not the same. One participant at Looking Well commented:

> I go to lantern making at Looking Well, chat to others and through this give and receive support. I gain enjoyment from creating lanterns and from the company of others. It provides an environment I have not found anywhere else.[21]

19 Angus J, *A Review of Evaluation in Community-Based Art for Health Activity in the UK*, 2002, Health Development Agency.
20 Ibid.
21 Everitt and Hamilton, op. cit., p 67.

The expectations are of mutual support, enjoyment and engagement in creativity rather than therapy that may lead to cure. Participants expect to feel better from the projects and this feeling derives partly from the fact that they themselves must participate and contribute to what goes on. This fulfils the 'bottom up' aspirations of the health promotion movement, which are based on the ethical ideal that individuals and communities should make their own health decisions rather than have policies imposed on them from above (see pp 103–106). At Looking Well that contribution is to the life of the community producing health promotion materials that are designed around the needs of the town. This gives participants, who may not have felt that they have much to offer, a sense of self-worth and usefulness that can lead on to re-emergence into the social world and the world of work. Such projects can, therefore, prove to be stepping stones for individuals, such as single mothers or people who have suffered from depression, back into work.

The participants as makers of 'art'

The projects offer the socially excluded individual a way back into society and the socially fractured community a chance to develop social capital through events such as the Happy Hearts Procession in Wrekenton and the Harvest Lanterns (associated with Looking Well) in Bentham. In this way the 'therapy' offered in these projects is as much a social therapy as a medical one. We may, however, legitimately ask, granted that the main benefits accrued from engagement in these projects are social ones, why is the making of art a crucial part of the activity? At Looking Well, for example, participants gather round a table to make their work and the main point of this is that it enables social interaction to take place in a congenial atmosphere. Could the participants just as well be playing bingo or eating a meal together? From the comments of participants it appears that the making of art is a crucial part of the activity. There is something about being engaged in a creative activity which is particularly effective at making people feel good about themselves. As one user of Looking Well commented, 'art releases something inside you and boosts confidence'. The implication is that being creative is in some way essential to human flourishing.

This may seem an attractive and uncontroversial view, but there is a problem with it. Most of us who are in paid employment do not participate in the creative arts as makers of art. Our involvement consists rather in being passive consumers of novels, plays or as viewers of art in galleries. We do not regard participation in art as essential to our humanity, although we may feel that being consumers of it enhances our existence and lends interest and depth to our lives. There is, therefore, a risk that participation in creativity through an arts in health project is seen as something only for the unemployed, socially excluded and mentally ill. To paraphrase Marie Antoinette, 'Let them paint paintings – we who have lives that are fulfilled through work and good personal relationships don't need to'.

Part of the problem here lies in how the participants in arts in health projects are encouraged to think of themselves. In most cases, as in the above example from Looking Well, the participants do not come to regard themselves in any way as serious artists: the work provides a chance to get out of the house and meet people and to find ways of exploring themselves and what they are good at. On the other hand, art – to be regarded as art – requires a certain context. For example, it requires a viewer and a formal context for display. Now, the work produced by arts in health projects often does go on display. When this happens the work becomes part of a larger more critical system that may not take into account the disabilities or illness problems of the artists when judging the value of what is presented. There is an example of an arts in health project involving a group of learning disabled people who had their work displayed in a public gallery and were dismayed by some of the adverse comments made. But if work is displayed in this kind of context then it is quite legitimate that viewers would assess it as they would any other art work – but vulnerable patients may find this very difficult to take.

It is clearly important that these projects involve participation in the making of art and this is central to their success. But it is also essential that participants are able to contextualise what they do and are able to relate it to the specific aims of the project, and most projects achieve this successfully.

The context

Lastly in this chapter we will discuss the ethical and moral issues that arise for those in charge of the contexts in which arts and health projects take place. Playing host to arts in health projects confers certain responsibilities on those who are in charge of the building in which they take place. We have discussed some of these already in relation to the artists and participants involved. If the project takes place in a school or hospital, the head teacher or hospital administrators have well-recognised responsibilities to protect their pupils or patients against harm. But equally, as employers, they have less well-recognised obligations to the artists to support them and to attend to the proper promotion of the artists by acknowledging them in publicity that may result from the project or in any work that goes on display. In addition, employers of artists in these contexts should be aware of the knock-on financial effects for self-employed artists of delays which affect the timing of projects and commissions.

A more fundamental consideration for those who may wish to set up arts in health projects, particularly in health contexts, is whether money should be spent on them in the first place. Those who run our health services, particularly NHS in the United Kingdom, are expected to exercise wise and judicious control over the resources at their disposal and as yet there are no studies that prove the economic supremacy of arts in health as against usual medical care for any condition. Richard Smith, a previous editor of the *British Medical Journal*, has suggested that diverting 0.5% of the health-care budget to the arts would improve the health of people in Britain.[22] This contention was based on the notion, already discussed, that engagement in the arts is essential to human flourishing and health, in its widest sense. But, as we have already suggested, most people do not regard the arts in this way. Smith quotes a survey in which only 7% of respondents agreed that increased spending on arts would be good for the health of the country as a whole. The patients and staff at JCUH also tended to express this view:

> There has been a lot of money spent on theming it around James Cook [and] it is a waste of money because people are too ill to say 'that's nice', they want to get themselves better. The hospital is there to help them to get better not for a day out.

What the sceptical population and the funders of such projects need, of course, is evidence that they work. But social interventions, such as arts projects, suffer in our highly medicalised society from being unable to provide the 'right' answers to the kinds of questions medicine asks. A recent research project carried out by public health clinicians in Newcastle illustrates the problem.[23] The researchers wanted to find out if giving people in a deprived community more money as a result of reviewing their benefits status actually improved their health. They approached the issue in two ways. First, they used quantitative measures including 'validated' scales to measure health status. These showed no improvement at all in health from the increased money. This was not at all surprising as many of the respondents were on benefits to which they were entitled on account of chronic health problems which are more likely to become worse rather than better over time. The second method was semi-structured interviews where the respondents were able to express their more subtle psychological responses to having more money. Here there were marked improvements to be found. In particular, respondents valued the fact that more money allowed them to exercise greater choice, even if it was only between taking the taxi rather than the bus home from the shops once in a while, or gave them the freedom and happiness to help out a son and daughter who had got into financial difficulty.

Thus, one of the problems for arts in health is that the kinds of proof medicine asks for are not easy to provide. Smith's contention that diverting 0.5% of the health budget to the arts would improve health may well be true – but only if our conception of health is broad enough to include 'well being' and is not narrowly medical (see p 98ff). Nevertheless, those in charge of commissioning arts in

22 Moynihan R and Smith R, 'Spend (slightly) less on health and more on the arts', *British Medical Journal*, 2002, 324, pp 1432–1433.
23 White, Martin, 'Evaluation of the health effects of welfare advice in primary care', Medical Anthropology Research Group Seminar, University of Durham, February 2006 (unpublished).

health projects face a tough task of justifying such spending to a sceptical workforce and an even more sceptical public. The root problem is that the public have been encouraged by the medical profession to perceive all the set-backs of life as medical problems with medical solutions. But perceptions of this kind generate attitudes towards health and its enhancement which are narrow. It is a central function of bioethics to regulate the health-care professions. But we wish to supplement this by suggesting that the humanities can recommend broader perceptions of and attitudes to health and how it may be enhanced.

Conclusions

The ethical problems that arise in relation to the practice of arts in health are both practical and philosophical in nature. Practical problems include the risks to vulnerable patients and participants when they are supervised by artists who are not qualified 'therapists', and also the risks for artists of patients raising problems with which they cannot cope. Philosophical problems arise when we consider the value of art in such contexts: can – or should – artists produce art with a therapeutic purpose, and indeed what is the value of art work produced by participants in the projects. Lastly, we considered the problem of funding such projects and how this funding is to be ethically justified in an increasingly hard pressed health service. The arts can release latent creativity which can improve self-esteem and change our attitudes to ourselves and society.

Chapter 8

Teaching and research

We have stressed throughout the book that the humanities can have a role in the teaching of medical ethics but that they are no substitute for knowledge of medical regulations – of basic medical law and of the various booklets on ethics produced by the GMC, BMA and similar bodies. Such booklets instil the wisdom of the profession on a wide variety of ethical issues.

Our message has been that what the humanities can do is provide a wider critical look at the practice of medicine, its identity and meaning at a given point in time. They can provide a supplement to the rules of the profession and medical law by raising the consciousness of students and doctors to matters which might pass unnoticed but are of concern to patients, and society more generally.

Despite these positive contributions however there are problems attached to the use of the humanities in medical education. They derive from three sources: the idea that every medical student or doctor should be exposed to the medical humanities, that is, that the medical humanities should be a compulsory component of the curriculum; uncertainty and problems about who the teachers of such courses should be; uncertainty about research in the medical humanities.

Medical humanities: choice or compulsion?

As we have said, we have no doubt that the teaching of medical ethics should be compulsory, meaning by that that students must be made familiar with the guidelines of governing bodies of the profession. Of course, if a literary example is given to illustrate a point then well and good, but the medical humanities involve much more. Our view is that they should not form a compulsory part of the medical curriculum. To illustrate this point we shall use our experience of three different contexts in which medical humanities were taught over a period of 15 years at Glasgow University.[1]

---

1 Macnaughton J, 'The humanities in medical education: context outcomes and structures', *Journal of Medical Ethics: Medical Humanities*, 2000, 26, pp 23–30.

A voluntary course

In 1985 a group of students was involved in a voluntary course on literature. The students were in the third year of their medical course and met in the early evenings of the summer term. The course was run by a number of interested teachers in the medical faculty, including a general practitioner, some consultants, the postgraduate dean, and a philosopher. The aims of the course were to introduce the students to literature in its broadest sense, to suggest how it is possible to learn about life by reading the views, insights and feelings of others, and to encourage them to examine their own attitudes and prejudices. We read poems and extracts from medically relevant literature and discussed them in groups with the tutors. The evaluation suggested that 80% of the students felt that the course aims had been met. Students' reasons for attending included 'I came to broaden my views' and 'to try to stay human as well as being a doctor'. They were keen that the course be run again, as long as it remained voluntary.

This course was very successful and popular with the students, but attendance was sporadic and it felt more like a club for interested people than something integral to the students' education as doctors. Despite the involvement of the postgraduate dean for education (who left the university soon after the course was finished), the course did not run for a second year, as there was neither financial nor moral support for it amongst other members of the medical faculty. The group has, however, continued outwith the university and is still running, over 20 years later. It now consists of practising doctors from different specialities, dentists, philosophers and interested others. We meet two to three times a term to discuss a book, poems, a play or film we might have seen. The discussion ranges widely but often touches on how these works might have helped those of us who are clinicians. The involvement of people who are not clinicians is extremely helpful in clarifying the patient's perspective.

The seed planted by this voluntary course flourished, and it was greeted with excitement and enthusiasm by both students and teachers. It continues to flourish as a voluntary club but it did not become established as a part of the medical curriculum in any form because there was no support from the official medical educators. Even the students who attended and enjoyed the group did not regard it as a central part of their education.

Compulsory final year session

From October to February 1997/98 we attempted an experimental course with the final year students in general practice. In a 90-minute session they were introduced to the ideas of medicine and literature and were given reasons why broader reading might help them in their education. They were then split up into groups and set to read a passage from *The Trick is to Keep Breathing*, a novel by the contemporary Scottish writer, Janice Galloway, which gives an account of the experience of depression.[2] Some groups discussed three contrasting poems on old age, including the humorous poem by Jenny Joseph, *Warning*.[3] In the groups the students were asked to discuss questions such as 'How might these poems help us to understand our elderly patients?'

Some groups (the minority) took the whole exercise very seriously, entered into the spirit of it, and became quite animated; for a few, their excitement derived from the fact that they could recognise a patient they had seen in what they were reading. But the evaluations of the majority showed that although the students' interest had been aroused (and, from what we observed in the groups, they had made a connection between the material and their clinical work) they did not rate the course very highly in terms of usefulness to their medical practice. Here are some of the comments of the students who were not interested: 'Some [of us] just read the back page of the *Sun*, which is fine cos we are all different'; 'woolly'; 'less of the literature: not very useful'.

This course differed from the first in that it was compulsory. Perhaps because of the compulsion, it was less successful than the voluntary course. The comments and the poor rating for usefulness reveal an attitude that is a problem in vocational courses such as medicine: the students tend to regard as important only those classes which they see as being directly relevant to the job of being a doctor. Medical students have traditionally looked down on subjects such as psychology or sociology, which they see as being at best common sense and at worst unimportant to their future clinical work. This problem may be compounded with subjects such as literature and philosophy, which have even less obvious relevance to them. The moral of this type of structure is that it will be impossible to interest all medical students in the humanities as part of their medical education, even if we feel that it would be of benefit to them all. If students are to respond they would have to be open to, and interested in, what they are reading. If they read literature or philosophy on sufferance it will be of no value to them at all.

In this course the seed scattered by the humanities fell largely on stony ground. We can only speculate that for some of the majority who did not respond well to what they had read, a shoot might stir in the future when they see a depressed or elderly patient. They might then begin to understand the relevance to them of the insights of literature.

From these first two examples, we can derive two structural conditions for courses in humanities in medical education. First, they should be freely chosen options; and second, they should have some integrity as part of the medical degree. With the advent in 1993 of the GMC's new structure for undergraduate medical education in the UK – of 'core' and special study modules (SSMs), (now updated to be called Student-Selected Components or SSCs) – it became possible for humanities courses

2 Galloway J, *The Trick is to Keep Breathing*, 1989, London: Minerva.
3 Joseph J, *Rose in the Afternoon*, 1974, London: Dent.

to satisfy both conditions. Moreover, the new structure permitted, indeed required, a third condition, and for medical students this may be the most important of the conditions for a successful course: the SSM must in some way be examinable. The final course we will describe had the advantage of all three of these conditions: the students were self-selecting, but the course was also, as an SSM, regarded by them as part of the degree, and they had to achieve a pass in it.

Special study module in philosophy

February 1998 was the first time SSMs had been run in Glasgow and the students were offered a module in philosophy entitled 'The individual in society; an introduction to social and political philosophy.[4] This module was the product of a collaboration between the Departments of General Practice and the Department of Philosophy and enabled the medical students to take part in a course which was being taught to first year students of philosophy. We shall describe the course – its aims, structure and assessment – and go on to show how the three main aims are related to the education of doctors. The question of whether the course succeeded in its long-term purpose of broadening the outlook of future doctors cannot yet be answered, but we shall describe the initial evaluation by the first group of students and their assessment of whether the course was valuable for them.
The course had three main aims:

1   to read and discuss Plato's *Republic*;
2   to encourage the students to adopt the techniques of philosophical analysis in their approach to an argument; and
3   to expose them to the broadening experience of an academic culture different from their own.

The module provided ten second-year medical students with the opportunity to spend five weeks studying Plato's *Republic* in the context of a course of lectures on political philosophy.[5] As offered in Glasgow, SSMs have the advantage that they are five-week blocks set aside from the rest of the course, during which students can concentrate solely on their module subject. The medical students were, therefore, able to fit in with the pre-existing course on political philosophy which was about to start at the same time as their module. The lectures and reading material from this course became part of the module. Our medical students were therefore taught alongside the arts faculty students and were taught by philosophers who were not specifically angling their material at a medical audience – an important point in terms of the third aim, that of exposing the students to a different academic culture.

4 Downie RS and Macnaughton J, 'Should medical students read Plato?', *Medical Journal of Australia*, 1999, 170, pp 125–127.
5 Ibid.

What is the justification of the three aims in the context of medical education? Of what benefit is five weeks of philosophy to medical students, and why should they learn about Plato?

The justification of the first aim is that *The Republic* deals with fundamental issues relating to society, such as the reasons why people live together in communities in the first place. Humans are frail beings and need the protection of a group, and there is a need to share human resources in the form of the diverse range of talents that people have. Without reference to religious morality, Plato deals with the moral values which, of necessity, must rule human societies. This approach opened the students' minds to a deeper understanding of the origins of our society's make-up and of the values which allow it to function. From this point of view the module had a non-instrumental educational value. As it happened, the students had just completed their family project in the medical course, so they were challenged by Plato's rejection of the family as the basic social unit. This was an unexpected educational bonus.

The justification of the second aim is in terms of its use in developing transferable skills and attitudes. Clinical diagnosis requires that doctors be able to sort out information about a patient, order it and construct arguments for or against certain conclusions (diagnoses). Philosophy can teach students how to go about this; a major part of the module focussed on learning about argument, and students were taught the steps to take in constructing arguments. Besides learning how to do this for themselves, the students also learned to recognise when others were making arguments and when these arguments might be valid or invalid. This was a particular revelation to them (as we will show in the evaluation) as they had been used to accepting much of what they were told. Most of the students commented that by the end of the module, they had begun to question received wisdom with much more confidence.

The justification of the third aim is that it distanced the students from the pervading culture of their medical education and medical class and placed them in the arts faculty (physically and intellectually) and amongst philosophy students and teachers. This provided a broadening academic experience, a 'counter culture', and one that the students would recognise and value as different.

From the practical point of view placing the medical students in an arts faculty context was also a help. It was fortunate that there was a course on political philosophy going on in the philosophy department at the same time which enabled us to do this. This 'piggy backing' idea helped us to overcome the problem of getting arts teachers involved in the course. Other solutions might include joint teaching between the faculties and getting colleagues from other departments interested in teaching the medical students. However, in the current climate in universities, it is important that structures are devised to give collaborating departments equal credit for participating in such courses.

There were three parts to the assessment of the module. For the class essay, consisting of 70% of the marks, students were given a choice of two titles: 'Do we have a moral obligation to obey the laws of the state?' and, 'To what extent can one justify the criticisms of democracy which Plato makes in *The Republic*'? Students also had to complete two seminar papers, contributing a total of 20% of the marks, and two analytical exercises contributed the final 10%. One analytical exercise was handed out at the start of the module and one at the end, to see how their analytical skills had progressed. The exercises consisted of two paragraphs of contrasting arguments, the first relating to lie-telling and the second, to the relative moral value of doing voluntary work out of a sense of duty or for enjoyment. The students were asked to identify the arguments and suggest whether they were valid or invalid.

Evaluation was carried out in two ways: first, by a conventional questionnaire, which asked the students about their reasons for taking the module and what they thought of the structure, content and educational value of the module; and second, by comparing the two analytical exercises that the students did at the beginning and end of the module, to see how their analytical skills had progressed. These results relate to our 1998 groups of 10 students.

In their responses to the questionnaire most of the students said they had taken the module because they were keen to do an arts subject again, having missed the opportunity to study the arts since leaving school, and nine out of ten wanted a complete change from medicine. Again nine out of ten students felt stimulated by the discussion in seminars and by the new ideas that were introduced. They were keen for more discussion time and for more time spent on clarifying issues they did not understand from their reading and lectures. The group seemed to have handled the content of the module well and most felt that they were better able to analyse argument by the end of the course. Most (7 out of 10) also said that they would be able to describe the major arguments of *The Republic* to a friend.

In the second half of the questionnaire, the students were asked about their views of the educational value of the module for themselves. All had discussed the module with their colleagues, indicating that the students had become interested and engaged in what they were doing (an important prerequisite for an educational activity). Most of them, indeed, wanted to do more philosophy in the future and had ideas they wished to pursue. We asked them specifically about the value of the module in medical educational terms and the most frequent comment here was that they would now be less inclined to accept things they were told without justification and they would be more critical of what they were told.

The second part of the evaluation involved a comparison of the first and second analytical exercises as a more objective measure of whether the students had succeeded in learning the skills of analysis. In the first exercise, the students were unable to identify specific arguments and they had no idea what constituted validity. Most of the analysis consisted of whether they agreed or disagreed with the arguments presented. By the end of the module, 6 out of 10 of the students had reached quite a high level. They were able to list the arguments used in the passages, and outline their logical sense, separating premises from conclusions. All of the students attempted to analyse the arguments for validity and most succeeded.

This module was designed to broaden both the students' education and their views of society and its structures – a non-instrumental role for the humanities.

The process by which it helped them to do this enabled them to learn the technique of philosophical argument and how to apply it themselves – an instrumental role. The initial evaluation would imply that the seed we have planted has taken root but it will be a rather longer term exercise to prove that it will flourish and will make any difference to these young people in the future.

Having discussed these courses we may conclude that arts and humanities subjects may be valuable in medical education but not all medical students respond enthusiastically to this teaching. There are three possible responses – and here the metaphor of seed planting is relevant. First (as with the literature group and philosophy module) some students will delight in the opportunities offered by studying literature and philosophy and such opportunities will produce an immediate flowering of the imagination and the understanding. Second, many students, such as the final year class, will be left cold until, perhaps, an encounter with an individual patient germinates one of the seeds we have planted, as they remember something they have read and discussed, which enhances their understanding of their patient's problem. Third, some students, perhaps the majority, will never see the value of the broader educational base and skills that arts and humanities subjects can bring to them – and there is nothing wrong with this as medicine is a discipline which requires many different sorts of people.

It is clear that the students need both the freedom to choose to take up the opportunity of broadening their educational experience by taking humanities subjects, and the impetus to work that comes from these subjects being an examinable part of the curriculum. We are fortunate in the undergraduate arena that we have the SSM/SSC structure which allows humanities subjects to be introduced for students who wish to take them. We can also make use of skills and ideas from philosophy, history and literature to illustrate and illuminate teaching in other areas of medical education – such as in communication skills and behavioural science – and thus suggest their instrumental value to all medical students. Medical practice consists of a wide range of different jobs requiring many different sorts of people and the educational benefits of the humanities may not be appropriate for them all. We must avoid expecting an enthusiastic response from all medical students.

Who should the teachers be?

In a perceptive paper entitled 'Medical humanities: a vision and some cautionary notes' Stephen Pattison advises the practitioners of medical humanities to take a warning from what, he alleges, has happened to medical ethics. To make his point he traces the history of medical ethics in the period 1960–70.

> In the 1960s and 1970s a few medical professional and arts academics such as philosophers became interested in the lack of medical ethics teaching and discourse. By definition, all these people were amateurs in a field whose edges and parameters were not yet established. They were driven as much

by interest as by necessity and were all equally motivated to find ways of enriching a discourse around medicine and health care. Necessarily, they had to make the effort of trying to understand different disciplinary perspectives and to be committed to working together. The early pioneers of health care ethics were theologians, philosophers, doctors, nurses, health care chaplains and others. Medical groups in different centres of health care education were similarly diverse and health care ethics teachers and researchers might come from a variety of disciplinary backgrounds, practical and theoretical. There was, if I recall correctly, a real sense of mutual exploration and excitement as interdisciplinary health care ethics research and education made its first tentative steps towards inclusion in the curriculum, and towards becoming more central to health care in general.[6]

He goes on to point out that 25 yeas later medical ethics has developed in a manner which has limitations; something has been lost.

Because health care ethics is now a recognised disciplinary speciality, there is little room now within it for enthusiastic amateurs who do not know its sources, forms and conventions. Increasingly, health care ethics teachers and researchers have specialised in it at post graduate level over years. It has therefore become professionalized, creating a contrasting 'laity' of people who cannot be recognised or defined as health care ethicists. Indeed, this jargon and the conventions of health care ethics are now so well-defined that many people would recognise it as a specialised language which they cannot and do not speak, rather like legal jargon and concepts. Health care ethics has acquired the dignified paraphernalia of formal journals and an 'official' literature. This announces that it has become 'academic'. The loss here may be a failure to recognise that non-academic perceptions, approaches, utterances and performances can have real value. The jewel in the 'crown' of centrally established health care ethics is the creation of defined agreed curricula for students and trainees. However, it is this kind of clarity that may cut health care ethics off from interdisciplinary messiness and open-ended exploration. Health care ethics is obviously closely related to matters of law and procedure in health care. But focusing in a procedural, componential way on well defined decisions and problems separates this discipline from curiosity about wider, more complex issues of human existence.[7]

We agree with a great deal of Pattison's critique of medical ethics, and have tried to show that medical ethics as it is currently practised would be enriched

6 Pattison S, 'Medical humanities: a vision and some cautionary notes', *Journal of Medical Ethics: Medical Humanities*, 2003, 29, pp 33–36.
7 Ibid.

by the critical and supplementary contributions of the medical humanities. Our question here however is whether the medical humanities are likely to go the same way as medical ethics and become a specialised discipline with its own professionals, vocabulary and journals.

If it does happen it will have the disadvantage that medical humanities professionals will be at some remove from the clinical concerns of their target students or readers. Indeed, they may become figures of fun. We have observed before (p 128) that an obsession with the term 'narrative' has come to dominate the vocabulary of medical humanities professionals. But recently doctors have come to notice this and make fun of it. Consider, for example, the following 'opinion' in the *BMA News Review* (5 May 2006). Dr Flora Tristan, an inner-city GP, writes as follows:

> You know they say medicine is all about stories? I am not sure if that is all there is to it, but certainly today in the practice we have had enough narrative, humour, pathos, complexity and satire to keep all those clever people in the narrative medicine seminars happy through several workshops.

Among various 'narratives' from general practice she recounts the story of Grace (28) who is applying for a Disability Living Allowance.

> The benefits advocate who had helped her apply had clearly done what we urge medical students to do, namely write down verbatim what the patient said. So in the section on activities of daily living we had:
> 'I do not cook mostly as I cannot be bothered.... It is difficult to get out of bed or get dressed. Thinking about work makes me tired.... I have not been able to clean up as no one has brought me any Flash.'
> You see? It is all there – simple narrative, complex meaning, pathos and humour. Worthy, almost, of Dr Chekhov.[8]

The point here is that enthusiasts for the term 'narrative' have turned the medical humanities into a joke. This is likely to happen when the practitioners of medical humanities develop a specialised vocabulary and see everything in clinical practice through the lenses of that vocabulary.

Who then should be the teachers of medical humanities? They can be anyone with an interest in and enthusiasm for ideas, for different perspectives and different conceptual structures in terms of which human beings can be seen. The teachers of medical humanities may enable students and doctors to escape from the strait-jacket of 'evidence-based medicine', but this is not much of an escape

---

8 Tristan F, 'Opinion', *British Medical Association News Review*, 5 May 2006, p 62.

if they are immediately imprisoned in the strait-jacket of 'narrative-based medicine'. To quote Pattison again, medical humanities should be

> a loose coalition of concerns people, disciplines, approaches, practices and methods that are engaged in a fairly open-ended dialogue and exploration of where humanities approaches etc can be illuminative of, or even obstructive to, health and health care.[9]

This kaleidoscope approach to medical humanities can enliven the teaching of medical ethics. Medical ethics must remain mainly a matter of regulation, but if it does not go beyond that it will ossify.

Medical humanities: research

Research into the medical humanities can be divided roughly into two kinds. First, research into the subjects which comprise the medical humanities, such as medical history, the philosophy of medicine, the influence of their medical problems on creative writers, artist or composers, or the insights of creative artists deriving from the fact that there were also doctors. Second, research on the students and others who are the participants.

The first sort of research is best carried out by those who are knowledgeable and skilled in the first-order discipline. Sometimes the researchers ought to be clinicians, and sometimes they ought to be humanities specialists. For example, clinicians are best placed to comment on (say) Beethoven's medical problems (especially if they have first studied his letters, notebooks and other recorded comments). But medical historians (rather than clinicians) are best placed to comment on (say) the development of GP research. Of course, it helps if they are also clinicians.[10]

As far as medical ethics goes it takes a historian rather than a clinician to examine medical ethics in the Greek world, or the influence of Thomas Percival on medical ethics in the nineteenth century.[11] Studies of this kind make a useful supplement to contemporary writings on the subject which are written from what might be called a Whig perspective, that is, the perspective that suggests that medical ethics has brought about a steady ethical improvement in the relationship between doctor and patient. For example, it is widely believed in medical ethics circles that it has been an ethical improvement to change the doctor/patient relationship into a consumerist one with competition, league tables and patient choice as the key to the best medical ethics. But a medical historian with a broader perspective might be able to show that this is less an

9 Pattison, op.cit., pp 33–36.
10 Macnaughton J, 'The St Andrews Institute for Clinical Research: an early experiment in collaboration', *Medical History*, 2002, 46, pp 549–568.
11 Leake C (ed), *Percival's Medical Ethics*, 1927, Baltimore, MD: Williams and Wilkins.

ethical improvement than a cultural change brought about by the rise of consumerism since 1980. This is just one example of the way in which the medical humanity of history might inject some realism into the doctor-bashing, self-righteousness and self-congratulatory tone of some writings on medical ethics.

The second sort of research concerns research into the effect of the medical humanities on the participants, including those in undergraduate and postgraduate medical education, and also those in the target groups of the 'arts in health' movement (see Chapter 7). Here the misunderstandings are found among the medical authorities who talk the language of 'measurable outcomes'. This must be resisted. If medical faculties wish to recognise the humanities they must also accept the methods and approaches of the humanities. Evaluation is important, but it is not the same as 'measurement'. We have already exposed the inappropriate use of numbers (p 82ff), and suggested examples of more helpful qualitative types of evaluation (p 87ff). The effect of film, role play, short stories and so on can be evaluated in terms of the testimony of those taking part, but the use of numbers in this context reveals a sad misunderstanding not only of the humanities but also of numbers. In a similar way we should look to the testimony of those taking part in 'arts in health' schemes, rather than impose the absurd template of numbers upon them.

Conclusions

Any new movement in education attracts zealots. For example, the supporters of problem-based learning have introduced enormous and costly changes into medical training with little evidence that it is more effective than traditional methods. The same kind of ideology can be found in the supporters of the medical humanities. We have tried in this chapter to be more realistic about this. Not all students or doctors respond well to the humanities, at least when they are seen as part of medical education, even of ethical education. But when offered on a voluntary basis they can contribute an enrichment of the staple diet of bioethics. Likewise, research in the medical humanities is best conducted by the specialists in the specific disciplines involved. There is nothing more embarrassing than a distinguished clinician taking a brief respite from his professional labours in order to instruct us on the history of philosophy.

Part IV

General conclusions

Chapter 9

A humanistic broadening of bioethics

In his discussion of the shortcomings of contemporary bioethics Stephen Pattison argues as follows:

> One cannot easily imagine Aristotle or the great humanistic therapeutic philosophers of Greece being very impressed by health care ethics today. Their questions about life and practice were developed out of a total view of human existence and its possibilities. It is difficult to think of their being content to deliver or take a module in procedural health care ethics, however well they might be paid, however grandly titled their chairs and however exalted their place in the academy. For such thinkers, the particular and the problematic had to be situated within a much larger picture about potential and meaning that covered all of life and the entirety of social and institutional arrangements. This breadth of vision seems to be singularly, if inadvertently, lacking in established health care ethics today.[1]

In this passage Pattison is not so much dismissing contemporary medical ethics as claiming that it is lacking some important elements. We agree with this position. We have argued that, whereas every doctor and medical student should be familiar with the regulations currently in force for medical practice, at least some doctors and students should be encouraged to become interested in the bigger picture. For example, they should be encouraged to engage critically with the assumptions about measurement and evidence-based medicine and the views about human nature implied by them, to examine (cynically as well as critically) the claim that doctors are uniquely and by definition altruistic, to consider the politics of health, and to become aware of how doctors are depicted in literature. Some doctors in literature are presented in an idealistic manner, but others more cynically. Yet it is possible to learn ethical lessons even from cynical depictions.

---

1 Pattison S, 'Medical humanities: a vision and some cautionary notes', *Journal of Medical Ethics: Medical Humanities*, 2003, 29, pp 33–36.

The argument can be put in a different way. We can say that medicine is regarded as a 'vocational' qualification at a university in that it prepares the students for a particular job at the end of their degree. We talk of students being 'trained' to be doctors, rather than being 'educated' in medicine. It would also be true to say that they can, and ought to be, trained in medical ethics in the sense that they ought to be familiar with the regulations concerning what doctors should do in certain contexts. For example, if a daughter says, 'I want you to attempt to resuscitate my 90 year-old mother if she has a respiratory arrest', and the doctor knows that such an attempt will certainly fail, is he bound to obey the relative? The answer to that question is not a matter of opinion; it is a matter of knowledge. It is important that doctors should have the knowledge of medical regulations and guidelines which will enable them to make decisions in such situations.

But it is another matter entirely how the doctor communicates that decision to the daughter and family. Ability to do so in a compassionate manner is not a matter of regulation but derives from the kind of person the doctor is, from a humane perception of the situation and attitude towards it. It may be that some people have this attitude and others simply don't. But if anything can help to nurture the germs of fellow-feeling which we all have it is the humanities.

It is in this context that we can return to the distinction which has been touched on in several contexts in this book. It is a distinction which is crucial to the contribution which the humanities can make to medical ethics. The distinction is between training and education. Here we shall draw on the work of educational theorist RS Peters.[2] In a medical context, similar distinctions are drawn by Calman and Downie.[3]

First, to be educated is to have a broad prospective, as distinct from the narrow focus of training. Second, education is a process, not a single objective. As Peter says: 'to be educated is not to have arrived; it is to travel with a different view'.[4] Peters' final point is that an educational process should be valuable as an end in itself and not just because it enables someone to do something else.[5]

By contrast, when we speak of training it always makes sense to ask, 'Trained in what, or for what end, or to do what?' Such questions do not have the same sort of relevance to an educational process. Education seems more like something worth having for its own sake. If someone insists on a purpose for education (as distinct from training) we find ourselves using phrases such as, 'It creates a rounded human being' or 'It conduces to personal development' or 'It provides a broad and humane perspective on life.'

2 Peters RS, '*Ethics and Education*', 1966, London: George Allen and Unwin.
3 Calman KC and Downie RS, 'Education and training in medicine', *Medical Education*, 1988, 22, pp 488–491.
4 Peters, op.cit., p 34.
5 Ibid.

Points of this nature were clearly in the minds of the GMC when they wrote *Tomorrow's Doctors*. Commenting on the deficiencies of current undergraduate medical education they said that the current system results in

> a regrettable tendency to underprovide those components of the course that are truly educational, that pertain to the proper function of a university and that are the hallmark of scholarship.[6]

Clearly, the curriculum for future doctors will rightly and predominantly involve training. But some educational components are desirable in addition, and the GMC here pointed out that the latter have tended to be neglected. By allowing the study of literature, history or philosophy in the medical curriculum, we shall at the very least introduce breadth. But, more importantly, these subjects can challenge the students by introducing them to some of the great thinkers, writers or artists, and will encourage them to consider different ways of perceiving the world. This will assist in the development of a critical and questioning attitude and help refine judgement. And sound judgement – technical and humane – is the most important attribute of the good doctor. We have stressed this in every chapter.

Turning to the value of the humanities in personal development, we can say that the educational process touches the student more deeply at a personal level than does the training process. Education is concerned not just with what someone can *do*, but with what *kind of people* they become as a result of their education. Sound ethical practice requires not only knowledge and skills but also a humane and sympathetic approach to human beings. JS Mill writes:

> It really is of importance, not only what men do, but also what manner of men they are that do it. Among the works of men, which human life is rightly involved in perfecting and beautifying, the first of importance is man himself.[7]

It is here that a study of the humanities is best justified in the context of ethics. As we have suggested, plays, poems and novels, music and the fine arts demand an emotional response and in doing so they will allow the students to discover their own hidden values and prejudices, and to challenge them. This will encourage the kind of self-understanding ('fine awareness') which is essential for the development of mature human beings who are attuned and sympathetic to the perspectives and values of other people.

The final point about the educational value of the humanities is their role in providing the experience of a 'counter culture' to medicine. Medical students

---

6 General Medical Council, *Tomorrow's Doctors: Recommendations on Undergraduate Medical Education*, 1993, London: GMC, p 15.
7 Mill JS, *On Liberty* (1859), in *Utilitarianism*, 1962, Mary Warnock (ed), Glasgow: Collins, p 188.

often have the impression, and are encouraged in it by medical teachers, that they have an intellectual and moral superiority over other students. This is further encouraged by the facts that entrance requirements for medicine are amongst the highest in the university system, and senior doctors seem to believe that, unlike the occupations of the rest of the world, the practice of medicine not only displays the moral quality of beneficence but is actually supererogatory or altruistic. These attitudes are mutually supported by the university experience of medical students, which tends to be rather insular, in that everyone follows the same course. The opportunity to take a humanities subject will allow medical students to meet teachers and students in other disciplines, will help reduce this isolation and may ultimately foster better relationships between doctors and the 'outside world' by affecting perceptions and attitudes. This can only be a good thing from the point of view of ethics.

Index

public health services: ethical problem in
    106–107; health promotion ethics in
    98–101; justice and utility in 92–98;
    through community participation
    101–106
public health specialist 92

qualitative research: effects of number
    distorts 86–87; and generalisability
    87–89; use of numbers and scales 82–86
qualitative researchers 89
quality of life 109, 120–124

Randal, Felix 57
randomised control trials 3
'randomly attached characteristics' 66
reductivism 86, 141
regulatory ethical rules 17
Reid, Thomas 50
respect 42, 43
Ross WD 34
Roswell, Hanger 84 (poem) 132–133
rule-utilitarianism 10

Saunders, Dame Cicely 87
scientific understanding, of madness
    139–143
Scottish Enlightenment 49
screening programmes 97–98
self-awareness 18, 136–137
Shakespeare, William 57, 79, 131
Shaw, Bernard 72
Smith, Adam 13, 45–47, 50, 114–115
social well-being 9, 99
Socrates 80
spirituality scale 9
supererogation 36–41
Sydenham, Thomas 71

taxonomy 46
Taylor F 122
The Duties and Qualifications of a
    Physician (lecture) 15–18
'the exertion of genius' 15
theory of knowledge 9
therapeutic processes 3
The Tenth Man (book) 1–2
Thurber, James 77
Tolstoy, Leo 77–79
Toulmin, Stephen 32, 45
Trick is to Keep Breathing, The
    (book) 168–169

UN Declaration of Human
    Rights 96

vaccination programmes 95
value judgements 32–33, 70, 100,
    122, 146–147
visual aids 23

Wagner, Richard 76
War and Peace (book) 77–79
Warning (poem) 169
Wealth of Nations, The (book) 114
Whig perspective 176
WHO 67, 75, 98, 101–102, 124
Wilks, Michael 62
Wittgenstein L 60, 67
Woman in White The (book) 147
Wordsworth W 142
World Health Organisation
    (WHO) 8
Wrekenton lanterns, *see* arts, in
    health projects

xenotransplantation 12